D0374360

Geocaching

Third Edition

by The Editors and Staff of Geocaching.com

A member of Penguin Group (USA) Inc.

ALPHA BOOKS

Published by the Penguin Group

Penguin Group (USA) Inc., 375 Hudson Street, New York, New York 10014, USA • Penguin Group (Canada), 90 Eglinton Avenue East, Suite 700, Toronto, Ontario M4P 2Y3, Canada (a division of Pearson Penguin Canada Inc.) • Penguin Books Ltd., 80 Strand, London WC2R 0RL, England • Penguin Ireland, 25 St. Stephen's Green, Dublin 2, Ireland (a division of Penguin Books Ltd.) • Penguin Group (Australia), 250 Camberwell Road, Camberwell, Victoria 3124, Australia (a division of Pearson Australia Group Pty. Ltd.) • Penguin Books India Pvt. Ltd., 11 Community Centre, Panchsheel Park, New Delhi—110 017, India • Penguin Group (NZ), 67 Apollo Drive, Rosedale, North Shore, Auckland 1311, New Zealand (a division of Pearson New Zealand Ltd.) • Penguin Books (South Africa) (Pty.) Ltd., 24 Sturdee Avenue, Rosebank, Johannesburg 2196, South Africa • Penguin Books Ltd., Registered Offices: 80 Strand, London WC2R 0RL, England

International Standard Book Number: 978-1-61564-194-9
Library of Congress Catalog Card Number: 2012930861

14   13   12   8   7   6   5   4   3   2   1

Interpretation of the printing code: The rightmost number of the first series of numbers is the year of the book's printing; the rightmost number of the second series of numbers is the number of the book's printing. For example, a printing code of 12-1 shows that the first printing occurred in 2012.

Printed in the United States of America

Note: This publication contains the opinions and ideas of its authors. It is intended to provide helpful and informative material on the subject matter covered. It is sold with the understanding that the authors and publisher are not engaged in rendering professional services in the book. If the reader requires personal assistance or advice, a competent professional should be consulted.

The authors and publisher specifically disclaim any responsibility for any liability, loss, or risk, personal or otherwise, which is incurred as a consequence, directly or indirectly, of the use and application of any of the contents of this book.

Most Alpha books are available at special quantity discounts for bulk purchases for sales promotions, premiums, fund-raising, or educational use. Special books, or book excerpts, can also be created to fit specific needs.

For details, write: Special Markets, Alpha Books, 375 Hudson Street, New York, NY 10014.

Publisher: *Marie Butler-Knight*
Associate Publisher: *Mike Sanders*
Executive Managing Editor: *Billy Fields*
Acquisitions Editor: *Brook Farling*
Development Editor: *Jennifer Bowles*
Senior Production Editor: *Janette Lynn*
Copy Editor: *Daron Thayer*

Cover Designer: *William Thomas*
Book Designers: *William Thomas, Rebecca Batchelor*
Indexer: *Tonya Heard*
Layout: *Brian Massey*
Proofreader: *John Etchison*

ALWAYS LEARNING   PEARSON

From Brad Simmons:

To my friends and family for their patience and understanding during the long hours away and to the muses who kept me focused and distracted during this process.

From the Groundspeak Lackeys:

To all those who are searching: keep it up! We know you are not lost since there is an adventure in every location.

Contents

Part 1: Welcome to a New Kind of Adventure 1

1   What Exactly Is Geocaching? 3

Geocaching 101 4

How It All Got Started 8

    GPS Users Get an Instant Upgrade *8*

    The Original "Stash" *9*

    The Origins of "Geocaching" *11*

The Birth of Geocaching.com 11

If You Hide It, They Will Come 13

Timing Is Everything 14

Is Geocaching a Hobby, Game, or Sport? 15

Variety Is the Spice of Geocaching 15

The Geocaching Community 17

The Geocacher's Creed 17

2   The Basics of the Game 19

Getting Started 19

    Take Something *20*

    Leave Something *21*

    Sign the Logbook *21*

    Cache In Trash Out *21*

    Share Your Experience Online *22*

    Posting Photos *22*

Learn the Language 23

Log On Before Heading Out 24

Trinkets Can Be Treasures 25

    Geocacher Signature Items *25*

    Prohibited Geocache Items *26*

Where Are Geocaches Hidden? 27

    Wide-Open Spaces *27*

    Parks *28*

    Cities and Suburbs *29*

Packing Your GeoBag 29

Longer Hunts Need More Gear 31

    Gear Checklist for Overnight Trips *32*

    Dress for Success *34*

    Geocacher Communication *34*

Part 2:   Time to Get Out and Play 37

    3   Your Adventure Begins at Home 39
        Creating Your Geocaching.com Account 39
        Searching for Nearby Geocaches 40
        Paperless Geocaching 42
           Downloading Coordinates 43
           Pocket Queries 45
        Selecting a Geocache to Seek 46
        Cache Difficulty Ratings 47
           Difficulty 47
           Terrain 48
        Using Maps and Clues 49
        Watching a Geocache 52
        Temporarily Disabled and Archived Caches 53

    **4   What You Need to Know
        to Play the Game 55**
        Get Out and Play 55
           Coordinate Entry 56
           Searching for Clues Before You Hunt 58
           Hitting the Trail 59
           Navigational Tips and Tricks 60
        You Found It! Now What? 62
           Sharing Your Experience 63
           Logging with Field Notes 64
           A Picture Is Worth a Thousand Words 65
           A Souvenir of Your Adventure 65

    5   Geocaching Tips and Tricks 67
        Good Advice 67
           Before You Leave 68
           On the Trail 70
           Map Considerations 70
         Do Your Homework 71
        Search Techniques 72
           Cloverleaf 73
           Triangulation 74

Be Careful Out There!..76

Environmental Concerns 77

Poison, Stingers, and Fangs 78

Lions, Tigers, and Creepy Guys, Oh My! 79

Blending In and Getting Along 81

Environmental Ethics and Stewardship........................... 83

6   The Different Types of Geocaches.................85

Standard Geocache Types 86

Traditional Geocaches... 86

Multi-Caches 87

Mystery or Puzzle Caches 88

Letterbox Hybrids.. 89

EarthCaches... 90

Wherigo Caches 91

Unusual Cache Types...91

GPS Adventures Maze Exhibit 92

Project A.P.E. Geocaches..................................... 92

Groundspeak Headquarters Cache 92

Geocaching Gatherings....................................... 93

Grandfathered Cache Types and Events 94

**7   Creating and Hiding
        Your Own Geocache 97**

Hiding a Geocache... 97

Container Considerations..................................... 99

Ask Permission 101

Placing Your Geocache and Saving the Coordinates........ 102

Submitting Your Geocache to Geocaching.com...............103

The Geocache Review Process............................. 104

Care and Feeding of Your Geocache 105

Do's and Don'ts 105

**8   Travel Bugs®, Geocoins,
        and Trackable Treasures 109**

Twenty-First-Century Message in a Bottle..................... 109

Travel Bugs Are Born 110

Finding Travel Bugs...112

Relocating Travel Bugs......................................115

Creating Your Own Trackable Item 116

The Travel Bug Goes Big 118

The Evolution of the Travel Bug 119

Geocoins: Trackable Meets Collectible 120

Tracking Geocoins and Other Trackables *122*

Trackables Go Mainstream 123

Travel Bug Stories 124

Darth Vader TB1 .... *125*

Sysop's Traveler *126*

Tigger *126*

Part 3:   Get in Gear 129

9   Understanding How GPS Works 131

Evolution of the GPS Receiver 132

Top Secret Tech—Declassified *133*

Military Technology Goes Mainstream *133*

New Tools for Work and Play *134*

Satellite Signals 135

Features of GPS Receivers 136

How Accurate Is Accurate? 137

WAAS, EGNOS, and MSAS *138*

Factors That Affect Accuracy *139*

Getting a Fix 139

Initialization 141

GPS Limitations 142

10   Choosing a GPS for Geocaching 145

GPS Receivers 146

Primary Features 146

Device Types and Application 150

Handheld Without a Basemap Database *150*

Handheld with a Basemap Database *151*

Full-Featured Handhelds *153*

Vehicle-Based Receivers *155*

Laptops, PDAs, and Tablets *156*

Smartphones *157*

Batteries *158*

Special Considerations for Geocaching 159

**11   GPS Setup and Understanding
      All Those Features.................................163**

Learning Your Way Around Your Receiver 163

Which Button Does What?..165

Common Pages..166

    Active Route Page *166*

    Compass Page *166*

    Highway Page *167*

    Information or Position Page *167*

    Map Page *167*

    Satellite Status Page *168*

    Checking Out the Features *168*

Setup 169

    Alarms *169*

    Backlight Timer..*169*

    Battery Type *170*

    Coordinates *170*

    Distance Measurement *170*

    Map Datum *170*

    Map-Page Orientation *171*

    North *171*

    Time..*171*

    Timers..*172*

    Conserve Your Battery...*172*

Saving Waypoints..173

Track Logs...177

Routes..179

    Saving Routes *179*

    Auto Routing *180*

**12   Smartphones: The Next Step
      in Geocaching....................................183**

The Official Geocaching App.. 184

    iPhones and iPads *185*

    Android Phones and Tablets..*187*

    Windows Mobile *190*

Geocaching Challenges App 192

Third-Party Geocaching Apps.............................194
    Trimble Geocache Navigator............................. 194
    CacheSense..195
    CacheBox 195
    NeonGeo 195
    GCBuddy..195

13   **Geocaching with Computers**
       and Software.................................... 197
    GPS with Computers 198
      Computers as GPS Receivers...........................198
      Map Databases 199
      Data Transfer and Management 200
      Real-Time Tracking...................................... 200
    Mapping Software 202
      GPS Company Software................................... 203
      Aftermarket Software..................................... 203
      Online Map Services...................................... 205
    Terrain Analysis 205
    Thousands of Geocaches at Your Fingertips!.................. 207
    Geocaching Software to Enhance Your Game 207
      Geocaching Swiss Army Knife (GSAK) 208
      GPSBabel...208
      EasyGPS 208
      Google Earth 209
      CacheMate..209
    Geocaching Live Products and the Official API.............210
    Some Final Computer Bytes.................................210

14   **Going Old School—Using Analog Maps........ 213**
    Map Basics 214
    Map Scales 214
    Topographic Maps..215
    Map Reading..216
    Reading Topographic Maps................................217
      Check the Datum 218
      Grid Lock 219
      Map Colors and Symbols.................................219
      Contour Lines 219
      Pacing..221
    Navigation Tips..222

Part 4:   Beyond Basic Geocaching 225

**15   Getting Involved in
         Geocaching Communities................................227**
        Online Interactions 229
            Latitude 47: The Official Geocaching Blog.......................229
            Online Sharing for the Masses 230
            *Podcasts and Blogs Unite
                the International Community..................................... 230*
            Geocaching.com Discussion Forums 230
            Regional and Local Forums and Websites...........................233
        Local Clubs and Geocaching Organizations 234
            National Groups Get in the Game 236
        Geocaching in Education 237

16   Geocaching Goes Social 241
        Geocaching Events...241
            Meet and Greet Fellow Cachers.................................243
            Geocaching 101—Educational Events 243
            Camping with Cachers—Multi-Day Events 244
        Mega-Events 245
            GeoWoodstock, Where It All Started................................245
            Mega-Events Grow and Go Global...................................... 248
        CITO Events—Giving Back and Having Fun................ 249
        Organizing Your Own Geocaching Event 249
        Adding Geocaching Games to Your Events......................252

17   Hitting the Road: GeoTourism........................255
        Exploring Your World with GeoTourism....................256
            Take a Tour with the Locals 256
            GeoTours Help Explore History..................................257
            E.T. Phone Home: It's All About the Experience.................259
        Destination Caches 260
        Planning Your Trip.. 264
        Finding Caches Along Your Route 266
        Geocaching Vacations.. 266
            Local Treasures 267
            Packing for Vacation Geocaching.............................. 268
        International Considerations...............................270
            Flying with GPS.. 270
            Use Some Discretion 270

18   Geocaching Evolves: The Variations............273

Geocaching Challenges— The Newest Addition
to the Game 274

Adding Challenges to Your Geocaching Adventure 274

Photo Challenges 276

Discover Challenges 277

Creating Your Own Challenges...278

Waymarking—A New Way to Hunt 279

A New Game with Deep Roots... 280

Person, Place, or Thing? 282

Searching for a Waymark 282

Wherigo—Redefining Location 283

What Is Wherigo? 284

Get in Gear—Equipment for Playing 285

Wherigo: Getting into the Game 286

How to Play 287

More Than Just a Game 288

Wherigo Geocaches... 289

Benchmark Hunting.. 289

Searching for Benchmarks.. 290

Finding a Benchmark 291

Logging a Benchmark... 292

19   What the Future Holds for Geocaching.......295

Geocaching Grows and Evolves..295

Next Steps in Geocaching 296

The Ever-Changing GPS Constellation 296

Geocaching and Augmented Reality 298

Reconnecting with Nature in the Digital Age................ 300

Technology Brings Us Back to Our Roots...........................301

The Geocaching Community Goes Mainstream................. 303

It Is a Brave New World: Go Outside and Play 305

Appendixes

A   Resource Directory 309

B   Glossary 317

C   Navigation and Map References 327

D   Geocaching Sample Log Sheet 329

E   Geocache Notification Sheet 331

F   Travel Itinerary 333

     Index 335

Introduction

Congratulations for taking the time to find this book, *The Complete Idiot's Guide to Geocaching, Third Edition*. In your hands is an opportunity to learn about one of the most exciting and fastest-growing recreational activities in the world; it is the official book of Geocaching.com. Since the release of the first edition of this book in 2004, recreational use of GPS technology has continued to grow significantly on a global scale.

Why has its popularity skyrocketed? Perhaps it's because the geocaching adventure began up there in outer space—some 12,000 miles above Earth. That's where GPS satellites orbit and direct treasure-hunting, playful geocachers to within feet of hidden containers and exciting outdoor locations. Along the way, they also find community, creativity, exercise, and a world of adventures. And there is no need to leave the cool gadgets at home; this activity embraces both technology and the outdoors.

Jeremy Irish, Elias Alvord, and Bryan Roth, Founders of Geocaching.com, circa March 2001.

Our goal in writing this third edition was to create the next version of the ultimate book on geocaching: one that makes learning about the activity enjoyable and easy to understand. Whether you are new to geocaching or a seasoned veteran, we trust you'll find that we've covered the topics necessary to keep you geocaching successfully and safely every time you hit the trail. This is no easy endeavor. Although this is the third version of the original, the activity has changed significantly throughout the years and even changes from one week to the next. It has been a gratifying task to cover innovations in the activity that were not present at the time we wrote the first and even the second edition.

How This Book Is Organized

In our effort to make this book user-friendly, we have divided the chapters into four parts.

Part 1, Welcome to a New Kind of Adventure, covers the basics of what geocaching is and how it all got started. We go over the basics of the game and offer information and advice to help you get started. We also explain how to participate and prepare for outdoor geocaching adventures.

Part 2, Time to Get Out and Play, gets down to the business of playing the game. We explore how to use the Geocaching.com website to choose geocaches to seek. Then, we teach you how to get outside and find geocaches in the real world. We cover everything you need to know in order to find the most difficult of geocaches, and then discuss how to hide your own for others to find. In Part 2, you'll also discover the fun of Travel Bugs and other trackable items.

Part 3, Get in Gear, teaches you all about Global Positioning System (GPS) technology, which makes geocaching possible. You will get a solid understanding of GPS devices, including their features and functions. Part 3 also covers several of the more popular available GPS receiver options so that you can purchase the right device for your use, and we explain how to set up your device so that you'll be ready to hit the trail. We also take a look at a phenomenon that is changing the geocaching world—hunting with smartphones.

Finally, we unravel some of the mystery behind GPS mapping, and using computers and tablets to enhance your experience.

Part 4, Beyond Basic Geocaching, introduces you to the world-wide geocaching community. We teach you about the tools currently used for community interaction and show you how to find answers to any questions you have. We introduce you to the discussion forums, geocaching organizations, and geocaching events around the world. We also provide you with some information on geocaching while traveling, including tips for fun and safety, GeoTourism, and practical considerations. This part also takes a look at geocaching-related games and the evolution of the sport as geocaching moves into the future.

Extras

We've added these extras to help you navigate through the world of GPS and geocaching. Keep a lookout for Signal the Frog, the Groundspeak mascot, for a fun way to learn important tips, geocaching language, and warnings.

EUREKA!

These provide tips, discoveries, and trivia.

GEO-LINGO

These define technical or slang terminology.

NAVIGATIONAL NUGGETS

These provide useful advice specific to GPS and navigation.

DEAD BATTERIES

These provide a caution or warning to help keep you out of trouble.

Acknowledgments

This project seemed a lot easier at the outset than it did during the actual doing of it. It took a lot of work and there are a few people to thank for helping to make this book possible. First, thanks go to Jack Peters, who authored the first edition, and Shauna Maggs and Bret Hammond, who authored the second edition. Very special appreciation goes to Brad Simmons (aka MonkeyBrad) who has contributed countless hours to this, the third edition of *The Complete Idiot's Guide to Geocaching*. With this new edition, we are pleased to share Brad's insight gained through many years of international geocaching experiences, and all readers will undoubtedly benefit from the tremendous context and perspective he brings to this book. We thank Jenn Seva (aka MissJenn), a geocacher and a Groundspeak Lackey, for reviewing this book and making sure Brad had everything he needed from Groundspeak in order to complete this project. Also, thanks to Damon Brown, for his technical contributions, and to Brook Farling and the rest of the staff and editors at Penguin Group (USA) Inc./Alpha Books. Their follow-through and patience made this book possible. Always, thanks to our family and friends for your assistance, patience, and support. We could not have done it without you. Finally, thank you to the dedicated volunteers and many geocachers around the world who have made geocaching possible. We are continually inspired by your passion and dedication to geocaching, and it is truly an honor to serve you.

Trademarks

All terms mentioned in this book that are known to be or are suspected of being trademarks or service marks have been appropriately capitalized. Alpha Books and Penguin Group (USA) Inc. cannot attest to the accuracy of this information. Use of a term in this book should not be regarded as affecting the validity of any trademark or service mark.

Welcome to a New Kind of Adventure

So you have heard a little about geocaching and now you are ready to get more involved. That's great, and we are here to help. Before you set off to find your first geocache, let's take time to learn about the activity. Geocaching has been around long enough to develop its own traditions, guidelines, and lingo. And even though GPS technology makes staying found easy enough, it's good to understand how it works before depending on it outdoors.

In Part 1, we cover the basics of geocaching—what it is and how it all got started. We explore some of the best ways to get into the game and the different kinds of caches you can expect on the trail. We explain how to participate and prepare for outdoor geocaching adventures, regardless of whether you're a newbie or a seasoned pro.

We also take a closer look at some of the best ways to prepare for your geocaching adventure. You find out what you should carry with you when you hit the trail and some basic advice about the outdoors.

What Exactly Is Geocaching?

In This Chapter

- An explanation of geocaching
- How it all got started
- Big family adventures on a baby budget
- Reasons to play and skills to learn
- The types of geocaches out there

When the U.S. Department of Defense developed Global Positioning System (GPS) technology they probably never thought it would develop into the backbone for a worldwide entertainment activity, but that is exactly what happened. Geocaching is one of the most exciting and quickly growing activities in recent history. But is it a game, a sport, or a relaxing family activity like sightseeing? It is all of these things, depending on how and where you play and the energy you put into it.

History has demonstrated that people have always had a desire to seek out hidden treasure. Books are filled with stories of lost cities and hidden gold, with people driven to cross oceans, deserts, jungles, and continents in search of the elusive "X" that marks the spot. In this regard, it is not surprising that geocaching continues to grow in popularity. Considered a modern-day treasure hunt, by marrying technology and nature, geocaching helps people experience the outdoors in a way that captures this historical desire for adventure while having fun with friends and family.

This chapter introduces you to geocaching, how it all got started, and how you can begin to participate in this growing, global activity!

A typical geocache with a logbook and its treasure stored in a watertight container.
(Geocaching.com)

Geocaching 101

Geocaching combines *geo* for Earth and *cache*, a term used for both hidden provisions and, in a more modern sense, data stored on a computer. Put them together and you have a unique outdoor activity. Enthusiasm for the game has quickly spread as participants combine their love of the great outdoors with their interest in modern technology. It isn't often when you can tap into an outdoor game that has a government budget of more than half a billion dollars a year!

The activity began after the Clinton administration removed selective availability from GPS in May 2000. That was the scrambling technique that made GPS receivers inaccurate up to 100 meters (300 feet). Now that receivers are accurate within 15 meters 90 percent of the time, it is possible to navigate to a specific location with more precision.

EUREKA!

Geocaching.com was established in September 2000 with 75 geocaches posted online. Twelve years later, there are more than 1,750,000 geocaches hidden around the world.

Geocaching is played all around the globe. As of this writing, there are over 5 million participants worldwide seeking more than 1.75 million active geocaches. The number of geocaches continues to grow at a rapid rate as more people share unique locations around the world. It's fun to have a look to see how many geocaches are located within your own neighborhood. You'll undoubtedly be surprised at the number out there just waiting to be discovered.

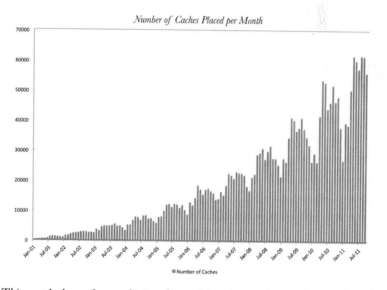

This graph shows the popularity of geocaching since its beginnings in May 2000.
(Geocaching.com)

The goal of geocaching is to locate hidden containers, called *geocaches*, using the latitude and longitude coordinates found on Geocaching.com. Geocaches must be watertight to withstand the outdoor elements. Items in a geocache are also sometimes stored in zippered plastic bags to provide additional protection from inclement weather. Geocaches are hidden in the wilderness, parks, or even urban locations accessible to the public. How geocaches are hidden depends on the skill and creativity of the one doing the hiding. Some are easy to find, while others take some work. They could be hidden on a cliff, in a hollow log, or even underwater. A geocache is even rated for how difficult it is to find and the type of terrain you must cover to get there. With such a large variety of geocaches and a creative geocaching community, there are unique geocaches of all types available for anyone to find.

GEO-LINGO

A **geocache** is a container that includes, at a minimum, a logbook for geocachers to sign. Geocaches are not buried but are hidden cleverly in plain sight.

Treasure (those items found within a geocache) can include nearly anything of value. Common items are books, toys, tools, games, camping gear, trackable items (more on these in Chapter 8), and sometimes even cash. Successful seekers take something, leave something else, and then sign the cache's logbook. As much fun as it is to find treasure, many geocachers find that the reward is more in the challenge and adventure of locating the geocache and the great locations they get to visit along the way.

What's the point, you may ask? Doesn't GPS take you to the exact location? Yes and no. Actually finding a location in the outdoors is often more difficult than it sounds. Going to a geocache's coordinates will take you to the approximate location, but not exactly, due to the system's inaccuracy. A modern GPS receiver is accurate to about 3 meters, or 10 feet, under optimal conditions. However, in thinking about accuracy, you must also consider the overhead conditions, satellite reception, and the receiver of the person who hid the geocache. How accurate was the other device and were there conditions that could further impact accuracy, such as weather or tree cover? The bottom line is that you may have more area to cover than you originally anticipate; even under the best of conditions you can expect to search an area about 30 feet across—and there can be a lot of rocks, trees, and benches to look around.

Geocaching.com provides you with the coordinates of the geocache, but not how to get there. The person who hid the first geocache of record, David Ulmer, reminds us that there are 360 ways to get to any one location. Roads on a map may not be accessible, and a map may not show the difficulty of the terrain.

After a geocache has been found (or not), seekers go online to post feedback, or logs, describing their geocaching experiences. These postings are fun to read, often provide clues for other geocachers, and are a way to document adventures. When logging a cache you should be careful not to post spoilers by giving too much information and making it too easy for the next person, such as saying, "We couldn't find it until we looked on the south side of the big tree!"

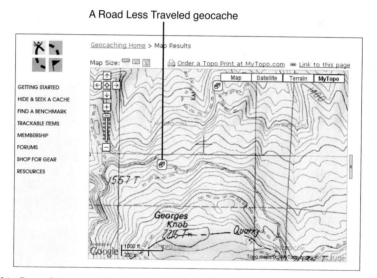

This Geocaching map shows a geocache located near a dashed line representing an unimproved road.

(Geocaching.com)

The map in the previous image is an example of the maps available from the Geocaching.com website. This map shows the "A Road Less Traveled" geocache (GCMXBR) placed in Oregon by a geocacher who uses the name "Odder." Finding this cache requires off-road driving or hiking to get to this remote location.

As geocaching has grown, certain standards and guidelines have come into place to protect players and the environment, while still allowing a lot of creativity on the part of geocache placers. The game is quickly making its way into the mainstream of outdoor activities with many outdoor groups and even tourism bureaus using geo-caching as a fun way to get people outside and exploring the world around them.

How It All Got Started

Geocaching is a product of the new millennium. With the limited accuracy of available GPS signals prior to 2000, geocaching would have been much too difficult. At that time a GPS receiver would get you within 300 feet or so of the cache and then you'd have to spend a lot of time searching a really broad area. After the removal of *selective availability* (SA) in 2000, the resulting increase in accuracy combined with some creative thinking on the part of some individuals led to the beginning of geocaching.

GEO-LINGO

Selective availability (SA) was an intentional error in GPS technology. When turned on, accuracy of GPS was only around 300 feet. It would be like trying to find and catch a hopping "You are here" sign in an area the size of a football field. Today's receiver accuracy typically ranges from 10 to 30 feet, producing a much smaller search area.

GPS Users Get an Instant Upgrade

On May 2, 2000, at approximately midnight, eastern daylight saving time, the system controlling selective availability was changed. The 24 satellites that made up the constellation at that time processed their new orders, and instantly the accuracy of GPS technology improved tenfold. Tens of thousands of GPS receivers around the world had a free instant upgrade.

The announcement a day before came as a welcome surprise to everyone who worked with GPS technology. The government had planned to remove selective availability—but had until 2006 to do so.

Now, said the White House, anyone could "precisely pinpoint their location or the location of items left behind for later recovery." How right they were.

The Original "Stash"

For GPS enthusiasts, the removal of selective availability was a cause for celebration. Internet newsgroups suddenly teemed with ideas about how the technology could be used.

Dave Ulmer, a computer consultant, wanted to test this accuracy by hiding a navigational target in the woods. He called his idea the "Great American GPS Stash Hunt" and posted it on an Internet GPS users' group. The idea was simple: Hide a container out in the woods and note the coordinates with a GPS unit. The finder would then have to locate the container with only the use of his GPS receiver. The rules for the finder were simple: "Take some stuff, leave some stuff."

On May 3, 2000, Ulmer placed his own container, a black bucket, in the woods near Beaver Creek, Oregon. Along with a logbook and pencil, he left various prize items including videos, books, software, a slingshot, and the now infamous, "original can of beans." He shared the location of his "stash" with a users' group in the online community:

N 45 17.460°   Latitude   W 122 24.800° Longitude

Within three days, the bucket had been found by two different individuals. The first was Mike Teague, who read about the stash on the Internet, used his GPS receiver to find the container, and shared his experience online, thereby garnering what may be the most coveted FTF (First to Find) in geocaching history. Throughout the next week, others excited by the prospect of hiding and finding stashes began hiding their own containers and posting coordinates. Like many new and innovative ideas on the Internet, the concept spread quickly—but this one required actually leaving your computer to participate.

Members of the geocaching community placed a plaque at the site of the Original Stash. Many players make pilgrimages to visit this location, which legend says will make them better geocachers.

(Brad and Liam Simmons)

EUREKA!

Due to the global nature of geocaching, there are various pronunciations of the term. However, the most common pronunciation is jee-oh-kash-ing, like riding in a Jeep and cashing a check.

Within the first month, Mike Teague, the first person to find Ulmer's stash, began gathering the online posts of coordinates around the world and documenting them on his personal web page. The GPS Stash Hunt mailing list was created to discuss this emerging activity. Names were even tossed about to replace the name "stash" due to the negative connotations associated with that name. One such name was "geocaching."

The Origins of "Geocaching"

Geocaching, first coined by Matt Stum on the GPS Stash Hunt mailing list on May 30, 2000, was the joining of two familiar words. The prefix, *geo*, for Earth, was used to describe the global nature of the activity, but also for its use in familiar topics in GPS such as geography.

Caching, from the word *cache*, has two different uses, which makes it very appropriate for the activity. A French word invented in 1797, the original definition referred to a hiding place someone would use to temporarily store items. The word *cache* stirs up visions of pioneers, gold miners, and even pirates. Today the word is still used to describe hidden supplies left along the way for deep wilderness hiking.

The second use of *cache* has more recently been used in technology. *Memory cache* is computer storage that is used to quickly retrieve frequently used information. Your web browser, for example, stores images on disk so you don't have to retrieve the same image every time you visit similar pages.

The combination of Earth, hiding, and technology made *geocaching* an excellent term for the activity. However, the GPS Stash Hunt was the original and most widely used term until Mike Teague passed the torch to Jeremy Irish in September 2000.

The Birth of Geocaching.com

For the first few months, geocaching was confined to existing, experienced GPS users who already used the technology for outdoor activities such as backpacking and boating. Most participants had an existing knowledge of GPS and a firm grasp of obscure lingo such as "datums" and "WGS84." Due to both the experienced player base and the newness of the activity, new players had a steep learning curve before going out on their first cache hunt. Tools were scarce for determining whether a cache was nearby, if one existed at all.

As with most participants, Jeremy Irish, a web developer for a Seattle company, stumbled upon Mike Teague's website in July while doing research on GPS technology. The idea of treasure hunting and using tech gadgets represented the marriage of two of his biggest interests. Discovering that one was hidden nearby, Irish purchased his first GPS unit and went on his first hunt the following weekend.

After experiencing the thrill of finding his first geocache, Irish decided to start a hobby site for the activity. Adopting the term "geo-caching," he created Geocaching.com and applied his professional web skills to create tools to improve the cache-hunting experience. The cache listings were still added by hand, but a database helped to standardize the listings, and features such as searching for caches around zip codes made it easier for new players to find listings for nearby caches.

With Mike Teague's valuable input, the new site was completed and announced to the stash-hunting community on September 2, 2000. At the time the site was launched, there were 75 known geocaches in the world. From these humble beginnings Groundspeak, the company formed to manage Geocaching.com, has grown to become the worldwide leader in GPS and location-based gaming. Groundspeak employees, know as "lackeys," serve as stewards for the activity, not only making the website better and easier to use, but working with the existing geocaching community and land managers to expand the game in a responsible manner. The game has grown so much in the last 12 years that today, there are nearly as many lackeys working to make the game better as there were geocaches worldwide when the site was started!

The Groundspeak "Lackeys" outside the Lily Pad in Seattle.
(Annie Love for Geocaching.com)

If You Hide It, They Will Come

Slashdot, a popular online magazine for techies, reported the new activity on September 25, 2000, introducing a larger group of technology professionals to the activity. *The New York Times* picked up the story and featured it in its "Circuits" section in October, starting a domino effect of articles written in magazines, newspapers, and other media outlets around the world. CNN even did a segment in December to profile the new hobby.

EUREKA!

Growth was slow in the early days of the game and it took nearly a year for Geocaching to spread to all 50 states. "SD #1" was hidden on March 3, 2001, in South Dakota, the last state in the United States to get a hidden geocache. Growth picked up steadily and by October 29, 2002, there were caches on all 7 continents. The last continent to get a cache was Antarctica.

However, because there were so few geocaches in the world, many would-be participants discovered they didn't have a cache listed nearby. Many wondered whether anyone would bother looking for a cache if they hid one in the area. The growing community chanted the mantra "If you hide it, they will come" to the newer players. After some reassurances, pioneers of the hobby started placing caches just to see whether people would go find them. They did.

Through word of mouth, press articles, and even accidental cache discoveries, more and more people have become involved in geocaching. First started by technology and GPS enthusiasts, the ranks of geocachers now include couples, families, and groups from all walks of life. The excitement of the hunt appeals to both the inner and outer child. Today you can do a search on just about anywhere in the world and be able to walk, bike, or drive to a nearby hidden cache.

Since Geocaching.com's creation, geocaching has doubled in participants approximately every year. When the website was launched, the pioneers of the game probably never imagined what an international phenomenon geocaching would become. The rest, as they say, is history.

Timing Is Everything

Sometimes, multiple factors have to come together in just the right way at just the right time for a new phenomenon to be created. How else could we explain the immediate popularity of geocaching? If you think about it, it all makes sense. Our traditional sports were created around 100 years ago in a low-tech, agricultural, and industrial age. Now, children grow up playing video games and operating computers. Most of the population utilizes technology for work, entertainment, and convenience.

As children, we grow up with a sense of adventure in finding something. From our earliest memories, we recall hunting Easter eggs and hearing stories of pirate's treasure. We enjoy games like hide-and-seek and capture-the-flag. We are lucky enough to live in a unique time when we experience technology that quickly develops from an obscure concept to a daily necessity. Consider the last 20 years, with the rise of personal computers, cell phones, GPS, and the Internet.

We can only imagine what's next, and we often wonder how we got by without this gadgetry before.

But along with the rise of technology, we have witnessed the rise of various extreme sports. Adrenaline junkies push themselves to the limits of their abilities and common sense for bragging rights. That is why the time is so right for a game like geocaching. We get to utilize the latest technological advancements in navigation and the web, and challenge our minds, bodies, and spirits with the childlike excitement of uncovering hidden treasures.

Is Geocaching a Hobby, Game, or Sport?

Geocaching can be played anytime, as often as you like. You can do it by yourself or with friends and family. After you get the hang of using GPS and finding caches, you'll enjoy sharing your adventures with fellow geocachers on the web, or better yet, in person. Geocaching events are held throughout the world and are a way in which people can get together to discuss geocaching.

Variety Is the Spice of Geocaching

Because this game is so innovative and continues to evolve, you cannot expect it to be a one-cache-fits-all kind of game. You need to be aware of a number of different kinds of geocaches before selecting one to find for yourself. Common geocache types include …

- **Traditional Cache.** This is the original cache type consisting of, at a bare minimum, a container and a logbook. Normally you'll find a Tupperware™ container, ammo box, or covered bucket filled with goodies. A smaller container (known as a "micro cache") is too small to contain items except for a logbook and usually requires you to bring your own pen. The coordinates listed on the traditional cache page are the exact location for the cache.

- **Multi-Cache.** A multi-cache involves two or more locations, with the final location being a physical container. There are many variations, but most multi-caches have a hint to find the second cache, and the second cache has hints to the third, and so on.

- **Mystery or Puzzle Cache.** The catchall of cache types, this form of cache can involve complicated puzzles you first need to solve to determine the coordinates. Due to the increasing creativity of geocaching, this becomes the staging ground for new and unique geocaches.

- **Letterbox Hybrid.** A letterbox is another form of treasure hunting using clues instead of coordinates. In some cases, however, a letterbox has coordinates, and the owner has made it a letterbox *and* a geocache.

- **EarthCache.** An EarthCache is a special place that people can visit to learn about a unique geoscience feature or aspect of our Earth. EarthCaches include a set of educational notes and the details about where to find the location. Visitors to EarthCaches can see how our planet has been shaped by geological processes, how we manage the resources, and how scientists gather evidence to learn about the Earth. The Geological Society of America (GSA) helps to administer the listing of EarthCache sites around the world on Geocaching.com.

As geocaching matures as an activity, new variations of geocaches continue to be created. At the same time, some cache types are no longer being developed but are still available to be found. These include virtual caches, where the goal is to find a location rather than a container, and webcam caches that use existing web cameras around the world to log a visit. These types of caches helped spur the development of new activities such as Geocaching Challenges, Waymarking, and Wherigo, which are discussed in Chapter 18.

The Geocaching Community

People who play this game—whether alone, with a family, or in a group—consider themselves part of the community. The geocaching community extends from a local bunch of friends and families to the wider group of geocachers across the country and around the world. Organizations and groups have sprung up everywhere. You most likely have a group nearby, or at least in your state. These groups often have elaborate websites, and the members get together frequently for all kinds of events.

The community is made up of adventurers from all walks of life, races, ages, and sexes, loosely bound to each other by their common interest: to enjoy and promote an activity they love so much. What that means to you is that no matter where you travel, if you are a geocacher, you can always make a new friend and have a geocache or two to find.

This is a player-driven and self-regulated activity in which participants take pride in its positive reputation. It is important to always obtain permission from the landowner or managing agency prior to placing your geocache. Also, never place a cache in any area that would be considered a potential environmental hazard, such as in a bed of flowers or rare plants. Caches that are hidden in potentially environment-damaging areas might tarnish the excellent reputation geocachers enjoy and make it more difficult for geocachers to work with park agencies and officials to obtain permission for future cache placements.

It is also important to remember this is a family activity, so nothing should be placed that is considered harmful, illegal, or in bad taste. Geocaching.com will not knowingly post caches that are in inappropriate areas or are filled with illegal or hazardous contents.

The Geocacher's Creed

The Geocacher's Creed was created by the geocaching community without direction from Geocaching.com and is designed to help orient new players to the ethos of the geocaching community and to guide experienced players in questionable situations, so that everyone can enjoy geocaching.

The Geocacher's Creed

When placing or seeking geocaches, I will:

1. Not endanger myself or others.

2. Observe all laws and rules of the area.

3. Respect property rights and seek permission where appropriate.

4. Avoid causing disruptions or public alarm.

5. Minimize my and others' impact on the environment.

6. Be considerate of others.

7. Protect the integrity of the game pieces.

For more information and detailed examples of these points please visit www.geocreed.info.

The Least You Need to Know

- Geocaching involves finding someone else's hidden treasure using a GPS receiver and your detective skills.
- Geocaching has only been around since 2000, but millions of geocaches have been hidden all around the world since that time.
- Geocaching is a great activity to get you outdoors, anytime, anywhere.
- Geocaching is fun for the whole family and can be played on a budget.
- Geocachers make up a community of participants from around the world.

The Basics of the Game

In This Chapter

- Grasp the fundamentals of the game
- Learn the lingo
- Find out where the game is played
- Grab the gear you really need

In this chapter, you'll learn the basics of the game and a little about how to speak the language. We'll familiarize you with website features to get you started with your first geocache adventure. We'll cover the environments you may encounter while searching for caches and how to prepare for a successful outdoor trip. Did you know that geocachers even have their own designated radio frequencies? Read on, you are getting closer to hitting the trail!

Getting Started

One of the great things about geocaching is it can be as simple or as complicated as you make it. If you're just interested in getting outside with your GPS or smartphone then you will have a great time. If you're heavily into technology and mapping then there are many resources you can easily employ to make the game what you want it to be. The guidelines that direct the game are written to maximize flexibility and fun for everyone.

The basics of the game are simple: The participants select a cache on Geocaching.com, download or enter the coordinates into a GPS receiver, and then it is up to the players to use their navigational and detective skills to seek out the hidden container.

This is all possible with help from above. Orbiting GPS satellites broadcast coded signals right to your receiver, which uses the signals from at least three satellites at a time to calculate its general location through a process called trilateration. Once the receiver knows its position, the receiver can calculate your speed, *bearing*, distance traveled, distance to your destination, and more. The more satellite signals the receiver reads, the more accurate the position it reports to you.

GEO-LINGO

A **bearing** (also known as azimuth) is a compass degree to be followed to find your target. When we go after a geocache, our GPS receiver provides a bearing as one of a compass's 360 degrees.

For example, the receiver might read "Distance: 2.8 miles, Bearing: 185°." But just knowing where the cache is located on the planet is only half the battle. It may sound easy, but as you will discover it often takes more work than you think. Not only might you have to navigate uncharted terrain, but when you reach the location it may take some serious searching, depending on the accuracy of the GPS receiver (both yours and the hider's) and the craftiness of the hide. With a little perseverance, though, you can find your first geocache—but once you find the box, what should you do?

Take Something

Congratulations! You've discovered your first geocache. Now what? Well, let's crack it open and see what you have found.

After pulling off the watertight lid, we find a bunch of items, or *SWAG*, stored in resealable bags. Items are stored in plastic bags to keep them clean, organized, and dry. Let's see: a logbook, a stress ball, a barrel of monkeys, a couple of silver dollars, and a "Best of the '80s" CD. You worked hard to find the geocache, now choose your reward.

GEO-LINGO

SWAG stands for "stuff we all get." It includes the trade items left in caches by geocachers.

Leave Something

If you do take something, be sure to replace the item with something else for the next lucky visitor to discover. The treasure can be almost anything you might feel is valuable, and be sure to "trade up" by replacing the item you found with something of equal or greater value. Because you planned ahead, you assembled your own swag in a plastic bag to leave behind. Placing a cool key chain that includes a compass, a minilight, and a carabiner in the cache, you leave a true treasure for the next person to find.

Sign the Logbook

The geocache logbook is the physical record of your visit. Be sure to sign the log with your name, the date of your visit, and the items you took and left. It's there to record not only your presence, but your experiences as well. Feel free to include details about your adventure, such as the weather and any interesting sights along the way. When the logbook gets full and the geocache owner swaps it out for a new one, he will have a souvenir of his own efforts for hiding the cache.

Sometimes the owner will provide a disposable camera. Take a picture of yourself and your group. The cache's owner will enjoy seeing who showed up at the cache. Who knows? Maybe your picture will be posted on a website and seen by people all over the world!

Cache In Trash Out

On your way back home, don't forget to give back to the outdoors and leave the area a little cleaner than you found it. *"Cache In Trash Out"* (CITO) is an ongoing environmental initiative adopted by geocachers to encourage good outdoor civic responsibility.

GEO-LINGO

Cache In Trash Out (CITO) is an ongoing environmental initiative supported by the worldwide geocaching community. Since 2002, geocachers have been dedicated to cleaning up parks and other cache-friendly places around the world.

While out geocaching, carry a trash bag to hold whatever trash you find along the trail. Doing so not only sets a good example for other hikers, it also improves the natural beauty of the area. Many cachers include "CITO kits," small containers filled with empty trash bags, as swag in their caches.

Share Your Experience Online

Now that you have signed the physical logbook, you also have an opportunity to share your experience with others online. You can wait until you get back to your computer or log your visit from the location using the Geocaching smartphone application. Either way, be sure to return to the cache page on Geocaching.com to post a log entry for the geocache listing. Your log not only informs the cache owner of your find, but it also lets you record the details of your adventure for yourself and the online geocaching community. We will talk about this more in Chapter 4.

The online log is also a great opportunity to thank the cache owner for taking the time and effort to place the geocache and to let him know how much you enjoyed the experience. Of course, this is also a good time to inform the owner of any issues with the placement. Is there construction going on in the area? Have wasps built a nest nearby? Is there a leak in the container? Is the logbook full and in need of replacement? Any feedback that can help update the geocache owner on the cache's status is always welcome.

Posting Photos

Posting photos to your log is a great way to share your geocaching adventures with the rest of the community. Just be careful to avoid giving away too much information in the pictures so others have the same challenge that you enjoyed in locating the cache.

Geocachers enjoy viewing the galleries of cache listings, often learning stories of participants from all over the world. Plus, uploading photos creates a gallery on your profile of all of your adventures that you can enjoy viewing for years to come.

EUREKA!

When writing your online log it's good to remember "The Four T's":

- **Trip:** Tell a little about your adventure, such as what you saw and what the day was like.
- **Traps:** Share any difficulties you encountered that might be important to pass on to other geocachers.
- **Trades:** Write about the SWAG you took and left. Were there any Trackable items in the geocache?
- **Thanks:** Just like your mom taught you—say "thanks" to the geocache owner for the experience!

Learn the Language

Over the years, geocaching has developed its own set of terms, slang, and abbreviations. If you play the game for any length of time, terms like "muggle" and "FTF" will become a natural part of your vocabulary.

You can check out the Glossary in Appendix B for a more complete list of caching and navigational terms, but here is a quick rundown of the most common geocaching slang you may find on a cache page or in a log:

- **BYOP.** An acronym for "bring your own pen/pencil," which is often used by cache owners to communicate to other geocachers that you will need to bring your writing utensil in order to sign the cache logbook.

- **FTF.** The first person to log a particular geocache as found is the "first to find." Sometimes there is an FTF prize left in the cache by the owner for this person. These special items can be as simple as a cash prize, an FTF certificate, or an elaborate collectible souvenir reflecting the theme of the cache. An FTF prize is a reward for being the first to locate the cache and does not require equal trade.

- **Geocoin.** A custom-minted coin stamped with "Track at Geocaching.com" and a unique serial number. Its travels can be followed through Geocaching.com. We will talk more about geocoins in Chapter 8.

- **Muggle.** A nongeocacher—someone who is not in on the big secret that there are treasures hidden all around them; based on the term "Muggle" from the *Harry Potter* series, for a nonmagical person.

- **Spoiler.** Information in a geocache log that gives away too many details of a cache location, spoiling the experience for the next geocachers who want to find it. Also used to describe a person who gives away details to other geocachers.

- **SWAG.** Stands for "stuff we all get." It includes the trade items left in caches by geocachers.

- **TFTC.** Geocaching shorthand for "thanks for the cache."

- **TNLN.** Stands for "took nothing left nothing." Usually written in cache logbooks by geocachers who do not trade for material contents in a cache.

- **Travel Bug.** A trackable tag that you attach to an item. The item becomes a hitchhiker that is carried from cache to cache (or person to person) in the real world. You can follow its progress online at Geocaching.com. You will find more info on travel bugs in Chapter 8.

- **Waypoint.** A reference point for a physical location defined by a set of latitude and longitude coordinates. These can be saved, stored, and recalled from a GPS receiver's memory. Cache locations are saved as waypoints.

Log On Before Heading Out

Now you know the basics of how the game is played, and you even know a little of the language, but before you head outdoors you need to go online and find a cache in your area.

Geocaching.com is the original and primary site for all geocachers worldwide. The website includes a great deal of information on how to get started and how to search for caches, and explanations about what GPS is and how it works. Geocaching.com also has chat forums, videos and downloadable resources. Surfing around the website is a great way to get up to speed on the activity.

From the website, you can find links to regional groups and organizations for nearly every U.S. state and even some countries. Many of these groups have websites full of informative local information. Many groups sponsor events, camping trips, pizza nights, and tournaments that make it easy to get involved and keep in touch with fellow geocachers in your area.

Trinkets Can Be Treasures

There are many rewards when geocaching, and everyone has their own personal favorites. Some thrive on the adventure and excitement of discovery. Others enjoy arriving at a destination they wouldn't have otherwise visited. But many, especially kids, are in it for the treasure.

You're not going to get rich from this treasure, but you're bound to find some unique items along the way. Caches are filled with just about anything that someone might find valuable, whether you think so or not! From dollar store finds to handmade items, a cornucopia of unusual treasure is waiting to be found.

For your own personal trade items, use your imagination and have fun. Consider the items you leave as a reflection of yourself. Items don't need to be expensive but will hopefully delight the next finder.

Geocacher Signature Items

The Lone Ranger had his silver bullets, Arthur Dent had his towel, and—in the same vein—geocachers have *signature items*.

GEO-LINGO

A **signature item** is a trademark object used as a geocacher's personalized calling card. These are often custom cards, tags, stickers, or geocoins bearing the geocacher's name and often a favorite phrase or graphic to sum up the geocacher's philosophy.

Signature items grew out of a desire to leave more than just a name in the logbook—to provide something tangible and personal for other geocachers. A signature item might be nothing more than a personalized business card with the geocacher's contact information. Sometimes they are an elaborate homemade item that shows off amazing creativity, or even a professionally minted geocoin.

Many of these signature items become collector items for other geocachers. For a diehard geocacher, finding a foreign geocacher's geocoin in a cache can sometimes feel like owning a Babe Ruth rookie card.

If you want to create your own signature item, think of something that reflects your own interests. Think of your own brand. If you're into snowboarding, you could design a stamp with a snowboarder and your username. If you study spiders, create a spider out of wire and attach it to a piece of cardboard with your username. You don't have to spend a lot of money to create a unique item to leave in caches. And other geocachers can get to know you by the items you leave for them.

Prohibited Geocache Items

Geocachers do their best to self-regulate their sport to keep the activity in a positive light. However, as with any activity, there can always be the occasional bad egg. Because this is a family activity, not only should we obey the local laws, we also need to apply common sense to the items placed in a cache. Some items that may seem harmless can be inappropriate cache items. The following are examples of inappropriate cache items:

- Ammunition, fireworks, explosives, lighters, and weapons (including pocket knives and multi-tools).

- Alcohol, drugs, and drug paraphernalia

- Food, candy, or highly scented items such as candles

- Suggestive or illicit materials

Food? We list food because animals can find food even faster than the best geocachers. Animals have been known to chew through caches to get to food and other items that smell strongly, including wrapped candy, candles, and lip balm.

Additional considerations when leaving items in a geocache are weather and seasonal changes. Liquid bubbles might seem like a great idea in the summer, but in winter they can freeze and break their bottles. Crayons might seem great in the winter, but during the summer they can liquefy in a hot ammo can and ruin the contents of the cache.

Where Are Geocaches Hidden?

Geocaches can be found almost anywhere, from remote mountain peaks, to city parks, to dense urban jungles. This is the beauty of the game: It can be played anywhere. You can discover caches in a park next to your neighborhood, in another city while on vacation, or in exotic locations requiring a passport. There are advantages to caching in these different environments.

Wide-Open Spaces

What makes geocaching truly special is that it can take you to beautiful, picturesque areas you might never seek out otherwise. We all enjoy a scenic drive in the country, but how often do we push ourselves to climb up and over that next ridge? Geocaching might involve a trip to a waterfall just off the beaten path, rock climbing, or a multiday hike. It is also not uncommon to hear, "Wow, this place is great, I never knew it existed!" Enjoy the discovery of new places and try to return to share the location with your loved ones.

Physical caches need to be kept at least 0.1 miles (528 feet or 161 meters) away from any other geocache to make sure an area doesn't get oversaturated.

Parks

Okay, so you don't always have time to take a day or two off work and pack up all your gear to venture off into the great unknown. In our fast-paced lives, parks are great places to take a breather and relax with the family or fun places to picnic and play with the kids on the playground. They are close to home and easily accessible. Because neighborhood green spaces are not far, even an hour spent in one feels like a rewarding outing. What's even better is that many of these areas include a cache or two. Park caches are typically easy to find, allowing kids of all ages to help take part in the search. These types of areas also enable people to go geocaching on their lunch hours!

NAVIGATIONAL NUGGETS

Outdoor navigation and travel is much easier if you are organized. Keep all of your essential gear in a "geobag" or pack. This saves time, helps to ensure you will not forget anything and, best of all, you are always ready for a geocaching adventure. Read on to find a checklist to help you pack your own geobag.

CurmudgeonlyGal reaches in for the find.
(Michelle Davison)

Cities and Suburbs

A good percentage of our world is made up of concrete and steel. Skyscrapers replace mountains, and wildlife tends to be of the two-legged variety. Don't let that stop you from taking part in geocaching adventures. Geocaches are hidden in all parts of cities. Smaller cache containers are often used to make them easier to hide. Statues and landmarks may also serve as clues in caches with several stages, called multi-caches. Remember: Do not let your location discourage you. Caches can be found nearly anywhere you may live or go.

Packing Your GeoBag

The best way to make sure you have everything you need for your geocaching adventure is to pack your geobag. You may have your GPS receiver ready, but a bit of planning and packing before hitting the trail will pay off in the long run.

Being prepared with all the right gear can help get you where you want to be.
(Brian Sniatkowski)

We recommend setting up a waist pack, small day-pack, or many-pocketed-vest with all the basics neatly organized and always ready to go. This way, when the phone rings and it's time to go play, you don't have to search the house, garage, and car for all of your stuff.

Here is the basic list of gear to take with you:

- **Batteries.** Bring plenty of extra batteries. Not only are they necessary food for your GPS receiver, they are also good to have for your flashlight or camera.

- **Compass.** Get one with a dial-in declination adjustment.

- **Extra clothing.** It is always wise to pack a change of clothes in case you get wet or dirty. You can also use these items to layer if the weather turns cool.

- **Flashlight.** It can get dark when venturing into the unknown.

- **First-aid kit.** It is always best to be prepared in the case of an accident. Don't forget to include items to deal with minor issues such as blisters or splinters.

- **Geocache repair kit.** It's always good to bring some items to help repair caches you find on your trip. Extra pens, log-books, sealable plastic bags, and duct tape are good to repair leaks, protect contents, and replace missing items.

- **GPS receiver or smartphone.** Don't forget the power cord so you can use it in the vehicle on the way there.

- **Knife.** Most outdoor enthusiasts agree that having a small sharp knife helps in many situations.

- **Maps.** Bring general maps of the roadways to get there, and a more detailed topographic map of the area. Waterproof map cases with marking pens are also helpful.

- **Matches.** We suggest that you carry waterproof matches and a striker, in case you become lost and it is necessary to light a fire.

- **Medications.** Be sure to pack any medications you may need if you end up spending more time on the trail than you originally planned.

- **Notepad and pen.** Keep them in a watertight bag.

- **Signal mirror.** These inexpensive mirrors can be used to signal searchers if you become lost and they can also be handy for peering into small areas or behind items when searching for a geocache.

- **Sunglasses/sunscreen.** Protection from the elements is of great importance when hiking or geocaching.

- **Water.** Always be sure to pack plenty of water when hiking; dehydration is a major danger out on the trail and drinking from natural sources is unwise.

- **Whistle.** This will help you signal other hikers or searchers if you become lost or injured along the trail.

Longer Hunts Need More Gear

It is not so much survival of the fittest as it is survival of the smartest. If you are going anywhere off the beaten path, there is always a chance of getting lost or injured, being caught in a storm, or, for whatever reason, getting stranded. Even on short hikes we recommend you bring the "ten hiking essentials." These are the ten most important pieces of gear that are the basis from which most outdoor enthusiasts begin when choosing what they need for their basic pack. Several companies even offer special compartments in their backpacks to hold these ten items:

1. Water

2. Map and compass

3. Flashlight/batteries/bulb

4. Knife/multitool

5. First-aid kit

6. Extra clothing

7. Matches/fire starter

8. Sunscreen/sunglasses

9. Signal mirror

10. Whistle

NAVIGATIONAL NUGGETS

If you do remote wilderness travel, consider using a personal locator beacon (PLB). Now available in the United States, these transmitters broadcast a satellite-based emergency beacon to allow rescuers to find your exact location anywhere in the world.

Be sure to pack your special medications such as insulin for diabetics or prescription eyewear. In any outdoor situation, the best food and water is what you bring with you. Take a little extra of both: if a hiking partner forgets his you can always share, and you are covered in the event you extend your stay a little longer than expected.

Be sure to tell someone where you are going. In your car, leave a printed copy of the geocache's information page, including the coordinates, or write this information on a travel itinerary—you can find one in Appendix F. Taking the time to do so will pay off well if you have a problem. By taking these precautions, search and rescue crews can provide assistance within hours instead of days.

Gear Checklist for Overnight Trips

Let's take a look at some of the things you might need if you are taking a longer trip. When hiking on longer trips, such as overnight excursions, it is important to make sure that you have all the gear you need to survive in the wild, in relative comfort. By creating a checklist and using it to pack your gear, you can hike comfortably in the knowledge that you have the right tools for the job, no matter what happens. Of course, no checklist is perfect for every situation, so you may want to edit this list to fit conditions in your area, but this example checklist will get you started off on the right foot.

- ❏ Batteries
- ❏ Binoculars
- ❏ Boots and socks
- ❏ Camera
- ❏ Cash/credit cards
- ❏ Cell phone, 2-way or CB radio
- ❏ Clothing, two sets minimum
- ❏ Compass
- ❏ Cooking kit, utensils, and food
- ❏ Dog stuff, including food (if traveling with your furry friend)
- ❏ Emergency blanket
- ❏ Energy bars
- ❏ First-aid/snakebite kit
- ❏ Flashlights
- ❏ Glasses, contacts
- ❏ Gloves
- ❏ GPS or smartphone and accessories
- ❏ Hat
- ❏ Insect repellent
- ❏ Jackets
- ❏ Licenses, hiking permits
- ❏ Lighter or waterproof matches
- ❏ Knife
- ❏ Maps, general and topographic
- ❏ Medications
- ❏ Notepad and pencil
- ❏ Rope
- ❏ Signal mirror and whistle
- ❏ Sleeping bag
- ❏ Stove and fuel
- ❏ Sun block, lip balm
- ❏ Sunglasses
- ❏ Tent or shelter
- ❏ Toiletries
- ❏ Water

DEAD BATTERIES

Hypothermia is one of the biggest threats to outdoor enthusiasts, even in warm climates. It is easy to get caught in a storm, and improper clothing can result in getting soaked through, resulting in the rapid loss of body heat. Most cases of hypothermia occur between 30° and 50° Fahrenheit. Keeping dry will go a long way to improve your comfort and survivability, so pack appropriately.

Dress for Success

It is said that there is no bad weather, only inappropriate gear. Just as with packing gear and supplies, having extra clothing is better than not enough. In hot or cold climates, it is typically best to cover up with long-sleeve shirts and pants. This protects the skin from scratches, insect bites, and sunburn. Wear clothing and a jacket that will shed water; your apparel should be made of fabrics that wick moisture away from your body. Also, wear layers you can remove to prevent overheating. Cotton clothing, such as T-shirts and jeans, absorb water and perspiration, sometimes taking days to dry. If you get wet and cold, it is difficult to regain heat, which increases the risk of hypothermia.

Don't forget a hat! Wide-brimmed boonie-style hats work great. They provide good cover from the rain and sun. Baseball caps leave the back of your neck exposed. Also, wear a good pair of boots that provide ankle support, and keep an extra pair of socks in your gear bag. Is all of this really important? Not if you're visiting a park for an hour or two, but it is in any wilderness environment. We want you to enjoy your outdoor geocaching experience, not be miserable because you're unprepared.

Geocacher Communication

Can you hear me now? If not, try the right frequency. Yes, geocachers use their own radio frequencies on the FRS (Family Radio Service) band in North America and the PMR (Private Mobile Radio) band in Europe. These bands are used with walkie-talkies, which are reasonably inexpensive and do not require a license to operate. The range is limited, however, often to a mile or less depending upon the terrain. On FRS, the geocaching community uses channel 2 with channel 12 as an alternative. On the PMR band, use channel 2 with channel 8 as the alternative. And for those who are into ham radio, the standard geocaching frequency is 147.555.

In our modern world, we often rely on our telephones to keep in touch, and that is a great option, but what do you do when there is no cell coverage? DeLorme offers their inReach technology that can send preselected text messages using satellite communication, or when paired with their PN-60w GPS unit can send two-way texts from anywhere in the world.

The DeLorme PN-60w and inReach 2-way satellite communicator.
(Image used courtesy of DeLorme Inc. or its affiliates. Copyright DeLorme, Inc. or its affiliates.)

The Least You Need to Know

- When you find a geocache, take something, leave something, and sign the logbook. Don't forget to share your experience online.
- Visit Geocaching.com to find geocache listings in your area.
- Geocaches are hidden in all types of outdoor environments.
- The probability of a successful outdoor experience greatly increases with the right gear and clothing.

Time to Get Out and Play

You've got a basic understanding of how to go out and find a geocache. Now it's time to go out and explore everything geocaching has to offer. You might be surprised to learn that there's more to it than just hiking in the woods: city dwellers can even geocache without leaving sight of an espresso shop! In this part, you learn about the many geocaching variations. Maybe you'll come up with one of your own!

Are you excited at the thought of finding your first geocache? Great! In Part 2, you learn how to find geocaches online before finding them outdoors. We cover everything you need to know to find even the toughest geocaches, and then we discuss how to hide your own. After that, we go over some potential hazards to avoid so that you can safely return from your geocaching adventures in one piece.

In Part 2, you also discover Travel Bugs, Geocoins, and other trackable geocaching items. These so-called Trackables represent their owners, often traveling from geocache to geocache accomplishing goals around the world.

Your Adventure Begins at Home

In This Chapter

- Learn how to search for geocaches
- Set up your own user profile
- What to consider before seeking a geocache
- Use maps and aerial photos to help you choose a geocache to search for

Now that you have learned some of the basics of the game, it's time to get you set up for your first geocaching adventure.

Before searching for a geocache outdoors, we first have to get online and identify a geocache to seek. In this chapter, you'll learn the many ways to select a geocache as well as how to get the maps and clues you need to ensure success. Do you use a personal digital assistant (PDA) or a "paperless caching" GPS receiver? We'll show you how to download lists of caches to take with you. You'll also learn about the maps, aerial photos, and other tools available to make your geocaching adventure the best it can be.

Creating Your Geocaching.com Account

As the official global headquarters for geocaching, Geocaching.com provides a great number of resources to support new geocachers. In an ongoing effort to support the worldwide geocaching community, the Geocaching.com site is also under constant development as new technology and user needs come into play. Spend some time cruising around the site and checking out the various features.

One of the first steps you can take to get involved in the geocaching community is to create your own account. This is your opportunity to provide your geocacher name, e-mail address, a photo or image, and other details you want to share with the community. This is also the opportunity to set your home coordinates, which you can then use to search for geocaches and events in your area. Other geocachers will be able to access your profile to learn a little more about you and what geocaches you may have found or hidden. With your new geocaching identity, you'll also be able to participate in the Geocaching.com discussion forums. And remember, you won't be able to see the coordinates for geocaches unless you are logged in to your Geocaching.com account. The best part is a user profile and basic membership on Geocaching.com is free.

Searching for Nearby Geocaches

Searching for nearby geocaches is easy. In fact, they are everywhere! You will be surprised to see the number of listings within 10 miles of where you live. The trick is to know how to select the interesting ones to find. Just head over to the search page at Geocaching.com and try one of these ways to search for the perfect cache to seek:

- **By address.** When you type in a street address the site will geocode the location and return a search based on the approximate latitude and longitude of that address.

- **By postal code.** Geocaches can be found by searching for postal codes in the United States, United Kingdom, Canada, or Australia. On the front page of Geocaching.com, simply type in a postal code and click Go. A list of caches will appear in order from the nearest to the farthest from the center of the postal code's region.

- **By state, province, or country.** Select a state, province, or country to search, and then a menu list of cities or states will appear to narrow your search.

- **By coordinates.** Search a radius around a set of latitude/ longitude coordinates.

- **By cache name.** Search for a geocache by its name. Don't worry if you can't recall the entire name as partial searches work, too.

- **By area code.** Search for U.S. listings based on the telephone area code of region.

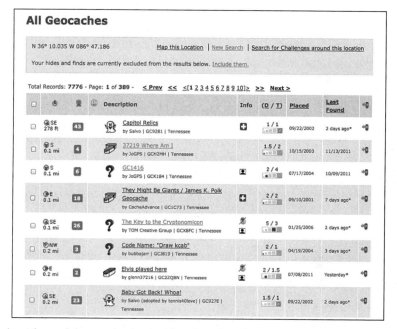

A quick search by postal code provides a long list of geocaches listed by the distance from the postal code's center.

(Geocaching.com)

- **By GC code.** When a cache is submitted for posting, the Geocaching.com website creates a unique code for the cache listing that begins with "GC" followed by letters and numbers, and is seven characters or less so it can fit in the waypoint title field on most GPS receivers. You can search by this code.

- **By username.** Search the database for fellow geocachers. Select a username and you can get a list of caches found or hidden by this person.

- **With geocaching maps.** Geocaching.com provides an amazing set of search tools on their maps. Simply enter an address or postal code on Geocaching.com and zoom in or out on the desired area. Switch from map view to satellite, and even check out the terrain and topography maps.

As you can see, there are many ways in which you can search for that perfect cache. All of these features make it easy to get a list of geocaches to find, no matter where you are.

Paperless Geocaching

Geocaching.com provides you with the abilities to download simple printer-friendly versions of cache pages that will save ink and Adobe PDF versions as well. The PDF version includes the ability to print out hints and the last five or ten logs for a little extra help on the search.

After a few geocaching outings, you'll likely want to switch to something less bulky than paper printouts. You will also soon discover how cumbersome it can be to enter a waypoint for every geocache you want to seek. Hand entering coordinates can sometimes result in accidental errors, perhaps causing your GPS receiver to show a geocache to be 100 feet to 100 miles from its actual location. Double-checking your coordinates before going out on a hunt helps, but fortunately there are alternatives to hand entering coordinates and carrying reams of cache listings along on your geocaching adventures. As the game has grown, so have the features for both enjoying a paper-free existence and downloading geocache waypoints directly to your GPS unit.

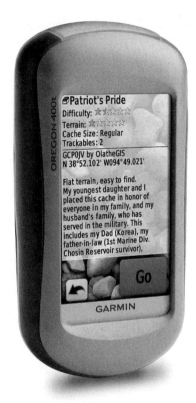

A geocache as it would appear on a Garmin Oregon.
(Image used courtesy of Garmin Ltd. or its affiliates. Copyright © Garmin Ltd. or its
affiliates.)

Downloading Coordinates

Transferring geocache coordinates from the Internet to your GPS
receiver is easier than you might think. You will need a data cable to
connect your GPS to your computer—in most modern units this is
a simple USB cable. If your GPS unit requires a specific cable, they
are available from many sources for most brands and models of GPS
receivers.

After you have a cable, you need to get a file of caches you want
to download to your GPS unit. Geocaching.com gives you several
options for how to do this. On the page of results, there is a check

box to the right of every cache listing. Select the caches you want to download to your GPS by checking the box next to each listing, and then click the Download Waypoints button at the bottom of the page.

If you haven't already agreed to the data license agreement, you will be redirected to another page, where you can do that. Otherwise your browser will prompt you to save a file named geocaching.loc to your computer. The LOC file format contains a list of coordinates for each selected cache, a web link for the location of each cache description, the names of the caches, and the waypoint names to be downloaded into your GPS unit.

Now that you have your waypoint file, you need a software application to open the file and upload the waypoint information to your GPS receiver. Fortunately, many GPS applications support the LOC file format. A list is always available at www.geocaching.com/waypoints.

The software application will ask you to choose your GPS receiver before uploading your cache list, because different units have distinct ways of downloading information. Now all you need to do is send the waypoints to your GPS receiver.

Coordinates on your receiver show each geocache with a name that starts with GC—this is known as the "GC code," which identifies the cache. You can use the GC code to look up the details about each geocache on the Geocaching.com website. If you prefer, you can change the name of each cache to something more descriptive before uploading it to your unit.

In addition to these features, if you have opted to become a premium member of Geocaching.com, you will also find the option to download individual geocaching.gpx files on each cache page. In addition, if you have a DeLorme, Garmin, or Magellan GPS, there is an optional plug-in that allows you to download coordinates directly to your GPS one cache at a time. There's also an option for transferring coordinates to a registered GPS-enabled phone.

NAVIGATIONAL NUGGETS

GPX (GPS eXchange format) files contain a great deal of information beyond just the coordinates for the cache. They also contain the information found on the cache pages, including recent logs, and can also include additional waypoints—that is, additional coordinates for parking, trailheads, and other locations pertinent to the geocache.

Pocket Queries

Pocket Queries are one of the best tools available for geocachers today. These customized search tools are a feature provided for premium members of Geocaching.com that enable you to receive a file that contains a listing of caches tailored to your interests. Pocket Queries can be set up to search by cache type, caches you haven't found, caches hidden between dates, and many other alternative searches. You can schedule five queries with up to 1,000 geocaches in each to generate on a daily basis. You can then download the resulting Pocket Queries into your GPS unit. It's like having a copy of Geocaching.com in your pocket.

If you own a GPS capable of paperless geocaching or a PDA, Pocket Queries can be your best geocaching companion. The files generated contain not only the coordinates for each cache in the query, but the information on the cache page, including recent logs and additional waypoints, which can load right into the unit. No more printing pages! You can also use several programs to display and manipulate the results of your Pocket Queries, but we will get into that in Chapter 4.

EUREKA!

Because Pocket Queries contain so much information, it's always a good idea to click the button at the bottom of the page to have the file compressed into a .zip format. These files are smaller and are much quicker to download.

Selecting a Geocache to Seek

As you can see, it is quite easy to find geocaches to seek. However, it may be challenging to select just one from all that are available. So you found a cache that looks interesting? Let's take a closer look to see whether this might be the one to find first. Depending on your needs, here are some important things to consider before packing up the crew and hitting the road.

- **Access.** Is the location next to a parking lot? Is it permissible to use bikes or wheelchairs?

- **Size.** How big is the cache? Geocaches come in all sizes, from as small as a fingernail to larger than a car. Larger caches are often easier to find than smaller ones and offer you the opportunity to trade swag.

- **Children.** Is the geocache location kid-friendly? Is it conducive to pushing a stroller, and is there a restroom or a playground nearby?

- **Cost.** Some parks charge for admission.

- **Distance.** Check out the distance so that you can plan how to best get there. Remember, GPS receivers return results as the crow flies (in a straight line) and it is up to you to determine the best navigational route.

- **Dog-friendly.** Check out any factors that might affect whether Rover can come along.

- **Special equipment.** Does the cache location require a special vehicle, like a boat or kayak, or other equipment to reach it? Some more complex caches may require rock climbing or scuba gear.

- **Terrain.** Get an idea about how far this cache might be off the beaten path. Can you wear shorts and sandals or should you don long pants with boots? Depending on the location, there could be hazards like poison oak or sticker weeds. Remember that for hiking in brushy areas, more clothing coverage is best.

- **Time consideration.** Is this a cache you can snag on your lunch hour or is it a weekend excursion? Travel time will be a factor in determining how long it will take. Be sure to add a little more time than you think you might need.

- **Environmental factors.** Caches in higher elevations could be snowed in for much of the year and access to coastal caches is often affected by the tides and may require wading.

Many of these factors can be found listed as cache attributes on the geocache detail page. These handy little attribute icons help you filter out conditions you would rather not tackle (like poisonous plants or difficult climbs) or filter in conditions you prefer (like caches that are available 24/7 or are in pet-friendly areas).

Cache Difficulty Ratings

Geocaches are rated in two categories, each designated on a five-point scale. Difficulty relates to the mental challenge of finding a cache and terrain describes the physical environment. A 1/1 difficulty/terrain rating would the easiest cache to find, while a 5/5 difficulty/terrain rating would be the most difficult.

Difficulty

★   **Easy.** The geocache is in plain sight or can be found in a few minutes of searching.

★★   **Average.** The average geocacher will be able to find this in less than 30 minutes of searching.

★★★   **Challenging.** An experienced geocacher will find this challenging, and it could take up a good portion of an afternoon.

★★★★   **Difficult.** A real challenge for the experienced geocacher. May require special skills or knowledge, or in-depth preparation to find. May require multiple days or trips to complete.

★★★★★   **Extreme.** A serious mental or physical challenge. Requires specialized knowledge, skills, or equipment to find the geocache.

EUREKA!

Adventurer Richard Garriott, known as LordBritish on Geocaching. com, has gone out of his way to place some of the most extreme caches imaginable. His International Space Station cache (GC1BE91) is literally "out of this world." It orbits the earth at 17,000 MPH at an altitude of 250 miles and holds the title of highest geocache. At 7,546 feet under the sea, his Rainbow Hydrothermal Vents cache (GCG822) holds the record for the lowest geocache. For more info on both of these extreme caches check out: blog.geocaching.com/2010/06/ geocaching-coms-lost-found-video-highest-and-lowest-caches

Terrain

★   **Handicapped accessible.** Terrain is likely to be paved, is relatively flat, and requires less than a half-mile hike. A good rule of thumb is that the geocache should be findable and retrievable from a wheelchair.

★★   **Suitable for small children.** Terrain is generally along marked trails, and there are no steep elevation changes or heavy overgrowth. Less than a 2-mile hike is required.

★★★   **Not suitable for small children.** The average adult or older child should be okay depending on physical condition. Terrain is likely off-trail. It may have one or more of the following: some overgrowth, some steep elevation changes, or more than a 2-mile hike.

★★★★   **Experienced outdoor enthusiasts only.** Terrain is probably off-trail. It will have one or more of the following: very heavy overgrowth, very steep elevation (requiring use of hands), or more than a 10-mile hike. It may require an overnight stay.

★★★★★   **Requires specialized equipment, knowledge, or experience.** This geocache may require a boat, a four-wheel-drive truck, rock climbing, or scuba gear, or is otherwise extremely difficult.

Using Maps and Clues

So you found a cache to seek out that fits your criteria. The distance, accessibility, and difficulty rating are just right. It's time to take a closer look at the cache's page for clues. There are descriptions offered that will probably provide useful information to its whereabouts. Clues might include details of the area and local landmarks. There might also be comments on what you need to bring along and what the cache itself looks like.

The geocache owner's hint will most likely be encrypted. To read the hint when in the field, you will have to decode it using a letter key system that is provided on the cache's web page. To make it even easier, you can click the Decrypt link to have the hint unscrambled before you set out for your adventure. Remember, this hint will probably tell you where the cache is hidden, so you may not want to decrypt it unless you really have to.

EUREKA!

To keep from ruining the surprise, Geocaching.com encrypts the hints on cache pages using a fairly simple substitution cipher known as ROT-13, which stands for "rotate by 13 places." This encryption scheme involves substituting each letter with the letter 13 spaces ahead in the alphabet and wrapping back to the beginning when necessary. The great thing about ROT-13 encryption is that it is easy to decipher along the trail.

The ROT-13 system means that the letter above equals the letter below, and vice versa:

A B C D E F G H I J K L M

N O P Q R S T U V W X Y Z

The cache details page includes the option to view the cache using a variety of maps. Street maps can help you select the most efficient route to begin your search. Topographic maps provide you information on the surrounding area—hills, valleys, rivers, and other information that can affect how you approach the cache.

Note the hints that can be provided on a geocache details page.
(Geocaching.com)

This cache was placed by the original three Gorilla Freedom Finders.

Trailhead and Parking Information

There are two trailheads for the Yanahli Trails System and either will work, depending on which caches you are hunting. The Northern trailhead and parking are at the boat ramp at the end of Old Railroad Bed Road, North 35 34.062 West 086 57.857. The Southern trailhead and parking, and my preferred entrance is just off Highway 50 at North 35.32.222 West 086 58.037 near the old quarry. The trail is not a loop, although there is a loop section near the river, check the uploaded pictures for a map of the trails.

Additional Hints (Encrypt)

At the base of a big tree uphill from the trail.

Decryption Key
A|B|C|D|E|F|G|H|I|J|K|L|M

N|O|P|Q|R|S|T|U|V|W|X|Y|Z
(letter above equals below, and vice versa)

Additional Waypoints (Add / Edit waypoints)
No additional waypoints to display.

Here is the same page with the additional hint decrypted.
(Geocaching.com)

One of the most useful tools available to you is the Geocaching.com full-screen map. This is a fairly new feature that combines several view options with the details of Geocaching.com. You can use these maps to display unlimited geocaches anywhere in the world, zoom in and out, drag the map to a new area, and switch between road maps, satellite photos (with or without roads highlighted), terrain and topographical maps, and a variety of other options from several providers. In addition, Geocaching.com maps track your hides and finds, and display trackables and favorite points, plus you can click on a cache to see its details or to go straight to the cache page. Premium members have access to filtering tools to customize which cache types they want displayed or to hide their previously found or owned caches from view. Plus you can use the Geocaching.com maps to display the results of your Pocket Queries.

As with Pocket Queries, access to some of these maps is limited to Geocaching.com premium memberships. Working with these tools will help you realize just how beneficial they can be, but they are not required in order to find geocaches.

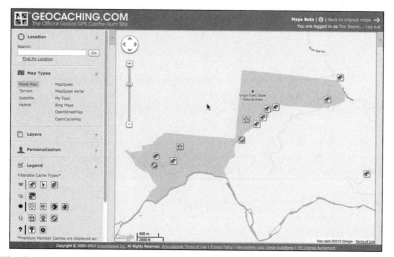

The Google map provided on a Geocaching.com cache details page provides general information about the landscape and area around the geocache.

(Geocaching.com)

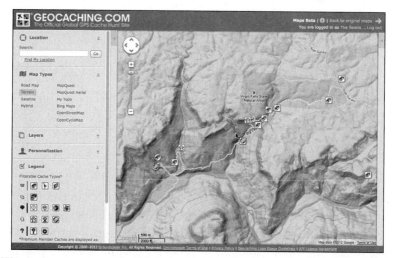

This is the same map zoomed in using the Google map on Geocaching.com. Notice that you can also switch to satellite or terrain maps for more information.

(Geocaching.com)

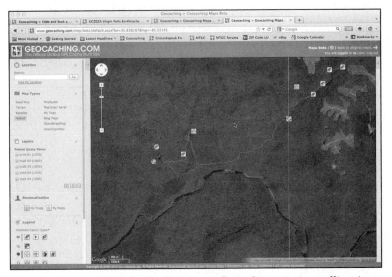

This is an example of the Google map on Geocaching.com in satellite view.
(Geocaching.com)

NAVIGATIONAL NUGGETS

Maps are an essential guide, but don't be surprised if the map does not exactly match the ground. Maps are sometimes inaccurate due to changes over time to roads, trails, waterways, and other features.

Watching a Geocache

Would you like to be notified whenever there is a change to a cache listing, or when a cache is found by another player? Perhaps the cache is in a unique location, or you simply want to relive the adventure vicariously through your fellow cachers' logs. Whatever your reason, if you want to be notified of changes to a cache listing you can add it to your watch list.

A watch list is a free feature on Geocaching.com that notifies you via e-mail whenever the status of a chosen cache has changed. When you are logged in, this option is visible for you to select on each cache listing. If you add a listing to your watch list, you can remove it at any time from your account preferences.

Keep in mind that if it is a popular geocache, you may receive a lot of e-mails. Also, there is no need for you to watch your own cache listings because you are automatically notified of changes. Sometimes you can tell the popularity of the cache listing by the number of geocachers who watch it.

Temporarily Disabled and Archived Caches

After a geocache is published, the geocache owner is responsible for updating the cache listing with any changes to the cache so that other geocachers are aware of its status. Whether a cache is temporarily disabled for maintenance, has gone missing, or is no longer being managed, it is important to provide up-to-date information to prevent geocachers from looking for a cache that cannot be found. Geocaching.com shows a cache is disabled by placing a line through the title. This means the cache is currently inactive. It can be made active again if the owner reinstates it or agrees to allow someone else to adopt it.

Geocaching.com relies on player feedback to keep the status of caches updated. If you discover a cache is missing, be sure to log on to the website to let the owner know the cache was not found. A cache owner should check out the location if there are an unusual number of Did Not Find log entries. The geocache can be temporarily disabled to allow the owner time to check on it. If the cache remains disabled or abandoned for an extended period, it will be archived and removed from the search list altogether. If, while hunting a geocache, you discover an issue that requires its immediate removal from the site, you can file a "Needs Archived" log to bring the listing to a reviewer's attention.

The Least You Need to Know

- Setting up a user profile allows you to join the Geocaching.com community and access geocache coordinates.
- Geocache data can be downloaded into your GPS receiver.
- Consider the geocache ratings and attributes before seeking a geocache.
- Maps and aerial photos help you analyze the terrain to determine the best way to navigate to a location.

What You Need to Know to Play the Game

In This Chapter

- Get ready, it's time to play!
- Hitting the trail to find a geocache
- Sharing your experiences online
- Adding photos to your log to create a gallery of your adventures
- Collecting virtual souvenirs of your travels

In this chapter, you'll learn how to go outside and find a geocache or two. After you get that down, it's time to share your adventures with the rest of the Geocaching community.

Get Out and Play

At last you've selected a geocache to find. You have a GPS receiver and other gear neatly organized in a pack, and everyone is anxiously waiting to go. But wait, you still have some homework to do. Actually, finding a cache is a little like detective work, a case that needs to be solved. After you select a cache, the sleuthing begins. First some research, as you comb the information page for clues. Then some CIA-type analysis, as you study maps and decrypt secret codes. Finally, it's time for gumshoeing as you seek to solve the mystery of the uniquely hidden geocache you've chosen.

Proper preparation before you hit the trail will ensure a fun geocaching adventure.
(Brad Simmons)

Coordinate Entry

The first step is to enter the geocache coordinates into your GPS receiver. This requires knowing how to save a waypoint. If you do not know how to do this, check out Chapter 11, which covers setting up a GPS receiver and entering waypoints in detail.

The standard geographic coordinate system used for geocaching is latitude and longitude. Latitude is the measurement of distance north or south of the equator, while longitude is the measurement of distance east or west of the prime meridian, located at Greenwich, England. Latitude and longitude lines are measured using degrees, minutes, and seconds. More specifically in geocaching, the standard coordinate type is decimal minutes. This means that coordinates are displayed using degrees and decimal minutes instead of a full address of degrees, minutes, and seconds. On the GPS Setup menu, typically under Position, the option usually appears as hddd°.mm.mmm. Also be sure that the map *datum* is in the WGS 84 format. On the same

Setup Position screen, the option will appear as [WGS 84]. You may need to consult your owner's manual to find the correct screen to enter this data.

GEO-LINGO

A map **datum** is a global survey system that is used to create maps. Each datum may take a slightly different measurement of the earth. Using the wrong datum can result in positions being off by as much as a mile. The most used datum for geocaching is WGS 84, but many older maps use NAD 27.

Sample Setup menu as shown on a Magellan 710 GPS receiver.
(Image used courtesy of Magellan Navigation, Inc. or its affiliates. Copyright © Magellan Navigation, Inc. or its affiliates.)

Okay, so you have the coordinates entered as a waypoint in decimal minutes. Once the coordinates are entered you can choose a name that references the cache's title or the GC Code to help you identify these coordinates. Print out the cache information page to take along. Use it first to double-check the coordinates to ensure every number is absolutely the same as listed on the sheet. Any data-entry error will give you a waypoint possibly hundreds of miles off.

DEAD BATTERIES

Be sure to double-check the coordinates when entering the data into the GPS receiver. Getting one number wrong could result in being 100 miles from the actual cache location. Don't put yourself through the frustration of searching in the wrong area.

Searching for Clues Before You Hunt

Remember that many times the cache owner will provide you with good information about the surrounding area of the cache, possibly even about the container itself. While this is helpful, the cache details page may also contain clues, the main hint being encrypted by the cache owner. Most people choose to wait until they have trouble finding the cache and need a little help. For your first find, however, you should strongly consider decrypting the hint before heading outdoors. Also, if the cache owner does not provide a helpful cache description, take the time to read recent logs and try to determine what kind of cache container is used. You want your first caching experience to be a positive one, so you might as well arm yourself with as much information as possible to ensure success.

Next, check out the many map links on the page and the map shown for the listing. It will be a general map, possibly showing the cache's location in reference to the nearest town or city. Geocaching.com provides you with links to various online map sites, some of which may provide you with turn-by-turn directions to the general area of the cache.

Reviewing the map is important because you have to find the general vicinity before getting out and actually finding the cache. Often there is more than one way to access the area. A little analysis may be required to figure out the best route to take. The road that gets you closest to the cache may not leave you at the best route to take when you get off the road.

When you know the general area where the cache is located, it's time to check out the topographic maps. They give greater detail of terrain features through the use of contour lines. Based on the location and potential difficulty, you can decide whether you need to buy an additional detailed topographic map. Topo maps are a great tool for navigating off road, especially when going on longer hikes. It is well worth the time spent learning how to read and use them properly.

Remember, even if your GPS receiver includes routing maps, getting to the actual geocache location can sometimes be difficult. There could be obstacles that lie between you and that elusive geocache. Waterways, mountains, cliffs, or simply no trail are all examples of potential challenges. Another consideration is the access road itself. A map's collar information should reveal the type of roadway going in. The collar is the section across the bottom of a map that contains the map's reference information. That way you'll know whether you can travel in a sports car or if you need something with higher ground clearance and off-road capabilities.

Finally, review the geocache details page and make sure that the cache owner has not already provided additional waypoints for the cache you are seeking. These waypoints might include information about the best parking location or trailhead near the geocache. Additional waypoints make it easier to know where to start your hike, which is a huge plus. Even better, they make sure you are using the correct trail and experiencing the area and the cache hunt as the hider intended.

Hitting the Trail

You've read the cache page, the maps are printed, and your group is confident they know where they're going. It's time to head outdoors and fire up the GPS. After the unit gets a satellite fix, you are ready to navigate to the additional waypoint for the correct trailhead for the geocache you have selected. Assuming you are using a basic GPS unit that does not route along roads, you will need to "follow the arrow" to the cache site. Remember two important things about GPS data: Distance is measured in a straight line directly from you to the target; and with the turns, hills, and *switchbacks* of ground travel, the actual distance to the cache may often be significantly farther than the distance indicated on your GPS receiver. The compass bearing and pointer arrow also give you a straight shot to the target, but it is rarely possible to follow an exact compass bearing unless flying or sailing.

GEO-LINGO

Switchbacks are areas on a trail that zig and zag up and down steep slopes. Although indirect, switchbacks help protect the incline from erosion and they create a more gradual climb to the top of the hill. Never shortcut switchbacks when hiking as this can damage the trail system.

You have successfully navigated to the trailhead and, sure enough, there is a trail heading off in the general direction of the cache as indicated on the GPS receiver. It is time to mark the location of your car in your GPS and grab your gear, including your geobag or daypack with plenty of water, supplies, and spare batteries. Half a mile down the trail you find a fork with two trails that will take you in the general direction of the cache. After careful inspection of your maps, you find that a creek runs between the left trail and the cache site. From the map it's difficult to determine how big the creek is. That thin blue line could be anything from a dried up riverbed to a raging river. You decide to take the right fork of the trail that requires hiking a little farther, but that's okay. It's not a race. It's all about the journey, the challenge, and enjoying the outdoors.

NAVIGATIONAL NUGGETS

A GPS receiver will not provide you with directions to a geocache, only distance and compass bearing. Remember there are 360 approaches to each location (one for each compass degree). The shortest distance may not be the most accessible or wisest path to travel.

Navigational Tips and Tricks

You continue to follow the trail with the compass page selected on your GPS to provide a large pointer arrow and the distance to the target. In this case, you are .75 miles away with a compass bearing of 290° west. Onward you go, down the dusty, twisted trail as the distance indicator slowly ticks down. For the person holding the receiver and watching its arrow, it may be tempting to walk in a direct line, following the pointer arrow, tripping over rocks and brush (even though a neatly groomed path runs right alongside the course), but that is rarely the best policy.

Geocaching point one: You probably do not need to bushwhack (travel off-trail). This might be necessary when you reach the cache's general location, but not three quarters of a mile away. It's time to start thinking like the person who hid the cache. Would they stumble over nature's obstacles for nearly a mile even though a trail leads to the same location? Besides not tripping and falling on your face, there are lots of other good reasons not to bushwhack. Staying on trails makes less of an impact on the local environment. Besides, it is not fun to get tangled in trees, thorns, and blackberry bushes. This across-land travel will get you scratched up and make it easier to get lost (as you wander in foliage that may obstruct your view). Even animals know this; that's why they use the trails, too.

This is especially true for off-road driving. Whether on a mountain bike or four-wheel-drive vehicle, traveling off the trail marks the ground and damages foliage. Off-trail travel often leads you to obstacles such as boulders or ravines, which make passage difficult, if not impossible. That is why someone else has already made a trail going to the desired location. Also, if you do need help, taking yourself off the beaten path only makes it more difficult for someone to find and assist you.

You are getting closer, less than a half-mile to the cache, but now the trail has switched back and is heading the wrong way. Excitement turns to confusion as the group questions whether you are on the right path.

Geocaching point two: Even though a road or trail veers off in a different direction, it does not mean you are on the wrong path. Often wilderness roads switch back and curve all over to reach their destination. When you are in this situation, you have a choice of two actions to take. One is to check your map to determine where the trail or road ends up. If your path is not mapped, continue to follow it out. Keep a close eye on the distance indicator to see whether you are walking closer to or farther away from the target. If you continually get farther away, it may be time to backtrack and reassess your direction.

NAVIGATIONAL NUGGETS

Check satellite reception often. This will give you a good indication of how accurate the gear is at any given time. Be sure to check the battery gauge at the same time. It is typically located on the same page.

In this case, you decide to follow the trail to see where it goes. Despite its curving, it does continue to lead closer to the geocache. Now, with 320 feet to go, your anticipation builds as you wonder what you will find. The arrow leads into a forested area filled with logs and rock outcroppings—many good places to hide a cache. You continue hiking until you get a reading of 35 feet. Going farther on the trail only increases the distance, so you turn around for another look.

No cache and no big "X" on the ground: this might be a little harder than you thought. Turning back around, you walk until there is a reading of 30 feet. While this is still not as close as you might like it to be, and the tree coverage is most likely affecting your GPS unit, it is still close enough to begin your search.

After walking around the area, searching first with your eyes you narrow the location to a likely area for your search. After hunting for a little while without any luck you decide to decrypt the hint, which says, "hollow log." You remember seeing a hollow log a few feet away and return to check it more thoroughly. Eureka! A plastic box is tucked away behind some leaves at the other end of the hollow log. That was a great hunt and you got to go for a hike and have an adventure looking around rocks and trees until you found the cache.

You Found It! Now What?

Remember the rules: Take something, leave something, and enter your name and experience in the logbook. You worked hard to find it; it's your right to leave a record of the experience.

After signing the log and trading any items, be sure to seal up the cache and place it back where you found it. If it was hidden in a stump or covered with rocks, place it back the way it was. Do not move the cache or leave it exposed. You want the next person to enjoy finding it just like you did.

He found it!
(Brad Simmons)

Sharing Your Experience

When you get home, log on to Geocaching.com and record your adventure for the world to see! A geocache log can be as detailed as you like. The cache owner is always happy to know about the condition of the cache and how well you enjoyed the experience. Also, if there were problems with the cache your log will tell the owner that cache maintenance is needed. This will allow future cache seekers to see when it was found and possibly learn from your experience. It may even help other geocachers decide whether this is the type of cache they want to visit.

There are five log types available when logging a cache:

> • **Found It.** Used when the cache has been found and the log signed. Logging a cache in this manner increases your find count by one in your profile on Geocaching.com.

- **Didn't Find It (DNF).** Used when a search has been made but the cache could not be located. This type of log is useful for alerting cache owners of potential issues.

- **Write Note.** Notes are often used on return visits to a cache, perhaps to pick up a trackable item or simply check on it. At times, a note is often used instead of a DNF if your geocaching adventure is interrupted and you don't want to give others the impression that the cache is missing.

- **Needs Maintenance.** Used if a cache is in need of attention from the owner. Maintenance can include replacement of a container, or the need for a new logbook. Use of this log type places a *Needs Maintenance* attribute on the cache details page, which remains until the owner posts an *Owner Maintenance* log. Keep in mind that you need to find the cache to know whether or not it needs maintenance.

- **Needs Archived.** Used when the cache cannot or should not be replaced due to outside forces, including new construction, land-management issues, or other dangers. When a log of this type is posted, the cache owner and the local cache reviewer receive notification of it and may take action to archive the cache. *Needs Archived* logs are rare and are used only in situations where you are certain of the problem at the cache site.

Logging with Field Notes

If you are hunting with a GPS unit that features paperless geocaching or the Geocaching smartphone application, you have access to Geocaching field notes. These small text files allow you to create your logs right at the cache site and then upload them to Geocaching.com. Using field notes makes it easy to keep up with which caches you found during your hunt and lets you upload detailed notes about your adventure. You can either post these notes directly to the cache page or to your profile where you can edit and post them to the cache page later.

A Picture Is Worth a Thousand Words

With your log entry, you have the ability to upload digital photos to share your Geocaching adventure, which are added to the photo gallery for that particular cache. Geocachers enjoy viewing the galleries of cache listings, often learning stories of participants from all over the world.

Even better, when you sign up for an account on Geocaching.com it automatically creates a photo gallery just for you. Now every photo that you upload to the site is placed in your account's gallery as a great way to record your adventures and memories. Many geocachers share the link to their gallery with family and friends as a way to help them share in the fun.

A Souvenir of Your Adventure

In addition to your great memories and photos, Geocaching.com also awards digital souvenirs to help you keep track of your adventures. Souvenirs are virtual pieces of art with some associated text that you can discover and display on your profile page. Think of it like patches that some travellers affix to their backpacks, or stickers that get stuck onto luggage. Some souvenirs are awarded for their geographical location, such as Groundspeak Headquarters, the Original Cache Location, or even a state, province, or country, while others are awarded differently. For example, you might get a souvenir for attending a specific Mega-Event, like Geocoinfest Europa or GeoWoodstock. We will discuss these huge geocacher gatherings in detail in Chapter 13. Still others are awarded for specific activities, like finding a cache on the third Saturday in August—International Geocaching Day.

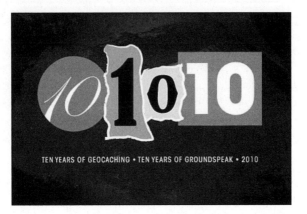

Geocachers who hunted on 10/10/10 were awarded this souvenir for their efforts.
(Geocaching.com)

The Least You Need to Know

- The decimal minute format is the most commonly used for geocache coordinates.
- Be sure to use the correct datum to avoid serious error.
- Know how to use maps and hints for assistance in finding geocaches.
- Geocachers should keep geocache owners up-to-date on the status of their caches by logging their experiences online.
- Online logs, photo galleries, and souvenirs are great ways to record your geocaching adventures.

Geocaching Tips and Tricks

Chapter 5

In This Chapter

- Advice for your geocaching adventures
- Techniques to help you find geocaches like a pro
- Ways to keep yourself safe while on the trail
- What to do when encountering non-geocachers

Now that you have learned the basics and been on your first geocaching adventure, it's time to sharpen your skills. You've created a profile, learned how to use the website, and gotten outside to experience the thrill of geocaching for yourself. If you are like so many others, this activity could go beyond an occasional weekend pastime and become a full-blown obsession.

Have you been bitten by the bug to the point that you try to find ways to sneak out to get just one more cache? At night, are you looking around ferns and rocks in your sleep? We thought so. There is just one reasonable thing to do, and it's not therapy or counseling. No, it's time to go pro by learning from the best! We have assembled the best advice we could think of to help you find them fast and get you home by dinner.

Good Advice

Since geocaching is still a relatively new activity, many participants are self-taught and have learned what does and does not work through trial and error. The online geocaching discussion forums and face-to-face exchanges at geocaching events have also served to distribute some of the best geo-wisdom, tricks, and tips. By learning from others you can transform yourself from a stumbling newbie to a seasoned professional in no time.

This chapter shares good, commonsense information about outdoor activities that will help you get out there and back in one piece. It also offers specific search techniques that will help make even the toughest geocache hides easier to spot. What do you tell non-geocachers you run into while on the trail? This chapter covers that topic, too.

Before You Leave

Tell someone where you are going before you take off. You can use the travel itinerary in Appendix F to leave vital information about the geocaches you are going after. Besides leaving the coordinates, let someone know whom you're traveling with, what communication gear you have, and what time you expect to return.

Bring a friend! It's always good to have someone with you when venturing outdoors. It's easy to have car trouble, get lost, or twist an ankle. Having someone with you can help overcome these challenges and get you back home safely. Besides, geocaching and the outdoors are always more fun when shared with a friend.

Bring along a notepad and camera. You may see awe-inspiring areas that take your breath away. You will likely visit locations you have never seen before, and may not again if you don't take some notes. In the excitement of the moment, it's easy to forget the names of parks, trailheads, and waterfalls, or the unmarked turnoffs to get you there. Make notes and save lots of waypoints in your receiver. Don't forget to mark the location where you parked your car before hitting the trails, as this will make it easier to find your way back out if you get turned around. It is also a good idea to grab some extra batteries and film or data storage for digital cameras. A lightweight tripod works great to allow everyone to get in the frame if no one else is around to take a photo for you. Taking pictures is a great way to document your trip and enjoy your travels again and again. It's also fun to post your photos in your online log to share with others.

Outdoor travel often takes longer than you might think, especially if you are venturing out to unknown territory. When planning your trip, be realistic and give yourself enough time to get there and back.

Geocaching can be more fun when you bring a friend.
(Bernard Voges)

The problem with being caught outdoors longer than you plan for is that it gets dark. A day trip with a wrong detour can easily turn into a night trip. Always make sure to bring at least one flashlight with a spare bulb and batteries.

There is nothing worse than leaving for a trip only to realize you forgot something. It helps to organize your navigation and outdoor gear in the same place, like a geobag. Be sure to use the suggested lists in Chapter 2 when packing for your adventure.

If your GPS does not allow for paperless geocaching, print out the geocache information page and maps to take with you. This is important in order to check coordinates and hints if you get stumped. Don't forget to bring something of value to leave behind in the cache and a pen for writing in logbooks. Also, be sure to bring along plenty of water.

On the Trail

Do not spend too much time staring into your GPS's screen when you're driving to or hiking on the trail. If you do, two things might happen: you will miss the beauty of the natural surroundings, and sooner or later you may have an accident. Have your passenger check out the screen while you're driving.

DEAD BATTERIES

Whether walking, riding, or driving, taking your eyes off the road to watch the receiver's screen too often could ultimately lead to an accident. Be careful or your friends will have to use the coordinates to call in the paramedics.

Before heading out on foot for a geocache, save your vehicle's location as a waypoint. It's easy to get disoriented, even when using GPS. Having your vehicle or the trailhead saved as a waypoint provides you a location to direct the GPS on your return journey.

Pay attention to where you're going and be aware of the surroundings. Occasionally, stop and make a 360-degree turn to study the landmarks around you and to get a reverse perspective of the landscape behind you. It's important to do this so that you know what the landscape will look like on your return trip. Besides major ground features, can you see the sun or moon? Recruit assistance from others to help keep track of where you're going as well as your location on a map.

Respect the land by treading lightly. Do not leave tracks or break foliage, and carry along a garbage bag to make it easy to pack trash out. Remember to practice Cache In Trash Out. The best way to travel through outback areas is by leaving no trace. You can find more information regarding principles of leaving no trace at www.lnt.org.

Map Considerations

Use the general map on the geocache details page and a road map to determine how to reach the cache area. When you're there, it's time to get serious with highly detailed topographic maps. Topographic maps are often referred to as 7.5-minute maps because the distance they cover is 7.5 minutes long and wide in latitude and longitude—approximately 55 square miles. Book, outdoor, and travel stores are all great places to find topographic maps. They're a great investment for about $4. The digital topographic maps found on the cache details page are based on these maps.

After you learn how to read a map, you'll enjoy the challenge of following your position on it. Wilderness roads such as those marked by the U.S. Forest Service use small numbered signs. With a little practice, you can easily spot and match those signs in the field to the roads listed on your map. This proves especially helpful if you're traveling in areas where satellite signals are blocked by overhanging trees or cliff walls. For lots more on reading topographic maps, check Chapter 14.

NAVIGATIONAL NUGGETS

There are special map rulers made especially for plotting coordinates and measuring distances on the highly detailed 7.5-minute topographic maps. Just make sure you are using the correct ruler for the scale of your map.

Do Your Homework

If you get stumped trying to find an elusive cache, double-check the hint posted on the cache details page. A bit of overlooked data might just solve the puzzle. You can find clues in the general information about the cache, as well as the encrypted primary hint. There may be photos to check and spoiler information in geocacher logs that will give you that extra advantage in tracking down the tough geocaches.

It helps to know the size, type, and possible color of the cache you are looking for. You already know you're looking for a container, but you gain a psychological advantage if you have a more specific idea of what type of container it is.

Search Techniques

More often than not, when you get close to the geocache, you're simply going to have to look around. Sometimes you can search for long periods of time and still not find a thing. Seasoned geocachers have been there. In the rain and in the heat, they have spent hours looking around rocks, trees, and foliage only to be stumped. Then when it all looks grim and they are ready to call it a day, their eyes catch something that doesn't quite fit in the natural environment—a glimpse of plastic or metal that loomed out from the flora and fauna. You'll experience the same thing when your eye is trained on what to look for.

It often helps to think like the person who placed the geocache. When looking for a cache, ask yourself, "If I was hiding a cache here, where would I put it?" Geocache hiders can get very creative, but luckily, most hides are in logical places, such as under rock outcroppings, under limbs at the base of a tree, or in hollow stumps.

Here are some helpful tips when closing in on a geocache:

- Check the satellite status page on your GPS receiver when you are within 300 feet. This will give you an idea of your accuracy for approach. Remember that the receiver may not direct you to the exact location. Depending on signal strength, 30 feet may be your closest reading.

- After you get close, your pointer function may be less accurate due to your slowing pace. Because of this factor, when you slow down, disregard the pointer arrow and focus on the distance reading. In fact, many experienced geocachers say that at this point their GPS becomes as much of a hindrance as it is a help, and they will lay it aside as they begin searching for likely hiding spots. You are now using your *geo-senses*.

GEO-LINGO

Geo-sense is when, after a little experience geocaching, you will begin to notice your eyes being pulled almost instinctively to a little pile of sticks here or an oddly positioned rock there.

Using your geo-senses means that it is far more important to be searching the area with your eyes than to be watching the screen on the GPS. When you approach "ground zero," take a good look around before diving in. A hiding location is, in many ways, similar to a crime scene—if you rush in flipping over rocks and disturbing the area, you are more likely to destroy "evidence" left by the hider and previous finders of the cache.

While searching with your eyes, make note of any signs of use: not necessarily a trail to the cache, but broken branches or flattened undergrowth leading to an area. Also, be on the lookout for rocks or sticks that are not disturbed, as I have found that while searching many hunters will take the utmost care to place the cache back the way they found it, but they will often leave stones and sticks from fruitless searches overturned. When you find an area where all of the stones have been overturned except for one, the cache is probably behind that one perfect stone.

This technique works just as well in an urban setting: if you watch, you will notice signs of wear on a pole from having a cover moved, or that a sticker is a little crooked, or even that a bush seems to have an opening on one side where the branches have been pushed back repeatedly. All of these indicators are clues that can narrow down your search area.

Cloverleaf

The cloverleaf is a search technique to use when you're close to the geocache and the pointer arrow feature is no longer accurate due to your slowed pace. The cloverleaf works by narrowing down the search area using the distance reading on your GPS receiver.

As you approach the geocache location, the receiver indicates a distance at the closest point, typically ranging from 40 feet down to 1 foot. If, as you move through the area, the distance increases, turn around and head back to the area where it decreases. Take off in a different direction until the distance increases, and then turn around and go back to the area that provides the smallest distance number.

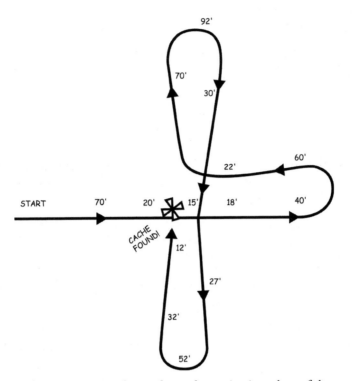

A cloverleaf pattern narrows the search area by moving in and out of the potential search location following the closest distance reading from a receiver.
(Groundspeak)

Circling around in a cloverleaf pattern narrows the search area by further confirming the location of the closest reading from at least four different directions. Found the geocache? We hope so. When searching for a geocache, remember to always be aware of your physical location; your search method should not negatively impact the environment.

Triangulation

Triangulation is similar to the cloverleaf search pattern, except you use a compass to take bearings on the search area. When you slow down or stop, the pointer arrow on your receiver will no longer work properly but the bearing to the waypoint should still be accurate. This procedure works great for dramatically narrowing down the search area.

> **EUREKA!**
>
> Geocaches in urban settings present their own share of challenges. Because of the location, they are typically small micro caches that can be difficult to find under the watchful eyes of non-geocachers. Be patient, take in your surroundings, and learn to pretend to tie your shoe while you are actually looking under things. After searching for a few of these you'll get the knack for finding the most likely hiding spots.

As you approach the geocache location, check the bearing degrees and distance. Using your compass, take a bearing. Be sure that the magnetic reading of both the GPS receiver and compass match, either true or magnetic north. The receiver will most likely be set as a default to true north, although the receiver can provide bearings on true or magnetic north (an option you can set through the Setup menu). Use the true north setting on your receiver if your compass can be adjusted for declination to indicate true north. If your compass cannot be adjusted, or if you do not know how to make the adjustment, set the receiver to provide bearings in magnetic north. It makes no difference what format you use as long as both the receiver and compass are set the same.

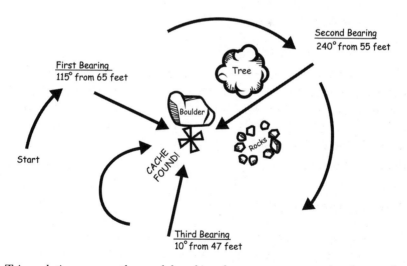

Triangulation narrows the search by taking three or more compass bearings on the target location.

(Groundspeak)

In our example, we approach the cache area and check the receiver data as we get close. We see the following:

> Distance 65 feet, Bearing 115°. Using a compass, we take a bearing in that direction. Looking carefully along the bearing, we see that it is just to the right of a large boulder.

> We circle the area clockwise to take a second bearing pointing west. The receiver indicates: Distance 55 feet, Bearing 240°. Along this bearing we see the path goes between a tree and rock pile, just to the left of the large boulder.

> The third bearing is from the south pointing north: Distance 47 feet, Bearing 10°. From this angle, the bearing is to the left of the tree and appears to be pointing at the large boulder.

> From these three bearings, all paths seem to point to the base of the large boulder. Sure enough, we find a plastic tube hidden in rocks exactly where the paths of the three bearings intersected.

Be Careful Out There!

Thankfully, there are still beautiful outdoor places where Mother Nature and the order of the food chain still rule the day. Most of us have become far too civilized for our own good and we can easily underestimate the power of nature. Safety should always be a major concern. Outdoor skills do not come naturally; they are acquired through education and experience.

It is your responsibility to have the knowledge and equipment to tackle the area you want to travel. This means being realistic about your limits to ensure you're not exceeding your outdoor abilities and putting yourself and others at risk. If you are leading a group, consider their limits, and remember they are relying on your knowledge to get them safely there and back. Make careful use of the terrain and difficulty ratings as well as the attributes on the cache page to eliminate any caches that might be beyond your or your group's comfort level. If you are unsure about more remote travel, take the time to educate yourself to build the skills and confidence necessary to make each excursion a successful one.

This section provides details about potential hazards and how to deal with them. Use common sense, think through challenges, and make the best decisions possible. This is done by not overestimating your abilities and by making cautious choices. Obviously, this book can't provide the exact solution to every potential problem, but here are some guidelines to help get you back from searching in good spirits and in one piece.

Environmental Concerns

The weather is typically the primary concern when geocaching. Being caught in a storm or in blazing heat unprepared and unprotected will definitely make you uncomfortable. Extended exposure can cause serious health problems and even death. Exposure is one of the leading causes of outdoor-related injury and death.

Hypothermia is caused by extensive heat loss, often a result of extended exposure to freezing temperatures, rain, and wind. The victim's body temperature lowers to dangerous levels, resulting in the body's inability to regain its own heat. It is estimated that hypothermia is responsible for 85 percent of outdoor-related deaths.

DEAD BATTERIES

Hypothermia kills because most people never realize they are experiencing it until it is too late. How can you tell if you're suffering from hypothermia while you still have time to treat it? Try touching your thumb to your little finger on the same hand. One of the first signs of hypothermia is trouble with dexterity. If you have difficulty passing this simple test, it's time to get inside and get warm.

Heat exhaustion and, eventually, heatstroke are risks in warmer climates. The body temperature rises to dangerous levels from ongoing sun exposure and dehydration. In cases of cold and heat exposure, victims are subjected to extreme weather conditions for much longer than their provisions allow for. They often find themselves in such dire circumstances because they are lost or stranded.

Here are some ideas that will help prevent you from finding yourself in a worst-case scenario with the climate:

- Tell someone where you are going; give that person your travel itinerary.

- Wear the right clothing for the environment and climate.

- Bring the right gear for the environment and climate.

- Bring communication gear appropriate for the area.

- Bring and consume adequate amounts of food and water.

- Have some form of shelter available that is capable of protecting you from the elements.

- Take the proper steps to avoid getting lost.

Poison, Stingers, and Fangs

Out of all the potential outdoor dangers, being bitten or stung is probably the most common and annoying. Okay, getting attacked by a bear would be worse, but animal attacks are rare. It's the insects and snakes that are more likely to give you fits. Mosquito bites on sunburned skin, tripping over a hornet's nest, a spider under a log, or even the dreaded snake in your boot … you get the idea.

EUREKA!

Gaiters are protective wraps that cover the lower leg from the knee down to the top of your boot. They are ideal for hiking through brush or snow to keep thorns, insects, dirt, and other crud out of your socks and boots. Some are armor-plated to prevent snakebites.

Here's some advice to keep you from scratching your skin away:

- Learn what poison oak and ivy look like and stay away from them.

- Wear pants and long-sleeved clothing, and use insect repellent.

- Carry a first-aid kit that includes a snakebite kit.

- Always watch where you're walking.

- Check your sleeping bag, clothing, and boots before slipping into them.

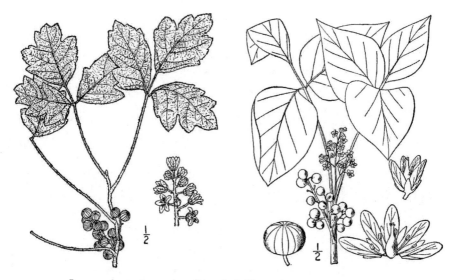

Learn what poison oak and ivy look like and stay away from them.
(Pbritt, N. L. & A. Brown, Kentucky Native Plant Society)

Lions, Tigers, and Creepy Guys, Oh My!

While wandering the trails enjoying nature's beauty, we have to remember to use some caution to avoid any unpleasant encounters with wildlife. Animal attacks are generally pretty rare, but it is still a good policy to remain vigilant and take some basic precautions. Although you will want to arm yourself with specific knowledge of the wildlife you are likely to encounter in your area, here are some good general practices to follow when you meet animals on the trail.

- **Never approach a wild animal.** Most healthy animals will avoid people if you give them the opportunity to do so. If they know you are coming, they will most likely get out of your way.

- **Never tease, threaten, or corner a wild animal.** Animals react instinctively to perceived threats and will often attack in order to escape.

- **Do not feed wild animals.** Feeding animals teaches them that humans are a source for food and will cause them to approach other people.

If you meet an animal on the trail, always back away slowly allowing it room to run from you if it feels cornered. Remember not to make any sudden moves. If the animal sees you as either a threat or a source of food it may attack, but most are scared of people.

Of course, the most troublesome animals you are likely to encounter on the trail are of the two-legged variety. Although most people you meet in the outdoors are friendly and would go out of their way to help you, there is a small percentage of people whose intentions may not be good. Maybe they are opportunists who might steal your gear or mess with you if they felt they could get away with it. An even smaller percentage of people are downright criminals who use the woods to hide out or for illegal dumping or drug operations.

As with other forms of wildlife, it is important to be aware of your surroundings and keep on the lookout for any signs of trouble. While geocaching, you might run across one or more people who appear to be a little shady. Long-term campers and land squatters often look rough, but might be perfectly harmless. If you are unsure about anyone you meet, the best thing is to just smile, wave, and leave. Don't be rude or tell them anything unnecessary like, for instance, that you're traveling alone. Regardless of what kind of jungle you find yourself in, criminals typically avoid people who do not appear to be easy targets or victims.

If you run across what looks like an illegal activity, immediately turn around and leave the way you came in. Remember the location and report it to the local authorities. Do not investigate the scene. Drug labs and dumpsites contain hazardous chemicals, and drug labs and marijuana crop locations are sometimes booby-trapped. Wilderness management agencies have their own law enforcement divisions for investigating such crimes. It is critical to report these crimes for a number of reasons. This activity is a serious threat to others and the environment. Such activity gives landowners and managers good cause to deny access to wilderness areas. Remember to keep the following in mind to stay safe:

- If you run across someone who you think may be unfriendly, just leave.

- Most criminals do not mess with people who look aware, confident, and capable of defending themselves.

- Immediately back out of any areas where criminal activities are taking place and report them to the police.

Blending In and Getting Along

When you're geocaching, you are on a serious mission. You have that cold look of determination in your eye as you shake off the elements and obstacles that get in your way. Others who are on a nice quiet scenic getaway might not share your enthusiasm—not because what you're doing is wrong, but because they have no clue as to what you're doing. Curious onlookers may wonder why anyone would so intently look around the same area when nothing appears to be there. You will undoubtedly run across non-geocachers. Though their ranks are diminishing steadily, they're still everywhere. At some point, depending on their interest level, you may have some explaining to do.

Some geocachers are happy to share the activity with everyone they meet, enthusiastically explaining what they are doing and how to play the game. Many people find the idea as interesting as you first did, and who knows, maybe you just created a new geocacher. Others like to be a little more discreet. For them, part of the challenge is to get in and out without anyone else even knowing they were there.

Whatever you do, keep a low profile. People visit outdoor areas for peace and quiet, and there is no reason to disturb anyone else's tranquility. There is also no harm done in explaining what you're doing. Even if you do not want to take the time to do so, it's better than having others become suspicious of your behavior. Some geocachers have developed creative ways to mask their activity. They've used excuses ranging from being agricultural inspectors to doing some kind of research that requires quite a bit of careful photography. Other geocachers have suddenly pretended that their GPS receiver is a cell phone and they are just having a phone conversation. Some even carry clipboards or wear hardhats knowing that such accessories can enable you to blend in and look like you belong there and are just doing your job.

Does this sneakiness help or just increase suspicion? Remember that what you're doing is a legitimate, family-friendly activity and that you do not want to cause anyone alarm. Here are some ideas when communicating with non-geocachers:

- Be prepared to quickly and politely explain what geocaching is. Most people receive the information with great interest.

- Remain low-key. There is no reason to disturb anyone or make anyone wonder what you're doing.

- Do not say or do anything that would make you appear as if you are doing anything suspicious or illegal. This is never more true than when you are approached by authorities. It is always best to be upfront and forthcoming about your activities.

- Be careful about how you use your receiver. In some areas, under certain circumstances, you could be considered a spy. Be sure to check local policies before hunting.

- Take out your trash bag and pick up whatever litter you find around the cache area as you search. Passersby will generally ignore you, and if you're approached the conversation will most likely start on a positive note.

Environmental Ethics and Stewardship

The issue of environmental ethics and access is critical for the ongoing development and survival of geocaching as an activity. Geocaching, as well as other outdoor activities, requires access to park, rural, and wilderness lands. Yet, there can be challenges inherent in sharing these lands. Those of us who enjoy venturing into the outdoors for almost any recreational activity are occasionally confronted with individuals and organizations that would prefer all wilderness lands be closed to public access.

Another challenge faced by outdoor enthusiasts lies in dealing with the small percentage of individuals who care nothing about the outdoors. Unfortunately, this small number of people who lack consideration for the environment sometimes use lands as dumping grounds for garbage or other ethically problematic activities. Although unrelated to geocaching, the actions of these people can sometimes lead to private and public land managers limiting land access to all, including responsible and respectful outdoor enthusiasts.

As a community, geocachers must practice good environmental stewardship and educate those who do not. If we continue to treat the environment with respect, outdoor and wilderness areas will likely be preserved and accessible for generations to come.

Like other outdoor activities, geocaching should be conducted with minimal or no impact to the environment. Generally speaking, as a group, geocachers are environmentally conscious and responsible. Geocachers are a global community composed primarily of individuals with a strong appreciation of nature. Through a demonstrated appreciation of nature and a lot of education, geocachers have worked with landowners and managers to open parks and other lands to geocaching around the world.

As geocaching continues to develop, we must continue working to overcome any negative preconceptions. Many people are unfamiliar with geocaching, while others have preconceived notions about what it is and is not. Some might have the image of geocachers digging holes and stashing junk. We need to work at educating the public, whether we are out on a trail as individuals or taking part in community projects within our geocaching organization. It's important to communicate that geocachers do not dig holes, leave garbage, or otherwise disrespect the environment. Our strength has always been our ability to take responsibility and hold ourselves and other geocachers accountable for all related actions as contributors to the global geocaching community.

To maintain its positive image, the geocaching community must regulate itself and remember that actions speak louder than words. Many people will judge the geocaching community, positively or negatively, based on what they actually see happening outdoors. Their perception will be based on how we conduct ourselves on the trail:

- Are we courteous and open or rude and suspicious?

- Do we leave garbage behind, or help take out a little extra (Cache In Trash Out)?

This is why working within groups and organizations can be so important, and all of these should be considered before you start geocaching.

Through positive volunteer efforts, we can be effective in cultivating relationships with land agencies while helping to preserve the outdoors. Groups can also help with community and outdoor projects, for instance, by taking youth groups to a park to teach them about GPS and geocaching or by repairing a hiking trail at a favorite park.

The Least You Need to Know

- Find geocaches like a pro by learning to think like a geocacher. Where would you place a cache in the same location?

- Take responsibility to learn outdoor skills and try not to exceed your abilities.

- Be polite and diplomatic with non-geocachers you meet on the trail.

- Always be a conscientious hiker—pick up any litter you see along the trail and help to foster healthy, positive relationships with land managers.

The Different Types of Geocaches

In This Chapter

- Examine the standard types of geocaches
- Explore rare and highly coveted geocache types
- Find out how to join in on geocaching gatherings and event caches
- Follow the evolution of geocaches

If variety is the spice of life, it is the soul of geocaching. Geocaches have evolved over the years into several types of caches that appeal to different interests. Each of these *cache types* was created to reflect a new direction in the game and sometimes a result of advancing technologies; some have been wildly successful and some have fallen by the wayside; others have even spawned their own games, such as Waymarking and Geocaching Challenges, that are enjoyed by players around the world.

No matter their differences, one thing is clear: each type of cache adds a little spice to the game. Start by looking for a traditional cache. As you become more comfortable with geocaching, you will want to try all of the varieties and find your favorite type of geocaching. This chapter is an easy guide to the different cache types and explains what all of those geocache icons on Geocaching.com mean.

Standard Geocache Types

Geocaches come in all shapes, sizes, and categories. The variety in geocache types and hiding places has grown due to the ingenuity of geocachers. As the game has evolved people have discovered new and innovative ways to share the excitement of the hunt with their fellow geocachers.

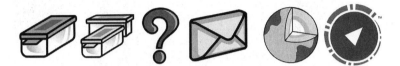

These icons represent the types of geocaches you are most likely to encounter.
(Geocaching.com)

Traditional Geocaches

In its most basic form, a geocache consists of a container and a log-book. This is known simply as a *traditional cache* in the Geocaching.com pantheon of geocache types. The finder follows a set of coordinates that leads directly to the geocache. While the process sounds straightforward enough, it's the individual creativity that each geocache owner puts into the cache placement and the location that makes finding the cache a unique experience.

GEO-LINGO

A **traditional cache** is the original type of geocache, consisting of, at minimum, a container and a logbook or logsheet. Larger containers generally include items for trade. Nano or micro caches are tiny containers that hold only a logsheet. The coordinates listed on the traditional cache page provide the geocache's exact location.

You should be able to find a traditional cache using the coordinates alone. This, of course, does not diminish the need for a good hint or other details on the cache page. Due to the clear-cut nature of this cache type, though, geocachers should know they're not going to have to solve any puzzles or do complicated compass work to get to the cache.

A smaller container, called a micro cache, is too small to contain items besides a log but is still considered a traditional cache.

(Georg Pfarl)

Multi-Caches

Multi-caches lead geocachers to two or more locations, the final location being a physical container. The intermediate locations can be either a physical item, such as a small (micro) container or a tag with coordinates to the next step, or a plaque or monument with numbers that lead to the final geocache. Multi-caches can also be "offsets," which provide compass points and directions leading from a chosen location to the actual hidden geocache.

Multi-caches can be as simple or as complicated as you like. While most of them range from 2 to 5 steps, there are some that contain 20 or more and take a lot of time to find. Putting a complicated multi-cache together can be a lot of fun but be aware that multi-caches of this kind may not be found as often as traditional caches. Also, make sure you will be able do the necessary maintenance on a cache with several steps.

As with all physical caches, multi-cache stages need to be kept at least 528 feet (161 meters) away from any other geocache or stages of another multi-cache. This is to avoid getting caches confused and oversaturating the area with caches.

When seeking a multi-cache it's a good idea to keep notes about what you are doing on each step. Make sure you read the clues carefully and change the coordinates when needed. It's very easy to miss one minor step in a multi-cache and find yourself searching in the wrong location.

Mystery or Puzzle Caches

As geocaching has grown, the challenge of the game has changed in many ways. Some geocachers love to go beyond the simple "follow the arrow to the hidden container" of the traditional cache and create mysteries and puzzles that not only offer finders a geocache as the payoff, but also offer the sense of accomplishment that comes with solving a puzzle.

You need only look at the number of people on the watchlist of a good mystery cache to realize what kind of attention these caches generate. They are often the topic of discussion at events and online. As you search out mystery caches you'll come to appreciate the experience and creativity that a good puzzle creator puts into his or her cache. You'll also come to realize that many mystery and puzzle caches are simply variations on themes:

- **Number puzzles.** These are popular due to how easily they lend themselves to establishing a set of coordinates for geocaching. You'll find a lot of puzzle caches built around number games, such as Sudoku.

- **Word puzzles.** Like secret messages sent from spies, word puzzles can lead you to a set of coordinates using particular words or phrases as the keys to the puzzle. Some word puzzles might use a simple alphanumeric substitution (a=1, b=2, c=3, etc.) while others can have you searching for much more complicated patterns within the cache page.

- **Picture puzzles.** Do you know the order of the U.S. presidents? Are you familiar with semaphore flags? How are you with the periodic table of elements? All these are fodder for some great puzzles that have people at home doing lots of research before they hit the road to find a cache.

The mystery and puzzle cache types are also a great catchall for a variety of challenges and requirements that cache owners place on their geocaches. By seeing the familiar question mark icon of the mystery cache, a geocacher knows that he or she is going to need more than just coordinates to find the cache and will need to consult the cache information page.

When hiding a mystery or puzzle cache, keep in mind that the posted coordinates are rarely the actual coordinates for the cache. Instead they lead to the general area of where your cache is hidden (usually within two miles). From there the seeker must use the clues you've provided to locate the cache.

Letterbox Hybrids

Almost 150 years before the first geocache was hidden, people in Dartmoor, England, were hiding little boxes along walking trails and leaving clues for others to find them. The boxes often contained postcards and letters from visitors, so they became known as *letterboxes.*

GEO-LINGO

Letterboxing is a hobby that combines elements of hiking, treasure hunting, and creative expression. Participants seek out hidden letterboxes by following clues that are posted on the Internet and record their discovery in their personal journal with the help of a rubber stamp that's part of the letterbox. In addition, letterboxers have their own personal stamps they use to stamp into the letterbox's log book.

Today letterboxing remains well liked; there are geocachers who are also letterboxers and find that both activities provide a great amount of fun.

Letterbox hybrids are geocaches that contain many of the same properties as a letterbox. Like modern letterboxes, these geocaches contain a rubber stamp so seekers can record their visits in their own personal logbooks. The instructions on the cache page often resemble the series of instructions for finding a letterbox (for example, "From the last fencepost, walk 17 paces northwest, turn 90 degrees") but also contain coordinates that lead directly to the container. Sometimes letterbox hybrids are cross-listed on letterboxing websites. This provides a great way for geocachers and letterboxers to be introduced to each other's favorite pastime.

EarthCaches

EarthCaches are a unique kind of cache that gets you outdoors and learning about the world around you.

While there is no physical container to be found, an EarthCache site is an exceptional place that people can visit to learn about a unique geoscience feature or aspect of our Earth. Visitors to EarthCaches can see how our planet has been shaped by geological processes, how we manage the resources, and how scientists gather evidence to learn about the earth.

An EarthCache might take you to a cliffside where it would be necessary for you to count the different layers of strata in the rock you see. Or you might visit an artesian well and need to use a measuring device to record the flow rate. Visiting EarthCaches from various parts of the world exposes finders to the wide variety of geological formations on Earth. They're not only fun, they're also educational!

EarthCaches are listed in conjunction with the Geological Society of America, and can be found all over the world—on land or at sea. Due to the distinct characteristics of EarthCaches, they are published under a modified set of guidelines from other caches. Be sure to read up and follow all the instructions before attempting to place one.

For more information on EarthCaches, please visit www.geocaching.com/earthcaching.

Wherigo Caches

As the capabilities of handheld GPS units have evolved over the years, geocachers have been presented with new tools and opportunities. One of these uses for GPS is an application called Wherigo, which guides players through a series of real world zones to complete tasks as part of a larger adventure. Players can download free cartridges from Wherigo.com, which can be run on a limited number of GPS units and PDAs. Wherigo is a toolset for creating and playing GPS-enabled adventures in the real world. By integrating a Wherigo experience, called a cartridge, with finding a geocache, geocaching can be an even richer experience. Wherigo allows geocachers to interact with a variety of physical and virtual elements that add to the adventure. These caches go beyond the capabilities of simple handheld GPS units and require specialized GPS units, which run the Wherigo player.

Unusual Cache Types

Now that you have learned about the standard caches you are most likely to encounter, let's take a look at a few of the more rare cache types. Many geocachers will travel long distances for the opportunity to log and receive the specialized icon on their profile for one of these unusual geocaches.

Some of the various geocaching icons that represent unusual geocaches.
(Geocaching.com)

GPS Adventures Maze Exhibit

The GPS Adventures Maze is a hands-on traveling exhibit created by Groundspeak, Development Sponsor Trimble, and Minotaur Mazes. Created for museums, it incorporates the history, current uses, and future possibilities of GPS, simulating geocaching by leading visitors of all ages through a 2,500-square-foot maze. Visitors must complete a series of challenges within the exhibit in order to "find" a cache. The maze was designed to illustrate the uses of geocaching and GPS technology.

Project A.P.E. Geocaches

In 2001, 20th Century Fox placed 12 geocaches, each with a Project A.P.E. theme, as a promotion for the movie *Planet of the Apes*. Each cache represented a fictional story in which scientists revealed an "Alternative Primate Evolution." These caches were made using specially marked and specially sized ammo containers holding original props from the movie as rewards for the first finders.

Only one Project A.P.E. cache exists today—in the jungles of Brazil—making it one of the rarest cache types of all. Dedicated geocachers travel from far and wide just to search for this last remaining Project A.P.E cache for the adventure and to receive this elusive icon on their user profiles.

Groundspeak Headquarters Cache

The Groundspeak Headquarters Cache is pretty rare, since there is only one in the world, located in the main lobby of the Groundspeak offices in Seattle, Washington. It is also known fondly as the Lily Pad or by its GC Code of GCK25B. Battling Seattle traffic is only slightly less dangerous than the Brazilian jungle. Visiting this one requires contacting Geocaching.com to receive an invitation, and they are happy to have guests come to visit, usually on a Friday. You even receive a specialized digital souvenir on your profile for logging it.

Geocaching Gatherings

Geocaching is a social activity, so there are several options to create events for people to get together and swap stories, attend educational sessions, or just hang out with people with similar interests. After attending an event you can come home and post an online log and pictures to share your experiences. We will talk much more about Geocaching events and even give you some great tips for hosting your own event in Chapter 16.

These geocaching icons represent the different types of geocaching events.
(Geocaching.com)

Here are some popular types of geocaching events. We predict that different styles of events will continue to be created as this social community evolves.

- **Geocaching Event Cache:** A gathering of local geocachers or geocaching organizations to discuss geocaching. The Event Cache page specifies a time for the event and provides coordinates to its location. In other words, it's a party. After the event, the cache is archived. Geocaching events are published at least two weeks in advance and are open for anyone to attend.

- **Cache In Trash Out Event:** An activity intimately tied to geocaching. While searching for caches, geocachers collect litter along the trails and properly dispose of it. Cache In Trash Out Events are larger gatherings of geocachers that focus on litter cleanup, removal of invasive species, revegetation efforts, or trail building.

- **Mega-Event Cache:** An Event Cache that is attended by 500+ people. Mega-Events offer geocachers a day of planned activities. There are often several days of additional activities surrounding a Mega-Event. These large events attract geocachers from all over the world and are usually held annually.

- **The Groundspeak Block Party:** This Mega-Event is held near Groundspeak Headquarters in Seattle, Washington. It's held annually on International Geocaching Day, the third Saturday in August. Not only can you can meet your friendly geocaching neighbors from around the world, but you can also log Groundspeak Headquarters, meet the Groundspeak Lackeys, and participate in several fun activities.

EUREKA!

On July 4, 2010, Groundspeak capped off the Lost and Found 10th Anniversary of Geocaching with a Mega-Event on the streets surrounding Groundspeak headquarters. This event went so well, it evolved into the annual Groundspeak Block Party.

Grandfathered Cache Types and Events

As the game has evolved, so have the types of geocaches published on Geocaching.com. In many cases the early caches have gone on to lay the foundations for new games and activities. Although some geocache types are no longer published on Geocaching.com, many have been grandfathered in and are still listed online for you to find—here are some of those:.

- **Virtual Caches:** Virtual geocaches are intended to bring the seeker to a unique location, not to find a cache container. The location itself is the reward in this type of cache. These sites are typically of a unique landmark or historical monument. Geocachers prove they were at the location by answering a question related to the area or by taking a photo of themselves. Virtual caches were also the inspiration for Geocaching Challenges.

- **Webcam Caches:** These caches use existing webcams that are available to be viewed by the public that were placed by individuals or agencies to monitor various areas like parks or roads. The idea is to get yourself in front of the camera to log your visit. The challenging part, however, is that you need to either use your smartphone to capture the camera image or call a friend to look up the website that displays the camera and save the picture to log the cache.

- **Locationless (Reverse) Cache:** These reverse caches could be considered the polar opposite of a traditional cache. Instead of finding a hidden container, you locate a specific object, such as an unusual type of statue or bridge, and log its coordinates. Locationless caches were also the inspiration for the Groundspeak GPS game of Waymarking.

- **10 Years! Event Cache:** To celebrate the tenth anniversary of the first geocache hidden, Groundspeak sponsored a series of celebrations around the world. This special Event Cache type was created specifically for events created as part of that celebration held April 30–May 3, 2010.

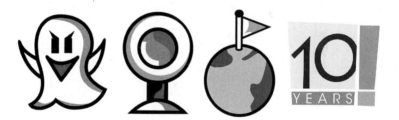

Some of the various geocaching icons that represent the different types of grandfathered geocaches.
(Geocaching.com)

More cache types may be added as Geocaching changes and continues to evolve. That is one of the great things about this community-inspired game. To make things better all you have to do is get involved and suggest new ways to improve the experience for everyone. Geocaching.com continues to grow the game by adding new variations as advancing technology and the creative community find new ways to expand the adventure.

The Least You Need to Know

- Geocaching continues to evolve as an activity; there are many different types of geocaches that appeal to a wide variety of people.

- Some geocache types have gone on to inspire entire new games like Waymarking and Geocaching Challenges.

- You may have to travel long distances in order to log some of the rare cache types.

- The social aspects of Geocaching and the desire to share the adventure with the community led to the creation of several types of Geocaching Events.

Creating and Hiding Your Own Geocache

In This Chapter

- What makes a great geocache hide
- Things to consider before hiding your first geocache
- Submitting your geocache to Geocaching.com
- Taking care of your geocache

Now that you know about the types of geocaches available, you may want to consider giving back to the community by hiding your own geocache. Once you've played the game for a while and found 20 or more geocaches, you'll realize that you know of unique or interesting locations that are important to you that you would like to share with other geocachers.

Hiding a Geocache

The first step in creating your own geocache is to read the Geocache Listing Requirements on Geocaching.com. The guidelines posted at www.geocaching.com help you in determining all of the information and resources you need in order for a cache to be published. The guidelines will also help you to place a geocache that you and fellow seekers will be proud of.

Here are some things to think about as you get started. Geocaching is just like real estate—the three most important factors in a cache site are location, location, location! It is common for geocachers to hide caches in areas that are important to them, reflecting a special interest or memory of the cache owner. When thinking about where to place a cache, keep these things in mind:

- **Does it meet Geocaching.com's listing requirements?** Make sure to review these during your research. Issues of concern include proximity to other geocaches, commerciality, solicitation, and long-term cache maintenance.

- **Did you consider accessibility?** If a cache is too visible or too close to busy roads and trails, there is a good chance someone may stumble upon it by accident. It is best to place a cache just off-trail to preserve the environment but keep it out of sight of people casually passing by.

- **Did you seek permission from the landowner or manager?** If you place a cache on private land, you must ask permission before hiding your cache. If you place it on public lands, contact the land manager to find out about any rules or restrictions.

- **Will the location placement cause unnecessary concern?** Please use common sense when choosing a location for your cache. Do not design your cache such that it might be confused with something more dangerous.

As the owner of your geocache, you are ultimately responsible for it, so make sure you know the rules for the area where you place your cache.

Finally, try to place a geocache in a location that is unique in some way—a location, possibly challenging and scenic, that will leave a lasting impression on its visitors. Ideally, the site itself will be as great of a reward as finding the cache. Use your imagination and think of some of your favorite outdoor spots. A prime camping spot, great viewpoint, unusual location, etc., are all good places to hide a cache provided no one has put a geocache there already.

Container Considerations

You have many options for containers; the primary requirement is that they hold up to the outdoor elements. Depending on your climate, the container will have to hold up to rain, snow, dust, and heat. Often, containers are camouflaged to blend in with the natural environment. This makes them more difficult to find, especially by someone who might stumble across one by accident.

Geocachers have had good success with clear, watertight plastic containers, ammunition boxes, and waterproof boxes often used on boats. Micro caches are often plastic film containers or some other type of small waterproof capsules, usually just large enough to contain a small logsheet. Others are made out of fake rocks, tins with magnets to attach to metal structures like park benches and signs, and waterproof match cases. To determine which type of container is most appropriate, consider where you will be placing it. Many geocachers believe that it is best to hide the largest container a location can support. While a micro may be the best choice in a city park, when hiding in the back country most geocachers will choose to hide a regular size container.

An example of clearly identified, watertight geocache containers.
(Geocaching.com)

You'll also want to invest in some plastic zippered baggies. These help you to organize the cache contents and help protect them if the container leaks. Whichever type of container you choose, be sure to identify your cache so that someone who doesn't play can figure out what it is. We suggest that you mark the outside of your geocache container with *Geocache* or *Geocaching.com*, and the name of the cache so that it is easily identified as a geocache and not something dangerous. It's a great idea to include an information sheet explaining what a geocache is and contact information for if it needs to be moved. This data may help keep it from being ransacked or removed by someone who is not familiar with the game. Check out the Cache Notification Sheet in Appendix E. Make your own copy to laminate or place in a waterproof bag. Geocaching.com has a list of cache notification pages that have been translated into many different languages for placement in a variety of different countries available for download at www.geocaching.com/seek.

EUREKA!

Geocache containers can be nearly anything that is durable and watertight. They can be as large or as small as you like and are often camouflaged to blend in to their surroundings. Be sure to properly label your geocache so it can be quickly identified if stumbled upon by accident.

Next you'll need a logbook and a pen or pencil. A small spiral notebook does the trick. If the cache is in an area that will freeze, use a pencil, since pens can freeze and refuse to work in the cold. Be sure to place the logbook and pen or pencil in a plastic bag. Now it's time to stock the cache with goodies. Chapter 2 includes lots of ideas about what to include in your geocache.

When you place the container, never bury it. However, it is okay to cover it up with rocks, bark, moss, and dead branches. Concealing the cache a bit helps keep it from being found by *muggles*. Place the container in a hollow log or stump, or secure it with a heavy log or rock to decrease the chances of it blowing, floating, or washing away.

> **GEO-LINGO**
>
> **Muggles** are nongeocachers, usually people on the trail who look suspiciously at a geocacher on the hunt, or who have accidentally found a cache. Geocachers borrowed the term from the *Harry Potter* series, in which it refers to a nonmagical person. Geocachers often try to avoid being conspicuous to muggles to keep the geocache safe from curious potential plunderers.

Ask Permission

Always ask permission before placing a geocache, especially on private property. Most sites have postings that indicate who owns or manages the area. Chances are they may never have heard of geocaching. It is up to you to explain the activity of geocaching, your role as a cache owner, and their potential positive contribution to the worldwide geocaching community. Obtaining permission from land managers is very important and helps ensure that geocachers will have a positive experience at the location.

Be aware that many public properties already have geocaching policies in place that you will need to comply with before submitting your geocache. When asking for permission, be sure to ask if there are any special requirements for geocaches on the property. For example, the U.S. National Park Service does not allow geocaching on the property it manages without specific permission from the park manager. In fact, it considers unpermitted caches violations of federal regulations. These strict regulations are intended to protect the often fragile, historical, and cultural areas they manage.

> **DEAD BATTERIES**
>
> As the geocache owner, it is up to you to ensure that its placement and the foot traffic being brought into the area do not cause problems or environmental damage. If you realize the geocache is in a poor location, discontinue the site immediately and relocate it to a better location, or remove it entirely.

Placing Your Geocache and Saving the Coordinates

Now that you have found a location, prepared your geocache for placement, and received permission from the property manager, it is time to place the cache and save the coordinates as a waypoint. If you haven't already, be sure to come up with a descriptive name for your cache. You'll use the name when saving the waypoint. You will need to consult your GPS user manual before leaving home to learn how to save waypoints. Not to worry, most manufacturers make this very easy and often even include shortcuts to save your position using a single button.

To ensure the most accurate coordinates possible for your geo-cache, be sure to have your GPS on, with good satellite lock as you approach your prospective cache site. After arriving at the site, set your GPS down with a clear view of the sky, and allow your GPS a couple of minutes to optimize its satellite lock. If your receiver has an averaging feature, use it to record the most accurate waypoint possible. This feature allows you to take the waypoint's reading over a span of time, usually a minute or two, to improve accuracy. Many modern units average their location automatically—just make sure to give it a few minutes to work its magic.

If your receiver does not have an averaging option, you can use a couple of tricks to do it anyway. One is to save multiple waypoints of the same area; however, this is more effective if done over several days and successive visits. Selecting the waypoint in the center aver-ages the position. Once you have several waypoints taken over 5 to 10 minutes, you can take all of those numbers and average them manually using good old arithmetic in order to come up with the best coordinates for your geocache.

After taking a few minutes to average the location, save it as a new waypoint. Just as when you entered a waypoint to find a cache, save your waypoint in the same format. At this point most experienced hiders will walk some distance, 200 feet or so, away from the cache site and then navigate back to it using this new waypoint. If it leads you back to the same approximate location, consider it "confirmed" and you are ready to go; if not you will want to try the process again. After you have your confirmed waypoint, it's a good idea to write it in permanent marker on the container and logbook, and make sure you have a copy to bring back with you.

Submitting Your Geocache to Geocaching.com

It's now time to go online to post your new geocache for the world to find. Some of the features required when posting your own geocache include:

- **Type, size, and name of geocache.**

- **Latitude/longitude coordinates in decimal minutes.**

- **Overall difficulty and terrain ratings.**

- **Short description.** Provide information about the location, including difficulty, terrain, and access.

- **Long description.** Provide details about the cache, including cache contents, what the container looks like, and the relevancy of the location. Is there additional educational or historical information you want to share?

- **Hints/spoiler info.** Hints will be encrypted on the site until a geocacher clicks a link to decrypt it, or decodes it on the trail. Keep your hints short so that decoding it on the trail is easier, and remember that no hint at all is better than a bad one. Imagine your frustration if after searching for an hour, you finally decide to decrypt the hint and it reads, "No hint needed."

- **Attributes.** These are characteristics represented graphically that provide helpful information to geocachers who wish to find specific kinds of caches. These graphics represent cache characteristics explaining what to expect at a cache location, like kid-friendliness, 24-hour-a-day availability, swimming requirements, camping conveniences, and more.

- **Trackable items.** Want to place a trackable item in your geocache? You need to add a log entry to your cache page in order for the Travel Bug to appear in the online inventory of the cache.

After you have compiled all of the information for your geocache, go to the "Play" tab on the front page of Geocaching.com and select the "Hide and Seek a Cache" option. Then, go to the "Hide a Cache ..." section and click the "online form" link. You can also reach this form by going to www.geocaching.com, logging in, and finding it on the website. Once you have completed all of the required information in the form, check the box marked "Enable Cache Listing" and click the "Report New Listing" button.

After posting your geocache listing, the cache is sent to the geocaching volunteer reviewer community, who reviews the cache submission to make sure that it meets the guidelines for geocache publication.

The Geocache Review Process

When a geocache is submitted on Geocaching.com it is placed in the Review Queue and marked for the volunteer reviewer of that particular area. Yes, an actual human being checks on each online cache listing before it is published. Volunteer cache reviewers are highly experienced geocachers who have been asked by Groundspeak to fulfill this role for the website. They are all geocachers themselves who love the game and have become familiar with the guidelines for placing a cache as well as special considerations in various areas as to land use and regulations.

Normally a cache reviewer examines your submission within three days (remember, though, that reviewers are volunteers with their own jobs and responsibilities that must come first). The reviewer examines the submission with a variety of maps and tools provided for the job and also keeps a keen eye on the guidelines that you read before submitting a cache. It's not uncommon for a careful reviewer to catch a mistake or omission on your page and ask you to make changes before continuing the review. When you post a cache, it is up to you to make sure all the information is correct. No one from a geocaching website will personally go outdoors to review the site before publication.

Many of the concerns your reviewer might raise can be addressed by the cache owner ahead of time by giving attention to the surrounding area and the maps. If there is now a trail system that used to be a railroad track but the maps still show it as a track, post a reviewer note with those details and any others that your reviewer might ask you about. Providing as much information about the hide and location as possible will greatly expedite the review process.

If there are any concerns, the reviewer will address them and wait for your response. Otherwise they will push the magic Publish button and your geocache will be available for the world to see! You will be notified by e-mail when your geocache is published; thereafter, you receive e-mails every time someone logs your geocache.

Care and Feeding of Your Geocache

After you place the geocache, it is your responsibility to maintain the cache and the area around it. You need to return as often as necessary to ensure that your cache is in good shape and is not having a negative impact on the area. After it has been visited, it is a good idea to check with the geocachers who found it to ask their opinion of its condition and placement. Have a look when you can to make sure it is in good condition and stocked with trade items. If you have concerns about the location, discontinue the cache site and move it to a better location. When the geocache is active, it can remain in place as long as you or someone you appoint will manage it.

Do's and Don'ts

As mentioned before, the geocaching community is a self-regulating group. There are no geopolice to ticket you for placing a bad cache or leaving behind inappropriate trade items. Something even worse would happen: the game and its participants would start getting a bad reputation for being careless with safety, or possibly damaging the environment. This type of reputation would do nothing but cause geocachers to be viewed negatively, resulting in bad press and the closure of areas to geocaching. Geocachers know this, and, with minimal exception, have gone out of their way to ensure that geocaching goes on without causing concern or problems for others. Here are some important points to remember:

- Read the guidelines (located at www.geocaching.com) for placing a geocache before actually placing one. This will also save you from a lot of extra work.

- Use common sense when thinking about a location for your geocache. Consider the possible impact it could have on the local area and its residents. Remember that your cache could attract a number of visitors.

- Clearly identify your geocache by marking the container with at least the cache name and GC code. This will help to avoid having the cache be mistaken as anything other than a geocache.

- Do not bury caches or place them in areas that will cause damage to the environment or wildlife.

- Do not place a geocache in any area that's home to rare or endangered species and plants. Also avoid areas with delicate ground cover: consider the number of people that may visit the site to find your geocache.

- Do not place geocaches on archaeological or historical sites. These areas could be negatively affected by the extra traffic the cache may cause.

- Do not leave behind any inappropriate material or items such as alcohol, tobacco, weapons, or drugs.

- Do not place a cache too close to an existing geocache. This can lead to confusion and oversaturation problems. Geocaching.com uses 528 feet (161 meters) as the standard minimum distance that must be maintained between geocaches.

- Never place a geocache in an area posted "No Trespassing."

- Do not place geocaches in areas that would be perceived to compromise public safety or cause unnecessary concern, such as near railroad tracks, public buildings, schools, or military installations.

- Do not place a geocache while on vacation; you need to be available to maintain it on an ongoing basis.

- Do not place geocaches that solicit customers or are perceived to be posted for religious, political, or social agendas. Geocaching is supposed to be a light, fun activity and not a platform for an agenda or advertising.

The Least You Need to Know

- You can give back to the community by placing and maintaining great geocaches.
- A beautiful location, hike, or view can make a basic cache a great adventure.
- Every geocacher has a part to play in maintaining the integrity and reputation of the game.
- Maintaining a geocache is the responsibility of the geocache owner.
- Always ask permission from the landowner or land managing agency before placing a geocache.

Travel Bugs®, Geocoins, and Trackable Treasures

In This Chapter

- An explanation of Travel Bugs and other trackable items
- What to do when you find Trackables
- Creating your own Trackables
- How Trackables have evolved

Like most adventurers and explorers, geocachers are fascinated by travel and love to explore new locations. Yet, even in geocaching there can be limitations to how much we can see and how far we can go. That's where Travel Bugs and other trackable game pieces come into play. These things are called "Trackables." When we can't go to a location ourselves, it's fun to send something that represents us out into the world, especially when you can track the travels of that something online. Think of it as traveling vicariously through inanimate objects.

In this chapter, you will learn how Trackables travel from geocache to geocache, picking up stories and photos along the way.

Twenty-First-Century Message in a Bottle

In the early days of geocaching, a unique phenomenon was observed. Players were leaving objects in geocaches not for trading but for traveling. Instructions were placed with these trinkets to keep them moving from geocache to geocache. Finders of the trinkets would send e-mails back to the owners letting them know which geocache the item was now in and how far it had traveled. These trackable items came to be known early on as "hitchhikers." They were hitch-hiking from one geocache container to another.

Like a bottle drifting in the ocean, Trackables are objects that find their way around by drifting from geocache to geocache. These items are usually some form of toy, symbol, or trinket that has meaning to the person placing the item. Trackables often include instructions for transport and final destination. Some Trackables want to wander aimlessly from geocache to geocache, while others desire to travel to a specific destination, sometimes even to perform a specific task, like having its photo taken by the Brandenburg Gate, the Eiffel Tower, or the Statue of Liberty.

It's up to the owner of the Trackable to give it a travel goal or mis-sion. Each journey is unique, and through the logs and photos on the website, Trackables take on lives of their own.

Unlike a traditional message in a bottle that is never seen by the owner again, the unique feature of each Trackable is that its adven-tures are tracked online. When a geocacher finds and relocates an item in the real world, she must also log the find online, sharing sto-ries and/or photos relating to its relocation and travel. Each time an item is logged, the owner of the item is notified via e-mail and learns of its adventures. A written log and map of all documented travels for each trackable item is maintained online for all to share and enjoy.

Travel Bugs Are Born

In response to the popularity of hitchhikers, the Lackeys at Geocaching.com came up with an idea to integrate this grassroots movement into the website and make it easier to follow these hitchhikers on their adventures. They created a system to track hitchhikers by having geocachers attach small "dog tags" with unique serial numbers to the items that move around. These serial numbers and tags provided a much more efficient way to track their travels, and so the *Travel Bug* was born.

GEO-LINGO

Travel Bug is a term that was coined by Jeremy Irish of Groundspeak in July 2001, inspired by a person's "travel bug," or desire to travel. Travel Bugs help you satisfy your own desire for adventure by living vicariously through inanimate objects.

A Travel Bug dog tag is a metal tag with a unique tracking number available for lookup at Geocaching.com. It is usually attached to a hitchhiker, but can be used as a Travel Bug itself. These bugs can be easily identified and viewed on the Geocaching.com site using their numbers. A geocacher who finds a Travel Bug logs information on how he found it and the new location so that the owner of the Travel Bug can check on its current whereabouts. Every time a Travel Bug or other Trackable is logged, the owner, and anyone else who chooses to subscribe to the bug by "watching" it, receives an e-mail notice from Geocaching.com. Those messages prompt readers to take a look at the dynamic map, read a bit about the new location, and check out any new photos. Those are the vicarious travels that cost significantly less than actual world travel.

A Geocaching.com Travel Bug dog tag.
(Groundspeak)

Each Travel Bug is marked with the Travel Bug bar code trademark logo and an individual tracking number. Brand new Travel Bugs, Geocoins, and other Trackables are available from the retail store at shop.geocaching.com as well as from a number of official distributors who usually attend geocaching events.

When you receive your Travel Bug, you will also find a duplicate tag and a chain. Owners can keep the duplicate as a memento and a reference to check up on their bug's status. The copy makes a neat necklace for hard-core geocachers, a great key chain, or possibly the ultimate accessory for your pet's collar. If you have lots of these duplicate tags, they make for a metal record-keeping catalog.

Travel Bugs are usually attached to an object the owner thought deserves to travel. Besides the object, which is often reflective of the owner's personality, each Travel Bug takes on an identity of its own. Each is named, has travel goals, and gets its own dedicated web page at Geocaching.com. Here is an example of a Travel Bug:

> Name: 50 State Cruiser (TB151EA)
>
> Released: Friday, 22 December 2006
>
> Origin: Kansas, United States
>
> Recently spotted in: Evasion (GC1HDW1)
>
> Current goal: My mission is to cruise from state to state, visiting *all* 50 states grabbing up pictures from cool state landmarks or oddities.
>
> About this item: This TB is a toy replica red and silver Honda 1000R street bike. Help it cruise along.

Finding Travel Bugs

If you find a Travel Bug, it is important to check to see whether the owner attached any instructions. Log on to Geocaching.com and go to the specific page for the geocache where the bug was found. Log your find, and then on the Inventory section on the page click the Travel Bug name link. Note that Travel Bugs are named. In the previous example, its name is 50 State Cruiser. Clicking the Travel Bug link brings up the bug's dedicated details page.

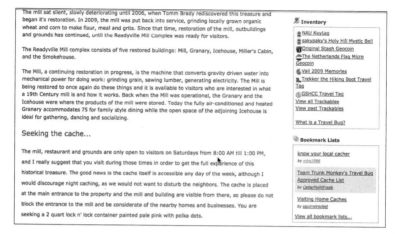

A Travel Bug link is shown in the geocache inventory.
(Geocaching.com)

You can also look up the Travel Bug by the specific Travel Bug tracking code at www.geocaching.com/track. This page works for looking up any type of Trackable.

There are a few options available for logging one of these game pieces. If the item has been properly logged into a geocache, you can simply retrieve it from the log for the geocache where it was found. However, occasionally Travel Bugs are misplaced or a previous geocacher has not yet logged it into the geocache when the new finder is ready to write her online log. When this happens, you have the option of writing a "Grabbed it from somewhere else" log. This enables you to inform the owner that the bug is no longer in the previously mentioned geocache but has been found elsewhere and will continue its mission soon.

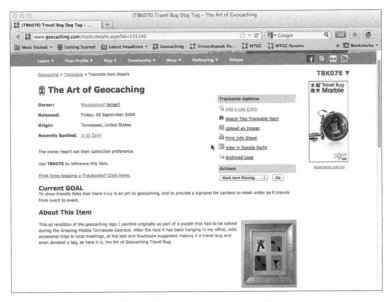

This page shows a Travel Bug's information, such as its name, owner, and travel goal.

(Geocaching.com)

Another logging option is to report that you have "Discovered it" on the Trackable's page. A "Discovered it" log means you can confirm that you have seen it in a specific geocache and you are not moving the item to a new location. This can be a very useful tool for the Travel Bug owner who might be concerned that the bug is missing if it has not been logged as having been moved from a geocache in some time.

"Discovered it" logs are also useful for Travel Bugs and other Trackables you might encounter at geocaching events. It's a nice way of saying "I saw you!" and lets the owner know that you appreciate her sharing her Trackables with you. Additionally, you retain a digital collection of these discoveries along with the creative graphic icons that represent each.

If you log a "Retrieved it" note, the Trackable will be shown in the online inventory on your personal account page. The next time you log that a geocache has been found, there will be an option to select the trackable item from your inventory list and post it to the new geocache location.

This page enables you to log a found Travel Bug after entering its tracking number.
(Geocaching.com)

Relocating Travel Bugs

When you move a Travel Bug to a new geocache, visit Geocaching. com and go to the new geocache's page. When you log the geocache as found, you'll see a menu on that page that provides an option to select the Travel Bug from your inventory list and "drop" it in the new geocache. When you submit your log entry, the bug will appear on the new geocache's page and others will know that it is in the geocache ready to be found again. Don't forget to upload an image, since most Trackable owners love to see photos of their items traveling "in the wild." These photos are also displayed in your own online photo gallery that is associated with your public profile page.

EUREKA!

The first Travel Bug, Deadly Duck: Envy, was placed on August 31, 2001. As of this writing, there are millions of Trackables in play all around the globe and even out of this world on the International Space Station.

Creating Your Own Trackable Item

Sending your own trackable item on its way is a lot of fun! The first thing you need to do is purchase a Travel Bug. You can purchase one online at shop.geocaching.com or from one of Geocaching.com's official distributors. Once received, it is time to activate the bug. Log on to Geocaching.com and select the "Find Trackables" option under the "Play" menu. Enter the bug's tracking number in the "Activate Trackable" box provided.

Geocaching > Trackables > Activate a Trackable

Step 1 of 3: Activation Code

Liam, congratulations on your Trackable purchase! There are only 3 simple steps to activate your Trackable. This screencast will walk you through the process.

First, you will need to enter your item's tracking number and activation code. The tracking number is the number stamped on your coin or dog tag.

* indicates a required field.

Enter Your Tracking Number: *

The activation code is a unique code located on the packaging for each Trackable. When activated, the Trackable will be assigned to your user account. This way you can modify its own personal page.

Enter Your Activation Code: *

Retrieve your activation code

Activate Your Trackable

Enter the tracking number and the activation code for new Travel Bugs.
(Geocaching.com)

The activation code is included in the Travel Bug package. Successfully entering the tracking number and activation code brings up the Travel Bug's information page. This is where the fun really begins. For the Travel Bug, you can now enter:

- A cool name
- Starting city
- Activation date
- Item description
- The traveling goal

Once complete, your trackable item will be activated and ready to go. Congratulations, it's all yours! Use the Edit link in the upper-right corner of the page to edit your Travel Bug's name, description, and travel goals at any time.

Whether you are relocating a bug or activating a new one, you have an opportunity to upload images to a Travel Bug page. Click the Upload Image link. If you are the bug's owner and have loaded multiple images, open the bug's Edit page and a drop-down box will appear with a list of the images loaded. Select your favorite picture and it will become the image for your bug's dedicated page and entry in the Travel Bug photo gallery.

Name your Travel Bug and list a description and travel goals on the edit page.
(Geocaching.com)

The Travel Bug Goes Big

As with geocaching itself, Trackables and Travel Bugs have evolved much through the creativity of geocachers. What began as a way to identify trinkets that move from container to container has grown into a means of self-expression.

There are a whole horde of oversized Travel Bugs in the world that won't fit into most geocaches. Rather, these "travel beasts" make their way from geocaching event to geocaching event, where they are displayed and discovered by geocachers. Some of these Travel Bugs are so well-known it's considered an honor and somewhat of a status symbol to log them. Here are some of them:

- **Cindy (the Cinder Block).** A standard 38-pound cinder block with instructions to be left near a geocache since it likely won't fit in the geocache. After nine years and over 13,000 miles, Cindy is covered in hundreds of signatures of the geocachers who have discovered or moved her.

- **Mary Proppins.** Mary is a propeller blade from a commercial aircraft. The owner gave her the goal of being moved by at least one geocacher. In nearly 9,000 miles of travel Mary has far exceeded this goal, but she better watch out. Her younger half-brother Iggy Prop is catching up quickly with almost 4,000 miles logged.

- **Chain Chomp.** A 15-pound bowling ball with a large chain attached. Considering the size and unwieldiness of a Travel Bug like this, it's amazing to realize it has traveled over 8,400 miles.

- **Pet Rock.** This 240-pound block of limestone has traveled nearly 2,000 miles since its launch in 2003. Most of those miles have been logged as the victim of several "bugnappings," all in good fun. It has become a bit of a local joke for a team to retrieve Pet Rock and transport it to an event or difficult cache where it must be rescued and brought back home by its owner.

The Evolution of the Travel Bug

It's not uncommon to attend events and see geocachers wearing T-shirts or even sporting tattoos with their own personal Travel Bug tracking numbers. You will frequently find geocachers with pets and vehicles as Travel Bugs. Rather than move these from geocache to geocache, they are available to simply discover as a way of saying that you've met or seen them.

Coffee Bug was released in Alaska in 2002. CYBret put it on his watch list simply because he loves coffee. Imagine his surprise in 2007 when he finally crossed paths with it and was able to have a cup of coffee with the Travel Bug.
(Bret Hammond)

It is clear that Travel Bugs have changed in the ways they are used since their early days, but there have been other changes as well. As the popularity of Travel Bugs increases, new styles are emerging to meet growing demand and changing needs. The classic Travel Bug is still going strong and is the main choice for most geocachers, but there are some other fun options out there today. From multi-sized, multi-colored Travel Tags to Hitchhiker container lids, the possibilities are nearly endless. The great part is that they are all trackable on Geocaching.com.

Geocoins: Trackable Meets Collectible

One of the biggest leaps in Geocaching Trackables came with the creation of the trackable Geocoin. In the early days of the Geocaching.com website, a Washington State geocacher by the name of "Moun10Bike" developed a new Trackable that would eventually spread like wildfire: the Geocoin.

Jon Stanley (a.k.a. Moun10Bike), an avid geocacher, became friends with the founders of the company. Stanley donated many of the original software licenses used to run the Geocaching.com website. Remember that he was in Seattle and so were the founders; it was a very small community at that time. After a few techie conversations about cool possibilities with software and our hobby, Geocaching. com worked with Stanley to have his "Geocoins" tracked on Geocaching.com, just like Travel Bugs.

As you might imagine, Stanley kept the very first Geocoin for himself. A decade later, he still has it in his possession. This coin traveled to Geocoinfest Europa in 2011, the largest Geocoin event to date, and to a select few other events. It gets "discovered" by many appreciative fans.

He bravely released the second coin in this series into the wilds of the game. It didn't travel very far, staying within Washington State. The geocacher who found it decided to keep it for himself as a collector's item, and he brings it out to local events occasionally.

The third coin in the series traveled as planned within the game until it got lost for a number of years in a dusty bin. Against the odds, it somehow resurfaced and eventually found its way into the capable hands of a Colorado geocacher named Joe Friday. After a brief reunion with Moun10Bike, that Geocoin left home once more to be part of the GPS Adventures Maze museum exhibit. To this day, Joe Friday happily escorts this coin to various gatherings. That little inanimate object has logged some 55,000 miles and hundreds of online records.

In no time at all, geocaches containing the elusive Moun10Bike trackable Geocoins were being sought after. The coins themselves were traded into other geocaches and passed around the community. Being able to log one and get that coveted icon on your geocaching profile was a rite of passage among geocachers.

Soon people weren't only moving them from geocache to geocache, they were asking Jon for permission to keep the coins as collector's items. It quickly became apparent that something very special was catching on.

A relatively short time later, mass-produced Geocoins with their own icons became available as an alternative to Travel Bugs. These popular Trackables started off as souvenirs for large events or as collectibles for local geocaching organizations, but eventually people started producing personal Geocoins and offering them to the community. Soon, geocachers were collecting and trading coins that reflected the distinct personalities of the geocachers who created them.

A collection of Geocoins created by individual geocachers, groups, and organizations.
(Groundspeak)

Today, Geocoins number in the tens of thousands with more and more being created each year. Most of them continue to have their own individual tracking numbers and custom icons. Collectors love them not only for their value, but also for their uniqueness and quality. If you would like to create your own Geocoins, you can learn more information at www.geocaching.com/track. There, you will find answers to frequently asked questions as well as a list of Geocoin manufacturers and resellers. If you attend a geocaching event you will often see the die-hard Geocoin collectors off in a corner showing off their collections and making trades for that next "must have" trackable Geocoin.

Of course, not every collectible is trackable on Geocaching.com. Some people choose to create limited-run nontrackable coins for events, as gifts, and for private trading. These nontrackable coins and tags are totally legit, but many cachers prefer being able to follow their Trackables' adventures through the Geocaching.com website.

Tracking Geocoins and Other Trackables

On the website, Trackable owners have the option to set the official status of their own trackable items as "Collectible" or "Non-Collectible." This is done from the "Edit this Trackable Item" link on the Trackable's listing page.

Collectible functionality allows the Trackable to be in a geo-cacher's collection rather than moving from geocache to geocache. Trackables that are in a collection do not show in the "inventory" field when logging a geocache. This is good because it shortens your inventory to Trackables that you've picked up to move. Trackables in a collection can only be discovered; they cannot be grabbed, dropped, or dipped into a geocache. You can allow another cacher to collect a Trackable that you own.

To move a Trackable to your collection, first visit the Trackable listing, and on the edit page, make the item collectible. This is a check box on the edit page. You can then move to collection as a log, available on the trackable listing page (not the log page). Or, once edited to collectible, you can visit "Your Trackable Inventory" page and select "Move to Collection."

To move a Trackable back to your inventory (giving it the ability to move to a geocache), visit "Your Trackables Collection" and select "Move to Inventory." This can also be done from the Trackable listing. If you leave its status as collectible, once in a cache and grabbed by another user, they can then move the trackable into their own collection—so if you want the item to move, you should revisit the edit page, and set the status to Non-Collectible.

Trackables Go Mainstream

From time to time Geocaching.com will host promotions involving trackable items. These promotions can be tied to awareness campaigns or centered around contests filled with great prizes, like GPS units or even brand-new Jeeps. No matter the prize, they promise new fun and adventure with unique trackable items. Here are just a few examples of these great promotions:

- **Unite for Diabetes Trackables:** Travel Bugs featuring the World Diabetes Day emblem and a special tag were distributed to commemorate the holiday. It was so successful, it spawned limited edition Geocoins distributed around the world. More than 5,000 were created and handed out at local International Diabetes Federation (IDF) events across the globe, bringing awareness to the more than 250 million people affected by the disease.

- **Geico's Find the Gecko Travel Tags:** 9,000 custom trackable travel tags were given for free to the geocaching community along with the chance to win one of twenty new Magellan GPS units. The tags were shaped like the insurance company's mascot: a friendly, green gecko. This "spokesgecko" had travelled well off the beaten path and geocachers were tasked to go find him.

- **Jeep 4X4 Geocaching Challenge:** For four years Jeep sponsored the 4X4 Geocaching Challenge, giving away over 30,000 custom diecast Jeep Trackables in the process. But the free Trackables were just the beginning of the fun: as part of the challenge, geocachers were invited to submit photographs of the Trackables in action with monthly winners receiving

GPS units and the grand prize winner receiving a brand-new Jeep Liberty. The associated Travel Bugs from each year—yellow Jeep Wranglers, white Jeep Rubicons, green Jeep Rescue Concepts, and red Jeep Commanders—are still out there traveling today! If you are lucky enough, you might even get to log one and share in the adventure.

This great photo titled "No Terrain Is Too Tough" was the Grand Prize Jeep Liberty–winning entry by Discovery Scout.
(Groundspeak)

Travel Bug Stories

Travel Bug and Trackable owners enjoy seeing their creations travel from place to place, each developing a story of its own. Unfortunately, some bugs get exterminated by being taken and never placed again, whereas others travel across many countries, for many thousands of miles.

Some of these bugs begin to stand out thanks to lofty goals or distances traveled. Following are examples of Travel Bugs that have found their way around.

Darth Vader TB1

Darth Vader TB1 is a typical-looking bug, a tag attached to a Star Wars toy. Its mission is also typical enough: "Darth is on a mission to find other Jedi out in the geocaching universe. Please help him get to as many states as possible by the end of the year. Alaska would be a really cool place to visit, as Darth's master has always wanted to go there, but he will take a trip to any exotic location anywhere in the geocaching world."

After the user "Captain Prozac" retrieved the bug, he took it along to the Gulf to fly seven combat missions over Afghanistan. After its share of combat service, it enjoyed a stop in the United Kingdom before returning to the United States. Of course, the bug accompanied the captain at a couple of pub stops along the way. The cool weather was a nice relief from the 100+ degree heat of Afghanistan.

After a whirlwind journey of an amazing 17,461.2 miles, Darth was returned to his owner and is now spending the rest of his days in retirement on the shelf.

Darth Vader TB1 on a combat mission over Afghanistan with a Navy fighter escort.
(The captain)

EUREKA!

Did you know that Travel Bugs are often used as teaching tools? From science and mathematics to history and geography, students can learn a great number of lessons, even predicting the Travel Bug's movements in the world!

Sysop's Traveler

When one of the founding members of the Little Egypt Geocaching Society (L.E.G.S.) in southern Illinois was killed in a motorcycle accident, the members knew they had to do something to honor the memory of their friend. Sysop loved wolves, so arrangements were made with a wildlife rescue organization to adopt a wolf. As a way of saying "thank you," the organization gave L.E.G.S. a certificate and a little stuffed wolf.

If there's one thing Sysop loved as much as wolves it was traveling, so the group struck upon the perfect idea for the little toy wolf. They attached a Travel Bug tag to it and sent it out on a mission to visit the kinds of places Sysop loved to visit. The geocachers who have picked up this Travel Bug really seem to want to honor Sysop's memory. The stories and pictures they have placed on the bug page truly do reflect the spirit of their friend.

DEAD BATTERIES

Use good geosportsmanship when it comes to Travel Bugs and other Trackables. It is considered bad etiquette to remove an item from a geocache and not move it along to another geocache. E-mail the owner if you keep an item longer than a couple of weeks. Also, do not mail items to a destination. If you do, what's the point? The point of Trackables is for them to experience the most adventure-filled journey possible.

Tigger

On September 14, 2001, only days after the September 11th tragedy, geocacher "bigkid" sent a Travel Bug on a special mission to the site of the World Trade Center. Its goal, "The wonderful thing about Tiggers is their power to heal and make fun. My name is Tigger

Travel Bug and I'd like to go to New York City and help the people around the WTC by making them smile. Can you please take my picture at the location of the WTC? Then perhaps I can make my way back to Seattle."

On February 16, 2002, after thousands of miles of travel through the goodwill of geocachers, Tigger stood at the memorial viewing platform at Ground Zero in the hands of geocacher Perfect Tommy.

Tigger's Travel Bug page contains many touching photos and logs from his journey. Tigger finally returned home to Seattle 16 months after he left. He was attached to a Ground Zero 9-11-01 NYC knit cap. Tigger had traveled 7,022 miles and touched the hearts of many. Tigger has since continued his journey, racking up nearly 19,000 miles along the way.

The Least You Need to Know

- Travel Bugs and Trackables are special trade items that are designed to move from geocache to geocache, picking up stories and photos along the way.
- The serial numbers on Travel Bugs allow them to be tracked on geocache and user profile pages at the Geocaching.com website.
- Releasing a Travel Bug of your own is as easy as registering its owner's username, the bug's name, and its traveling goals or purpose.
- Just "discover" rather than take a Travel Bug or Trackable if you cannot place it into another geocache soon.

Get in Gear

In the last few years, we've witnessed a revolution in the development and use of GPS receivers. Once deemed a high-tech toy for only the most avid of users, GPS devices are becoming an essential tool in navigation and outdoor recreation.

However, if you're a more casual user, chances are you haven't completely explored the features of your GPS receiver. In Part 3, we discuss important functions and features of devices to give you a better understanding of what the technology can do.

We explain the technology behind the Global Positioning System that enables us to find our way anywhere in the world and makes geocaching possible. We discuss its benefits and limitations so that you can learn to use your gear to its fullest potential.

You'll get the rundown on the GPS receiver options available so that you can buy the right gear for your needs and use. Then, it's time to set up your gear by finding out what all of those buttons are for.

We also explore the growth of smartphones and how integrating true GPS technology is providing some great new navigation options, right in your pocket. Several applications have been developed that make smartphones a viable option for all your geocaching and navigational needs.

As useful as GPS technology is, it doesn't replace the traditional map and compass. After you get your grid lines and true north figured out, it's time for some serious high-tech fun by exploring the use of GPS mapping and computers.

Understanding How GPS Works

In This Chapter

- Understand what GPS is and how it works
- Discover how accurate the gear can be
- Learn what satellite reception is needed for accurate navigation
- See the limitations of GPS technology

In many ways, geocaching is the latest incarnation of that age-old game of hide-and-seek, making use of the latest technology available. Letterboxers have been hiding containers in the moors of England using hints and puzzles to guide people to their locations for more than a century. Ham radio operators cleverly hide radio transmitters and search for them using the technology they've come to know and love. Now with GPS technology, the game has truly gone global.

In this chapter, you'll learn about the origins of the Global Positioning System (GPS) and how it works. You'll get a good understanding of how accurate the gear can be, as well as how to check and improve accuracy to make sure you're on track. After getting to know GPS, you'll understand why it can't completely replace traditional navigational methods like the map and compass.

Evolution of the GPS Receiver

In 1957, all eyes were on space. The Soviet Union had trumped the United States by launching the world's first artificial satellite, Sputnik. The world watched the night skies hoping for a glimpse of this modern marvel as it traveled in its orbit.

Scientists noticed that Sputnik's relative position in space could be calculated based on the length of the radio waves received from it. A theory was developed at Johns Hopkins University's Applied Physics Laboratory based on these observations and submitted as part of a proposal to the Navy Bureau of Ordinance. The proposal became Transit, which launched in 1960 as the precursor to the Navstar Global Positioning System, which is better known today as GPS.

The U.S. government, with an investment of billions of dollars, developed GPS. Now anyone with a GPS receiver can use it. Like mobile phones and Humvees, this is military technology that we civilians have adopted for uses both practical and fun, like geocaching. Read on to learn everything you wanted to know but were afraid to ask about GPS.

GPS is a gift from the U.S. Department of Defense. It currently is a system of 32 satellites broadcasting special radio signals down to Earth that are intercepted by GPS receivers. The receivers analyze the signals to determine the location of receivers anywhere in the world. There has not been such a quantum leap in navigation since the Chinese invented the compass 800 years ago. Imagine: we now have the ability to record our favorite locations and return to them again. Getting lost has never been so much fun. It sounds too good to be true, but, like anything electronic, there are limitations.

EUREKA!

Contrary to popular belief, GPS satellites are not in geosynchronous orbits, although the WAAS satellites are. Satellites in the GPS constellation make 2 orbits around the earth every 24 hours and can be maneuvered into different flight paths.

This is one of the reasons signal coverage may vary from day to day and your readings might be different from those taken on the day the cache was placed.

Top Secret Tech—Declassified

The origins of GPS began in the 1960s as a concept for a worldwide U.S. military navigational system. By the mid-1970s, it became a joint effort of various branches of the U.S. military and was referred to as Navstar. Despite the official name, GPS is the term that stuck.

On September 1, 1983, a series of preventable errors would become the catalyst that brought GPS technology to the civilian world. Korean Air Lines Flight 007 from New York to Seoul, via Anchorage, strayed off course and into restricted Soviet airspace where it was mistaken for a hostile aircraft and shot down, killing all aboard. Following this tragedy, President Ronald Reagan issued a directive that the US Global Positioning System be declassified and made available to the public, once completed, at no charge. Although performance would be degraded intentionally for civilian models using Selective Availability (SA), the navigation system developed for military use would now be available to the civilian world.

Military Technology Goes Mainstream

Over the following years the GPS technology would be expanded and improved, even though it was not widely known. The system's first major public debut was in 1991 when it contributed to the allied efforts in the first Iraq war, Desert Storm. With the system still in its infancy, only 16 satellites were utilized, with many specifically positioned over the Persian Gulf area. Hand-held receivers, primitive by today's standards, helped Allied forces navigate and maneuver around enemy positions in an unfamiliar, featureless desert. The system was considered fully operational in 1995.

In the late 1990s, improvements were made to allow receivers to track 12 satellites simultaneously, instead of the older single-channel units (which were not quite as accurate and much slower in getting a good satellite fix). Also at this time, the prices for GPS receivers began to drop, which allowed more people access to the technology.

All you need is a GPS and a sense of adventure.
(Brad Simmons)

New Tools for Work and Play

GPS obviously has many applications for the military, engineers, and emergency service agencies, but this was a major development for us technology enthusiasts who love the latest gadgets. Even better yet, this is something that is practical enough to actually use. For those of us who enjoy the outdoors, GPS provides us a little more freedom and confidence in backcountry travel with the reduced risk of getting lost.

With the ability to save locations as waypoints and create routes using road maps, this technology has, for the most part, removed the uncertainty and guesswork from navigation. For example, we can plot a course from our home to a geocache and the GPS will choose the best route for us to follow. Once there, we can save the location of a trailhead, venture off in a different direction to explore, and still return to the exact location of any saved waypoint. This could be done with traditional navigational skills through map reading and dead reckoning, but it's not nearly as efficient or fun as using GPS.

Satellite Signals

A GPS receiver is essentially a computer that receives signals broadcast from GPS satellites. That's why a GPS unit is referred to as a receiver, or GPSr. There are currently 32 satellites orbiting around the earth. Since the coverage provided is global, you can use your GPS to pinpoint your location anywhere in the world. Whether or not you have local maps in your device to help you navigate is a different matter we discuss later in this chapter.

GPS receivers need to read the signals of at least three satellites at a time to determine the equipment's exact location, a process known as trilateration. Four are needed for a more accurate three-dimensional fix, providing elevation and the precise atomic time. The more satellites the receiver can lock on to, the more accurate the position information.

Trilateration works by a receiver downloading radio signals broadcast from each satellite it can lock on to. The GPS receiver calculates its location by determining the distance from each overhead satellite. Satellites broadcast their radio signals in a sphere. The unit's computer determines its location by determining where all of the spheres intercept. This is why accuracy readings substantially increase with the more satellites a receiver can lock on to.

NAVIGATIONAL NUGGETS

GPS devices are known as receivers because they intercept special radio signals broadcast from GPS satellites to determine their location on Earth. There is often confusion over whether someone else can track the user's position. Very few recreational GPS units transmit data, and even then it only transmits your location if you tell it to. No one will know your position unless you have specialized gear and decide to tell others.

The government broadcasts two sets of coded signals. Military equipment can receive both the Precise (P) and Course Acquisition (CA) signals for highly accurate readings. Civilian gear receives only the slightly less accurate (CA) code. Despite this limitation, most receivers with a clear view of the sky are accurate within 33 feet (10 meters) more than 90 percent of the time and often achieve 10 feet (3 meters) of accuracy when using WAAS correction. We'll chat about WAAS and other technologies later in this chapter.

Features of GPS Receivers

Modern receivers offer many features, maybe more than you'll ever need or use. All of the buttons and screens can be a bit overwhelming. Despite being a high-tech electronic item, they are actually quite easy to use. The more you practice with the gear, the more your intimidation will turn into interest as your confidence grows.

Regardless of the brand, size, or price, GPS receivers are designed to provide the same basic functions. More expensive models provide a greater memory storage capability and provide at least one basemap to display on the receiver's screen. Even the least expensive models provide many of the following basic features:

- A color display indicating your position anywhere in the world, typically within 33 feet (10 meters) of accuracy. The current location is displayed on a view screen.

- Receivers record data that is displayed on the view screen and stored in the unit's memory. Such data includes saved points of interest known as waypoints, as well as an electronic breadcrumb trail indicating where you have traveled, known as a track log.

- Time of day, elevation, speed, bearing, distance, compass readings, and estimated time of arrival to selected waypoint destinations.

- More expensive models provide a built-in basemap provided from the manufacturer. A receiver's basemap may include a large area, such as all of North America or the United Kingdom. Additional basemaps can be added if memory space is available. Most basemaps make it possible for the unit to calculate turn-by-turn driving routes to your destination.

- Many of these more expensive receivers provide additional memory for map storage. This is used to enhance the basemap with topographical map data or other information selected by the user.

- More advanced units may also include a digital compass, altimeter, options to display geocache information (known as paperless caching), cameras, and even mp3 players.

NAVIGATIONAL NUGGETS

GPS receivers provide elevation information after acquiring a fix on four or more satellites. This altimeter function is usually not as accurate as the location data, but will most likely get you within 100 feet (27 meters). Some receivers have a built-in barometric altimeter to help ensure greater accuracy.

How Accurate Is Accurate?

Accuracy remains about the same regardless of the brand, size, or price of a receiver. Receivers work on line of sight to the overhead satellites, so the whole trick to accuracy is allowing the antenna to get a clear view of the sky. Because the government's Selective Availability is no longer in effect, a GPS receiver should be able to lock on to its location anywhere in the world within 33 feet (10 meters) more than 90 percent of the time. Not perfect, but somewhere within 33 feet will be close enough to find a cache, your camp, or anything else you might be looking for.

This was not always the case. In May 2000, U.S. President Clinton had the government eliminate Selective Availability (SA). SA was an intentional degradation of civilian GPS signals implemented for national security reasons. This military safeguard deliberately made the publicly available GPS signals inaccurate by 100 yards (91 meters). The removal of SA was the major development that allowed the accuracy necessary for caches to be hidden and found again, inspiring the game of geocaching.

Special systems have been developed for aviation and boating, for which absolute accuracy is required for autopilot features and for navigating around hazards in low visibility. Accuracy is improved by including radio signal broadcasts that help fine-tune the user's position. There are two systems that increase GPS accuracy: the original differential correction, known as DGPS, and WAAS. The DGPS system is primarily used around seaports and waterways and requires an additional differential beacon receiver.

WAAS, EGNOS, and MSAS

Fortunately, a system that considerably improves GPS accuracy has been developed. The United States uses a technology known as the Wide-Area Augmentation System (WAAS), which can typically improve accuracy from 10 meters down to 3. It was created for the aviation industry and includes 25 ground reference stations with a master station on each U.S. coast. These stations monitor and correct GPS signal interference caused by satellite drift and signal delay through the ionosphere. The corrected messages are then broadcast from one of two geostationary satellites. This corrected signal improves accuracy to less than 3 meters 95 percent of the time.

Currently, WAAS is available only in North America. However, since 2009 the European Geostationary Navigation Overlay Service (EGNOS) has provided a similar service to Europe, Eastern Asia, and North Africa. A Japanese satellite-based augmentation system known as Multi-functional Satellite Augmentation System (MSAS) provides similar functionality for Southeast Asia.

Almost all modern GPS units are capable of using the corrections provided by WAAS signals and many can use the EGNOS and MSAS systems as well. When using your receiver, check the satellite status page to determine whether the system is searching for, or has picked up, WAAS signals. There is no additional cost or equipment needed to use this system, but be aware that these features use more battery power. Your receiver can most likely be set to turn this feature off if battery use is an issue.

Factors That Affect Accuracy

The main cause of inaccuracies in civilian GPS equipment is ionospheric interference. This is caused by the delay of radio waves as they travel through electron fields in the ionosphere. Military receivers send two sets of signals that allow the ionospheric delay to be measured and compensated for. Nothing can be done for civilians to correct this inaccuracy other than DGPS and WAAS. Civilian GPS users must learn to accommodate for the equipment's inaccuracy.

A second problem is multipath interference. This is caused by error from a receiver picking up satellite radio signals that have bounced from terrain obstacles, such as buildings or cliff walls. Civilian receivers cannot distinguish the ricocheting signals from the ones traveling directly from the satellite to the receiver. Water droplets on overhead vegetation can also cause this problem. Be aware of your surroundings and understand that overhead vegetation, especially if it is wet or snow covered, will distort GPS signals considerably.

GPS signals can even be affected by solar flares and storms, which cause radio interference in the same range the satellites use. If you doubt the accuracy of your position, check the satellite status page to determine the current signal strength and quality. You may have to get into a clearing for a better view of the sky.

Getting a Fix

When you fire up the receiver by pressing the power button, the computer begins seeking out satellites. You have a satellite fix when the receiver picks up enough "birds" (satellites) to activate the navigation process. GPS radio signals work on line of sight, meaning they travel to the receiver in a straight line. So we know the signals will not bend around obstacles like heavy tree coverage or cave walls, but fog, dust, rain, or other extreme weather conditions do not affect them.

Depending on the quality of an antenna and a user's position, an average of seven or eight satellites may be locked on at any one time. Under ideal circumstances signals from 12 or more satellites may be received. Picking up only three signals will result in a two-dimensional (2-D) reading. This operation will provide location information that may be inaccurate by as much as several miles, and no elevation data will be provided. At a minimum, four satellites are needed to obtain a three-dimensional (3-D) fix. This will provide reasonably accurate location and elevation data. Accuracy is greatly improved with every additional satellite received.

When in doubt, check the satellite status page on your GPS receiver often to determine what kind of accuracy you can expect. This page provides a great deal of information, including the receiver's working status and the number of signals received at any given time. Through graphs, the signal strength will appear for each satellite. A satellite geometry graph will display how they are positioned overhead. This is important because satellites clumped together or arranged in a straight line provide poor geometry. The best satellite geometry is provided when there is at least one satellite directly overhead, with several others on the surrounding horizon.

Satellite status on the GPS.

(Image used courtesy of Magellan Navigation, Inc. or its affiliates. Copyright © Magellan Navigation Inc. or its affiliates.)

Two different accuracy readings are also provided. There is a signal strength indicator known as the DOP, or dilution of precision, number. The smaller the DOP number, the better the satellite geometry.

The other indicator is the EPE, estimated position error, number. This measurement also considers satellite geometry to determine the estimated accuracy in feet or meters. Check out these readings often to determine your level of accuracy and to ensure the antenna and gear are working properly.

Initialization

When you turn on the receiver for the first time, it will not be sure of its location and will need to initialize itself. This process is also necessary if the receiver has traveled a few hundred miles away from its home area with the power shut off, such as when you take it on vacation. The receiver may initialize automatically, although it may be necessary to point out your approximate location on the receiver's basemap.

DEAD BATTERIES

Is it your first time turning on your new GPS? Find an area with lots of open sky, turn your GPS on, and let it sit for about 15 minutes. This gives it time to download the almanac that will tell it where in the sky to look for GPS satellites.

This is also a good thing to do if you've left the GPS turned off and without batteries for a long period of time.

To initialize a receiver, go outside to an area with a clear view of the sky and turn the receiver's power on. The unit may prompt you to select an initializing method. If your receiver includes a basemap, choose By Map. Use the cursor arrow to zoom to your current location on the map page and press Enter. The receiver will now start to read satellites from the new location. After satellites are fixed, the present position pointer icon will appear in the center of the map page to show your exact location. When the receiver switches over to the map page showing your position, it is an indication that enough satellites are received for the equipment's navigation function to work properly. Now you're ready to go.

GPS Limitations

Wow, we can know exactly where we are at any time, anywhere in the world. With that kind of technological power, we can toss out the maps and compass and forget about paying attention to where we are going, right? Not exactly. There are still limitations to the Global Positioning System. For one, receivers are electronic just like your cell phone and computer. You wouldn't trust your life to one of those, would you? Gear can fail. It can also be damaged, lost, waterlogged, or stolen.

The other issue is that it needs power to operate. If you have the equipment set up in your vehicle, plugged into the accessory point, it's not a problem; you can leave it on all day. For hiking and geocaching, however, the gear has to rely on battery power. A receiver with dead batteries is nothing more than an expensive doorstop. Check the battery gauge. This meter usually looks like an E-to-F fuel gauge and is often found on the satellite status page. Always carry at least six or more spare batteries in a resealable plastic bag. Even if your receiver doesn't run out of power, you may need them for your flashlight or camera.

Even though GPS receivers include a compass feature, they do not replace the traditional compass. This is because unless it is an advanced model with an electronic compass, the receiver's compass will not work while the gear is in a stationary position. A receiver has to be traveling at least 4 miles per hour before its computer can accurately calculate the direction you are traveling. This is why, when you ask your receiver to navigate to a waypoint, the compass pointer arrow could be off in any direction, which we refer to as "loose bearings." When you start moving, the arrow immediately aligns to the correct bearing. Even if your unit has an electronic compass, it is always a good idea to keep a traditional compass on hand, either to augment your GPS unit or as a backup for navigation if your GPS unit fails.

As you can see, GPS still cannot completely replace the traditional map and compass. Equipment failure and dead batteries are not that uncommon, and getting lost or stranded turns a pleasurable outing into a serious nightmare. Because the consequences could be tragic, navigational skills are too important not to learn.

Knowing traditional navigational skills will greatly increase your confidence in backcountry travel and allow you to use your GPS receiver to its fullest capacity. Besides, you need to know how to read a map and compass to go geocaching! The rest of Part 3 covers using GPS, maps, and a compass in detail.

The Least You Need to Know

- GPS is a U.S. government technology that anyone can use.
- GPS devices calculate their positions by receiving satellite signals.
- GPS receiver accuracy is typically within 10 meters and can be improved to 3 meters with the aid of WAAS or EGNOS.
- GPS receivers need to lock on a minimum of three satellites to navigate accurately.
- GPS devices have limitations besides their accuracy: they can fail, be misplaced, and need battery power to function.
- Learning traditional navigational skills helps ensure that you can navigate to a geocache and safely return even if your electronic gear should fail.

Choosing a GPS for Geocaching

In This Chapter

- Learn about GPS receiver features and options before you buy
- Choose the right type of receiver for your use
- Find out everything you ever wanted to know about batteries
- Check out our recommended features for geocaching

Like any piece of gear, choosing a GPS for geocaching is a matter of personal choice and preference. If you ask 10 geocachers what is the best GPS receiver for hunting a geocache, you will likely be provided with 15 different answers. That's because the equipment you use may vary depending on the frequency with which you go geocaching, the typical terrain, the weather or season of the year, and the number of geocaches you usually seek in a single outing. Therefore, the equipment you choose is going to be a personal decision based on your needs and affordability. Many cachers have even found it helpful to have multiple units geared for different kinds of geocaching. For example, they may use one unit in the car to navigate to caches around town and another for when they are on the trail.

This chapter covers the basic options available and provides GPS receiver recommendations by type and cost.

GPS Receivers

GPS receivers are manufactured in various shapes and sizes, with as many features and prices. GPS technology is used for so many different recreational uses that it can be confusing to know which unit to buy and how much money to spend to get the features you need. Remember to keep your intended personal use in mind so that buying the right gear will be a worthy investment.

EUREKA!

Secure your gear with a lanyard. They are great for attaching GPS receivers, cameras, and radios. If you drop your gear, you will likely save it from crashing to the ground. They're effective in keeping gear from becoming lost or stolen. They're also just an easy way to keep your gear handy, conveniently hanging from your neck.

Fortunately, modern GPS receivers share many of the same basic features, regardless of price. While it is true that nearly any GPS receiver that can route off-road will work for geocaching, some will work better than others. Understanding the available features will enable you to make an informed purchasing decision. We understand that when you purchase a GPS unit, you will probably use it for more than just geocaching. Here is a list of the common features available. Learn how they may be applied to geocaching and other applications.

Primary Features

- **Accuracy.** Fortunately, accuracy is consistent in most receivers regardless of the style or cost.

- **Address finder.** Allows an exact address to be located within a basemap database.

- **Alarms.** An alarm notifies the user of an approaching waypoint. Text alarms flash a message on the screen; audible alarms sound a tone or make a voice announcement.

- **Altimeter.** A 3-D, four-satellite fix provides elevation information, although satellite-based altimeters are not known for being very accurate. Some GPS receivers provide a built-in barometric altimeter for more accurate elevation readings independent of a satellite connection.

- **Antenna jack.** This feature allows for a remote antenna to be attached. This works well for obtaining satellite reception if your GPS unit is mounted within a vehicle with no clear view of the sky. You can also bring it along while geocaching to get better signals under very heavy tree cover.

- **Auto routing.** Provides turn-by-turn directions to a waypoint. Directions may be in the form of arrows, automated voice commands, or both.

- **Basemap.** Most recent-model GPS devices include a map database stored within their memory. Basemaps include general information on cities, roadways, and waterways. Basemaps typically include such large geographic areas as North America or Europe.

- **Battery duration.** Battery life is important for extended hikes with no other power source available. Receivers are rated for battery life duration for both continuous use and power-saver modes. If the unit has an internal, rechargeable battery it is important to see if extras can be purchased and exchanged on the trail. You wouldn't want to run out of power away from recharging sources.

DEAD BATTERIES

Using a receiver without a basemap can be more challenging when geocaching in the backcountry. If you are hiking and do not have a basemap, bring along a paper map and try to plot the location coordinates. It is always wise to get a good sense of your final destination and best means to access the location before setting out to find a geocache.

- **Computer interface.** Data in/out capability allows the unit to receive (upload) data from a computer or send (download) data to a computer. This information includes digital maps, track logs, waypoints, and routes. NMEA, the National Marine Electronics Association, ensures that data can be exchanged with other electronic devices. If you plan to do more than a few cache hunts, make sure your receiver has this interface capability.

- **Durability.** It's not a question of whether or not you'll drop your GPS receiver, but of how often you'll drop it and what you'll drop it on or in. It's important that you choose a durable handheld model instead of something designed more for navigation inside a vehicle. Most handheld models come with rubber grips that will help you hold the device and cushion it slightly in a fall.

- **Electronic compass.** Although almost all receivers provide basic compass data, the feature will not work in a stationary position. An electronic compass is available to provide compass data independent of satellite reception.

- **Memory.** For receivers with a basemap, memory is used to store additional mapping data. GPS manufacturers provide greater detailed maps in CD-ROM and SD card formats exclusively for their brands. Map details, especially topography contour lines, use a great deal of memory. Some models have expandable memory, allowing virtually unlimited storage with high-capacity cards (or by storing multiple maps on more than one card). On some units, additional memory will enable you to store additional waypoints.

- **Routes.** A series of waypoints listed in sequence from start to finish. Designed to guide to a destination, they can also be inverted or reversed to track back from the destination to the starting point.

- **Sun/moon position.** Provides sun and moon positions, including sunrise and sunset time of day. This can be especially handy when planning a hike or when trying to decide whether to hunt "just one more" or head back to the car.

- **Tide page.** Provides times for high and low tides. Some caches are hidden on islands that can be accessed only by foot at low tide.

- **Track log.** Plots an electronic breadcrumb trail as a sequence of dots or trackpoints, showing a path traveled. Various brands and models provide different numbers of trackpoints that can be used. A backtrack feature automatically establishes a route from the last track log to provide a series of waypoints to follow on the way out.

- **WAAS, EGNOs, or MSAS ready.** Most modern receivers are capable of accepting broadcasts from one or more of these signal correcting systems. These signals can increase the accuracy of your GPS unit to within 3 meters. However, this feature drains batteries slightly faster than standard GPS use.

- **Water resistance.** Receivers are rated for their resistance to water. *Water-resistant* usually means the equipment can be splashed or briefly dunked (a rating of IPX4). *Waterproof* means the equipment can be submerged for a specific amount of time to a specific depth, such as 30 minutes at 1 meter, before damage occurs (a rating of IPX7). Regardless of rating, it is a good idea to use a watertight box or bag if you use your receiver around water—especially saltwater, which can kill electronics instantly.

- **Waypoints.** Specifically recorded locations stored within a receiver's memory. Saved waypoints enable you to return to exact locations. Various GPS brands and models enable you to store different numbers of waypoints. Most modern receivers enable you to store at least 1,000 waypoints and some will store up to 10,000.

- **Waypoint averaging.** A standard feature on most new GPS receivers. Waypoint averaging provides greater accuracy of saved waypoints because you actually record the position over a period of time. This is ideal when placing geocaches.

Device Types and Application

GPS receivers come in a variety of sizes and prices and provide various features. Devices can be generally grouped into the following categories:

Handheld Without a Basemap Database

These models are examples of low-cost, entry-level receivers. All work well and are capable of the same accuracy and provide the same features as more expensive models. These basic receivers are about the size of a TV remote control, with an approximate 2-inch view screen. They include built-in antennas and most likely do not include a remote antenna jack.

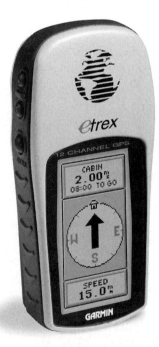

Garmin eTrex H.
(Image used courtesy of Garmin Ltd. or its affiliates. Copyright © Garmin Ltd. or its affiliates.)

- **Price.** $79 to $120.
- **Pro.** Low cost, small and lightweight, simple to operate.

- **Con.** No basemap. These models often do not include a data cable or data port for transferring information from your computer, although they can be purchased separately.

- **Application.** Ideal for geocaching, hiking, and biking where size and weight are important. This type of receiver has limitations but is a great choice if low cost is a primary consideration.

Handheld with a Basemap Database

The next step up, these receivers include an electronic basemap and expanded capabilities, such as paperless geocaching.

They may include other features such as memory or the capability to accept a memory card to store additional mapping data.

Magellan Explorist GC

(Image used courtesy of Magellan Navigation, Inc. or its affiliates. Copyright © Magellan Navigation, Inc. or its affiliates.)

Garmin Etrex 10.

(Image used courtesy of Garmin Ltd. or its affiliates. Copyright © Garmin Ltd.
or its affiliates.)

- **Price.** $120 to $249.

- **Pro.** Most have color screens. Electronic basemap provides a useful reference. Additional features include external jacks for a computer data cable. Memory storage capacity allows the use of the manufacturer's maps on CD-ROM or memory card. Some models may also include an electronic compass and altimeter capable of functioning independently of satellite reception.

- **Con.** Screen size works well for general handheld use, but the screens are difficult to read in a moving vehicle. While the basemap contains most major roads, many of the secondary roads you will be geocaching on won't be shown on your maps.

- **Application.** Ideal for all-around recreational use.

Full-Featured Handhelds

The next generation of handheld GPS contains all the features you will need for geocaching and any other outdoor adventure you might find yourself on. Expandable memory for extra maps and waypoints is just the beginning. These machines can load geocaching data directly onboard, making them the one tool you need for totally paperless geocaching.

Don't let their features fool you, these are rugged waterproof devices made to tackle the great outdoors.

Magellan Explorist 710.

(Image used courtesy of Magellan Navigation, Inc. or its affiliates. Copyright © Magellan Navigation, Inc. or its affiliates.)

Garmin Montana 650t.

(Image used courtesy of Garmin Ltd. or its affiliates. Copyright © Garmin Ltd.
or its affiliates.)

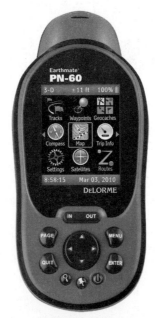

DeLorme PN-60

Image used courtesy of DeLorme Inc. or its affiliates. Copyright © DeLorme, Inc.
or its affiliates.

- **Price.** $250 to $699.

- **Pro.** Built-in worldwide color basemaps and topographic maps on higher-end models. SD card slots for more memory. Barometric altimeters for accurate elevation readings on many models. Some models feature built-in cameras and voice recorders, and many are capable of wirelessly transferring waypoints between units. Some models also feature touch screens, which means fewer buttons and larger screens. Integrated geocaching functionality.

- **Con.** For some people, price is a big factor in whether or not this is the GPS for them. Also, for the beginner, the wide variety of features can be confusing.

- **Application.** This is a geocacher's dream. As the game continues to grow and new features are made available, these devices will set the standard for the future of the game.

Vehicle-Based Receivers

Various models of vehicle-based receivers are available. Their larger screens are also ideal for car, RV, or marine use. They are typically mounted with a swivel bracket and can be plugged in to the vehicle, eliminating the need for batteries. At the top end of the line these receivers can be more expensive, averaging $500 to $1,000, but there are several less expensive options.

This type of unit works great for traveling around, but is not much good for geocaching if you can't take it with you on foot. Some of these models can be used for geocaching, but you will need to be sure that the model you choose is capable of off-road routing, with a compass arrow that can guide you to the geocache, and that the unit can be powered by batteries. The large color screen is great but it can be a bit delicate for field use. You might decide that a larger sized receiver is fine if you primarily use it mounted in a vehicle, but you can still take it with you when you go out on the trail.

Laptops, PDAs, and Tablets

If you're already packing around a portable computer, there are options to convert it to a GPS receiver. Digital assistants, PDAs, or laptop computers can be used this way through the combination of software and an antenna. Handheld PDAs use an adapter sleeve with an antenna that plugs into an expansion slot. Laptops use a dash-mounted remote antenna. Another option is to use them wirelessly in conjunction with a Bluetooth GPS receiver. Of course, many tablets, such as the 3G model Apple iPad, have GPS capability built in, which can be used with available apps as a GPS unit.

Real-time tracking is another neat way to combine the use of receivers and computers. Various brands of mapping software will accept a GPS receiver's signal to display a user's location indicated as an icon centered on a tablet, PDA, or laptop screen. Chapter 13 covers computers and real-time tracking.

- **Price.** $199 to $799 (software and antenna).

- **Pro.** Great way to utilize computer equipment and save money by using electronics already owned. Laptops accept high-quality mapping software. Larger screen size with a greater memory capability at a lower cost.

- **Con.** Often a poor choice for geocaching because they are not as durable or weather resistant as regular GPS receivers. Laptops are limited to vehicle-based use due to size and power requirements. Unless you rig up a stand, a passenger is needed to hold the computer; in addition, the power and data cords can be cumbersome.

- **Application.** Computers are an excellent complement to traditional GPS gear. They are great for trip planning and managing waypoints and routes. Ideal for vehicle-based use. Perfect for executives and road travelers who already use mobile computer equipment.

Smartphones

Over the past few years, we have witnessed significant developments in cell phone technology. Today, there are a multitude of cell phones out there with integrated GPS. With the addition of navigation software that uses the phone's built-in features, many cell phones can now be used as a primary tool for geocaching. We'll go in depth about smartphones in Chapter 12.

iPhone 4 running Groundspeak's Geocaching Application.
(Groundspeak)

- **Price.** $100 to $500 for the hardware, although cell phone carriers often subsidize the cost of a cell phone if you agree to a contract term. Geocaching applications can range from free to $25 depending on the feature set.

- **Pro.** Easy geocaching access without having to purchase a dedicated GPS unit. With data plans and associated coverage, you can have real-time access to geocaching information for spontaneous geocaching. If you already have the phone, spending $10 for the official Geocaching app is an inexpensive way to get involved. It's one less device to carry with you.

- **Con.** Cell phones are generally not as durable or weather resistant as regular GPS receivers. Navigation with GPS consumes battery at a high rate and makes full-day adventures difficult without recharging the phone battery.

- **Application.** They are great for spontaneous geocaching, which makes them perfect for anyone who is interested in on-the-go geocaching without significant planning.

Batteries

Batteries are the lifeblood of geocaching. Not only do you need extras, but when it's time to purchase them, there are more options than you might think. Some GPS units have built in rechargeable batteries, which can be a real plus, unless you don't have an extra when your batteries start to fade in the field. This is why most handheld GPS units use standard AA batteries. Choosing the right type will help squeeze a little extra mileage out of them and possibly save a little money, too. Here are the basics:

- **Alkaline.** These are typically the most common and economical to use. A quality set of these batteries lasts 12 or more hours in a receiver. They are also sold in bulk to reduce the cost further. Power is considerably reduced in freezing temperatures.

EUREKA!

It helps to use cameras, flashlights, radios, and other gear that use the same batteries as your GPS device. Active geocachers should also consider using rechargeable batteries.

- **Alkaline rechargeable.** They only last approximately 60 percent of the life of a regular alkaline, but they can be recharged effectively up to 25 times. Most rechargeable batteries have memory. Batteries last longer if they are completely drained before charging.

- **Lithium.** These batteries are more expensive, but may last more than 30 hours in a receiver. This style is ideal for low-temperature use.

- **Nickel-cadmium (NiCad).** These batteries may only have a life span approximately 33 percent of alkaline, but they can be recharged around 500 times. Economical to use, but plan on changing them more often.

- **Nickel metal-hydride (NiMH).** Similar to NiCads, but with an increased life span of approximately 75 percent of alkaline. The greatest benefit is that they do not need to be drained before recharging. NiMH batteries can be recharged from 500 to 1000 times under optimal conditions.

EUREKA!

Batteries can be lightly greased to prevent corrosion. This is ideal for longer-term storage applications, such as in flashlights, or any use where the gear is exposed to moisture. Dielectric silicone is a commonly used grease for these purposes.

To save batteries, turn the receiver off when you are not using it. Using the screen's backlight burns power faster. Backlights are typically on a timer that can be programmed to stay on a reduced amount of time. Check the equipment's battery-level gauge frequently to avoid having gear go dead. Many newer units such as the Magellan Explorist series have a "suspend mode," which turns off most features of the device, but continues GPS tracking, greatly extending battery life.

Special Considerations for Geocaching

Fortunately for geocaching, expensive and elaborate gear is not required. More importantly, gear should be easy to use, accessible, and durable. Outdoor gear gets seriously abused. Gear can get smashed in bags and packs, rained on, frozen, dropped in an icy river, and so forth. You get the idea. Luckily, most receivers are built to military specs to withstand a lot of electronic killing factors like moisture, dust, and vibration.

Here's a list of device feature considerations for geocaching:

- **Basemap.** This is highly recommended. The additional cost is marginal, and the increase in the equipment's usefulness is substantial.

- **External antenna jack.** With new GPS devices this has become less important, because the newer chips are sensitive enough to acquire signal under most circumstances. However, when it's not possible to obtain good satellite coverage because of an obstruction, an external antenna can help. Even backpackers will benefit from the ability to safely store the receiver inside a pack with an antenna attached to backpack shoulder straps. It can also help outdoor use in places where signals are weak, such as those under heavy tree cover.

- **Interface.** If you are using the receiver with a computer, be sure that the receiver includes an interface cable so you can quickly load maps and waypoints onto your device. Newer GPS units often support USB while older devices generally have serial attachments. If you purchase an older GPS device and have a newer computer, you may need to purchase a USB to serial port adapter as well.

- **Memory.** This is used to load detailed topographic maps, street-level maps, or additional waypoints into the receiver. Detailed maps can use a great deal of memory on your device. Consider internal storage capacity. Higher-end devices also usually accept a memory card for additional storage.

- **Power source.** It is preferable to have a device that can support external power, like a cigarette lighter power cable. Due to the power requirements the device should support standard batteries (AA or AAA) for easy replacement on the trail. Lithium batteries are recommended for newer GPS models to ensure a longer battery life, and power geocachers should consider rechargeable batteries.

- **Screen size.** For visual ease of operation, use a receiver with the largest screen that can be realistically carried. Screen size is measured diagonally. Color is great and helps define map features, and a backlight is important, although both features burn additional battery power. A screen protector is important in preventing scratches out on the trail.

- **Waterproof.** Sooner or later your gear will get submerged. Get gear that is at least water-resistant, although an IPX7 designation is preferred. Plastic bags and boxes can provide additional protection.

It is also important to note that an increasing number of handheld GPS devices now have functionality specifically created for geocaching. These devices can store detailed cache information, including cache details, hints, and recent logs. Some also store field notes to help you log your geocaches while outdoors!

The Least You Need to Know

- Consider how you will be using your gear and take the time to learn about all the various features and options available.
- Geocachers should shop for GPS receivers that are durable, waterproof, and compact.
- GPS receivers with built-in maps, external antenna jacks, and power cords are typically worth the extra cost.
- Making an informed buying decision will save time, money, and possible aggravation.

GPS Setup and Understanding All Those Features

In This Chapter

- Explore GPS device buttons and screens
- Learn how to set up a new receiver properly
- Use the simulator mode to program settings without wasting battery power
- Navigate with ease by learning how to use waypoints, track logs, and routes

In this chapter, we will learn to use basic device features to program your gear to play. After the basics are out of the way, we will get down to the specifics of using GPS by saving waypoints, track logs, and routes. The information in this chapter in no way replaces your GPS owner's manual, but provides additional explanation so that you can quickly and confidently head outdoors.

Learning Your Way Around Your Receiver

As much as we love high-tech gear, it can be intimidating. Most electronics have more features and buttons than you will ever use. That's fine, but you still need to learn the basics. Learning new functions and features opens up new possibilities, and familiarizing yourself with the device will quickly increase your confidence in navigation.

DEAD BATTERIES

This information is not intended to replace your equipment's owner's manual. Take the time to study the operation of your device to comfortably know how to use it. Read this chapter side by side with your receiver's manual before you head out, and you may even want to take the manual along in a waterproof bag. At the very least, bring the owner's manual in your car.

Fortunately, the major brands of GPS receivers share many of the same features and commands, although they may work a little differently. Studying this information in your product's instruction manual will provide a better understanding of how your device works.

Magellan Explorist Series GPS units were designed with many Geocaching friendly features.

(Image used courtesy of Magellan Navigation, Inc. or its affiliates. Copyright © Magellan Navigation, Inc. or its affiliates.)

Spend some time getting to know the purpose of each button and screen and practice using its features before relying on your device in the field.

Which Button Does What?

You can expect to find several kinds of buttons on most GPS receivers. With today's prevalent touchscreen technology the "button" may actually be an input on the screen instead. For ease of communication we will refer to these inputs as buttons. Here's a list:

- **Enter.** This button is used to select options from menus and to save waypoints. On some units this can be accomplished by pressing the center of the joystick control.

- **GoTo or Nav.** This button allows the selection of a waypoint from a list of waypoints saved within the receiver's memory.

NAVIGATIONAL NUGGETS

When using steering/guidance screens or pointer arrows, it is nearly impossible to maintain the exact bearing unless traveling by air or water. Roads and trails usually require you to track in different directions before reaching the destination. They are helpful, however, to determine if you're on track, and are the major indicator used in geocaching.

- **Menu.** This button scrolls through the receiver's set of data screens or returns to the top level of navigation.

- **Power.** This button turns the equipment on and off and may be used to adjust the screen's backlight.

- **Joystick or Rocker keypad.** This is used to move around on the map page and to select options from menus.

- **Zoom.** This button is used to change the viewing scale on the map page. "In" provides a more detailed smaller-scale view. "Out" provides a larger-scale view.

Common Pages

There are several types of pages you can expect to encounter on your GPS receiver. Here are some common ones:

Active Route Page

Once a route is selected, it displays the list of waypoints in the route and indicates which waypoint is currently activated.

Compass Page

Used for steering guidance, this page provides a compass ring and pointer arrow. If a waypoint is selected, the arrow will point to its bearing. An arrow pointing straight up indicates you are on course to reach the waypoint. The compass ring typically indicates the track (the direction actually being traveled). The compass reading will not be accurate unless the receiver is moving at least four miles per hour. In a stationary position, a bearing number should be accurate, although a regular compass is needed to determine the bearing's direction. Some units, like the Magellan Explorist series, are able to combine the compass and map screens into one easy-to-read view.

The compass page, with its large pointer arrow, is the primary screen used to find a geocache.

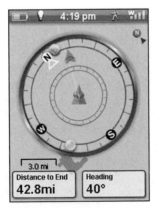

The Compass page provides direct bearing to a geocache or anywhere else you might like to go.

(Image used courtesy of Magellan Navigation, Inc. or its affiliates. Copyright © Magellan Navigation, Inc. or its affiliates.)

Highway Page

Also used for steering guidance. A picture of a moving highway runs down the page indicating an upcoming waypoint, or group of way-points if using a route. To stay on course, keep the highway down the center of the screen. This screen is most helpful when straight-line navigation is possible.

Information or Position Page

Multiple data fields providing whatever information is programmed to appear. A wide variety of data can be programmed to appear in a series of fields. Take the time to review the various information available to determine what data is the most useful to your application. The following are some typical data fields:

- Altitude
- Average speed
- Bearing
- Course
- Current coordinates
- Distance to next
- ETA to next
- Pointer arrow

- Speed
- Sunrise/sunset
- Time of day
- Time to next
- Track
- Trip odometer
- Trip timer
- User timer

Map Page

Primary display page that indicates your location with a present position pointer icon pointing to your direction of travel. The screen shows your movement in real time with a history in the form of a track log. The screen may be oriented to be displayed with the top of the page indicating north or the direction of travel.

Satellite Status Page

Provides the number and signal strength of the satellites received. Includes readings to estimate accuracy. Provides current navigation status such as: Searching, Acquiring, Poor Coverage, 2-D Navigation, or 3-D Navigation. It also typically includes a battery-level gauge.

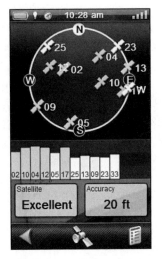

The Satellite status page makes it easy to judge your accuracy and whether you may need to get a better view of the sky.

(Image used courtesy of Magellan Navigation, Inc. or its affiliates. Copyright © Magellan Navigation, Inc. or its affiliates.)

Checking Out the Features

The best way to familiarize yourself with your device is to simply turn it on and check out the features. It helps if you are either outdoors or near a large window so that your device can begin to communicate with the satellites as soon as you turn it on. On some units, like the Magellan Explorist series, you can enter into a product demo mode, which will walk you through many of the features of the unit. Once you get an idea of how the unit works, get a good satellite fix outside, then scroll through and explore the pages.

One of the most commonly used pages is the Map page. Your current location will be displayed in the center of the page by a present position arrow icon.

If your receiver has a joystick, use it to move the cursor arrow around the map screen. A data field box will display changing heading and the distance from your current location. This is useful for finding approximate distances to nearby locations. Scroll to a nearby city and check out the bearing and distance. The distances provided are direct as the crow flies. Unless traveling in a straight line, mileage needs to be increased to estimate actual distance on the ground.

If your receiver includes an electronic basemap, you can view it in greater or less detail by using a Zoom feature. When initially viewing the Map page, the present position arrow icon will be in the center of the screen. The bottom of the screen will include a distance indicator that shows the scale of the current map. Zooming in will increase the map's detail. Roads and waterways and their names will appear as you zoom into an area of the map. The zoom range may go from 2,000 miles to less than 100 feet.

Setup

Before using the gear in the field, take time to carefully review the owner's manual to make some choices. The following sections summarize what to consider when selecting setup options.

Alarms

Alarms can be set for a specific time or waypoint arrival, and to notify if you are off-course. When the alarm activates, a warning will sound and a text message will appear on the screen.

Backlight Timer

The backlighting on the map screen uses a good deal of power. If operating on batteries, set the light to remain on just long enough to view the screen. When using a direct power source, it is helpful to keep the light on.

Battery Type

Different types of batteries, such as lithium-ion, alkaline, or rechargeable batteries, all discharge at different rates. On the battery type page you can enter the kind of battery used to ensure the greatest level of accuracy from the battery-level gauge. Installing new batteries also resets the battery-use timer.

Coordinates

The coordinates setting determines which system will be used and thus how coordinates will be displayed. There are various options available based on your location and preference. The two primary geographic coordinate systems are latitude/longitude and Universal Transverse Mercator (UTM).

Latitude/longitude is displayed in degrees, minutes, and seconds. The selection may look like HDDD° MM' SS.S". The standard for geocaching is the minutes displayed with a decimal point without the use of seconds. This display looks like HDDD° MM.MMM'.

UTM is metric and displays in meters. Its selection looks like [UPS/UTM]. The UPS is the UTM's system to grid the North and South Poles.

Distance Measurement

Distance and speed can be measured in statute or nautical miles. The receiver may also display metric kilometers. Note that a nautical mile is equal to 1.15 of a regular statute mile. A kilometer is equal to .62 of a statute mile, and a statute mile is equal to 1.6 kilometers. Based on your selection, altitude will display in either feet or meters.

Map Datum

The receiver will have been set as a default to one of the common map datums, such as the one used for geocaching, WGS 84.

Map-Page Orientation

Map-page orientation sets the direction of the map page. North Up orients the top of the page to north despite the direction of travel. Track Up changes the top of the page to the direction of travel.

North

The type of north can be selected for your preference. The following are the options available:

- **Auto Mag Var.** Magnetic north automatically adjusts for local declination (the same reading as a compass).

- **True.** True north.

- **User Mag Var.** Adjustable to any degree of declination.

NAVIGATIONAL NUGGETS

Remember, if working within a group, be sure everyone is speaking the same navigational language. Agree in advance on the following, and then set your GPS receiver to the correct values:

1. Map coordinates: lat/long or UTM? If lat/long, full address or decimal point?
2. Which north: true or magnetic?
3. Which map datum?

Time

Time of day is adjusted to display regular 12-hour time or 24-hour military time. The time provided is exact and set to your local time when you enter your time zone, or how many hours before or after UTC time (also known as Greenwich Mean Time or "Zulu time") your location happens to be.

Timers

A trip computer can be used to track average speed or minimum speed, or provide an odometer for your overall travels or for a particular trip. Timer features also include a user timer and a battery-use timer. Remember to reset these fields before setting off on a new trip.

NAVIGATIONAL NUGGETS

Most GPS receivers provide a Trip Computer feature. Reset the computer before your next outing to check out interesting data. This includes trip odometer, average speed, trip timer, and maximum speed.

Conserve Your Battery

Simulation, Demo, or GPS Off modes save valuable battery power by allowing you to review and program information without the receiver searching for satellites. This proves helpful when learning how to use the device indoors; you can learn without the device trying to obtain a constant satellite fix. Without the receiver searching for satellites, the battery power requirement is reduced by nearly half.

In these modes, you can review, demonstrate, and program the receiver's various functions and features. It is ideal for transferring data with a computer and for updating and entering waypoints and routes. Despite not using a satellite fix, navigation calculations can still be made. For example, waypoints can be entered as a route to determine the bearing and distance between waypoints.

Unfortunately, the Satellite Status page may appear as if satellites are being received. This is only an example of what the Satellite Status page looks like under normal operating conditions. The device's location will most likely appear as the last area for which the receiver obtained a real satellite fix. Be sure you are not in simulation mode during normal navigation operation.

Saving Waypoints

One of the primary reasons to use a GPS receiver is to save and travel to waypoints. This, of course, is the whole basis of geocaching; the geocache's coordinates are saved as a waypoint. Besides telling us the distance and compass bearing, the receiver's computer can provide neat information we have never had access to before. An estimated time of arrival (ETA) is provided based upon our current speed.

The first waypoint to save is your home. This is helpful, because regardless of where you are in the world, the waypoint can be recalled to determine how far in distance you are from home and the time to return there. Venture out to the yard for a satellite fix.

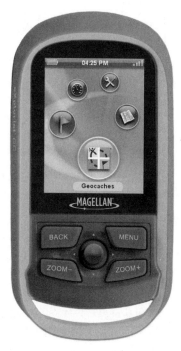

Magellan Explorist GC.

(Image used courtesy of Magellan Navigation, Inc. or its affiliates. Copyright © Magellan Navigation, Inc. or its affiliates.)

For the following examples we will be using the Magellan Explorist GC, a great entry-level GPS unit and the first created specifically for Geocaching. If you have a different GPS you will need to consult your user manual to discover the method for entering waypoints into the unit, but the principles discussed should be the same.

The best waypoint to save first is your own home location. This screen shows the waypoint name and symbol being selected on a Magellan Explorist GC.
(Image used courtesy of Magellan Navigation, Inc. or its affiliates. Copyright © Magellan Navigation, Inc. or its affiliates.)

Once the GPS has acquired satellite lock you are ready to create a waypoint for your home location. This is very simple to do:

1. Press MENU to bring up the Options menu.

2. Highlight 'New Waypoint' and press ENTER.

3. Now you will want to modify the waypoint.

    Change Icon: Highlight the current icon and press ENTER. Use the joystick to highlight the icon desired and press ENTER. In this case you will want to select the "Home" icon.

    Change Name: Highlight the name field and press ENTER. Use the joystick to enter "Home" as the new name. When completed, highlight the green checkmark box and press ENTER.

Add Description: Highlight the description field and press ENTER. Use the joystick to enter the description. When completed, highlight the green checkmark box and press ENTER.

4. Save the waypoint by pressing MENU and selecting Save from the menu.

After setting your home location, you may also want to go to the "Tools" Menu and enter your "Owner Information." This is very helpful because it will aid in getting your GPS unit returned to you in case it gets lost along the trail.

The waypoint screen shows a list of locations saved.

(Image used courtesy of Magellan Navigation, Inc. or its affiliates. Copyright © Magellan Navigation, Inc. or its affiliates.)

Saving waypoints is important because it gives you a perspective of your travel area. Save lots of waypoints; this receiver will allow you to store up to 10,000, and you can always delete old ones. Save your campsite, the trailhead, where you park your truck, and your favorite picnic area or swimming hole. If you ever do get turned around, select the nearest waypoint you need to navigate to. You can select the waypoint page and select a waypoint, and navigate straight to it. It's that simple; getting lost has never been so much fun. Even in a worst-case scenario with your batteries going dead, you can use your compass and hike out on the bearing provided with the selected waypoint.

Saving waypoints is a fun way to document your travels. Better yet, you can share them with others. There are a number of ways to save waypoints:

- **Entered manually. Enter** the numeral coordinates manually using the joystick. Be sure to double-check the coordinates to make sure you entered them correctly; just being one number off could put you miles from your intended destination.

- **Marking the current position.** This is one of the most common and easiest methods. Holding down the joystick while on the map page or going through the menus, as in the previous home waypoint example, saves the current position.

- **Selecting from a basemap.** Using the rocker keypad, move the cursor arrow to a desired location and then save it by holding down the enter function of the joystick.

- **From a computer.** You can load previously saved waypoints and routes from a computer to the receiver. This is done through selecting a computer interface data-transfer option within the receiver and the use of a data cable. This is the most commonly used method in geocaching today, especially when loading Pocket Queries into the unit.

- **Name search.** Most receivers provide the option for a name search of towns and cities. When the location is selected, you may choose to navigate directly to it.

- **Mark a MOB position.** On many receivers, holding down the GoTo button saves a "man overboard" waypoint. On the Explorist GC this is accomplished by holding down the joystick. This is a quick one-button method ideal for emergency situations, as indicated by the method's name.

- **Enter a projected position.** Enter the compass bearing and distance information in the reference fields on a new waypoint screen. This data can be entered from a current position or any other waypoint. From these values, the receiver projects the new location and saves it as a waypoint. Some of the more difficult geocaches require this function.

NAVIGATIONAL NUGGETS

Holding down the GoTo or Enter button on most receivers saves the current location as a "man overboard" (MOB) waypoint. This feature is designed as a one-button method for immediately marking and navigating back to a location.

After waypoints have been saved, the data can be modified at any time. You can manually change or delete the name, symbol, and coordinates.

Track Logs

A track log is an electronic "breadcrumb" trail that is stored and displayed by the receiver. This log indicates the path you have traveled, greatly reducing the chance of becoming lost. Following a previously stored electronic track allows you to literally retrace your steps to backtrack to a previous position. This feature requires two elements to work properly. First, there must be a continual satellite fix for the duration of the track. If coverage is broken, blanks will appear on the track, which will most likely be represented as straight lines. The second element is that adequate memory be available to record the track.

Of course, the amount of information your receiver can record is finite. Depending on the unit's setting, one of two things will happen if the track log memory becomes full. The receiver will stop recording or it will automatically delete older track data. Most receivers provide the option of programming the track log as follows:

- **Fill.** This option records track log data until the memory is full. A text warning message may appear when the memory is full. This option is useful when returning to a starting position is most important.

- **Wrap.** Under this option, data is continually recorded. This is done by recording over the earliest saved data. This option is useful when the latest saved data is most important.

- **Off.** This may be useful to prevent recording excessive tracks to be saved on a log. Shutting this feature off presents a risk because no tracks will be recorded if you fail to turn it back on.

NAVIGATIONAL NUGGETS

Track log data is valuable to geocachers because it does such a good job of documenting your travels. Zooming in on the Map page will show tracks in greater detail, which may help you to find a geocache by indicating that you have walked a specific area.

Another variable is how often a track will be recorded. This is known as the interval value. This adjusts the distance between each track-point to fit the user's application. Most receivers default to some form of automatic or resolution method where a track is recorded based on the user going into a turn or traveling approximately 80 feet in a straight line. This option works best for most applications. A user-defined distance or time can also adjust the interval.

Track logs are saved just as waypoints and routes. First, clear any previously saved unnecessary track log data. If necessary, adjust the interval value (the distance between each trackpoint) for your application. Select the Fill or Wrap option if the new track log may be longer than what the receiver can store. After the trip, select to record the track log. Most receivers will then save the track log in a reduced number of trackpoints and title the log with the current date. Like a waypoint, the log can be renamed at any time. To avoid a memory problem, users on longer-distance trips can record their travels with multiple saved track logs.

Remember the following when saving a track log:

- Clear the track log at the starting point of a new trip.

- Save the track log at the completion of a trip.

- Be sure that the receiver is operational during the entire time of the trip. Lost satellite signals or power will result in a discontinuous log. The log will still be recorded, although broken. Nonoperational time will be recorded as a gap or a straight line between recorded tracks.

Routes

A route is a series of waypoints that are listed in the order of start to finish. Routes may contain up to 30 or more waypoints depending on the capacity of the receiver. Each section between two waypoints is a leg. To create a route, select a series of waypoints in the sequence they are to be followed.

Routes are beneficial because, unless you're flying or sailing, it's difficult to travel in a straight line. Obstacles require us to travel indirect paths until we reach our destination. This feature provides direction by organizing waypoints in the flow of travel. Following a route not only makes navigation easier, it also reduces the risk of error. Multiple waypoints like cabin, stand, camp, and fish, may not mean much by themselves, but when saved in a route they are given order, making an easy sequence to follow. Routes also help designate points of interest, including locations to stop for camping, eating, or refueling.

NAVIGATIONAL NUGGETS

Routes are beneficial to geocachers because they allow a series of geocaches to be saved in a sequence. Those of you who like going after multiple geocaches in the same day can be easily directed from one to another, with the distance provided between each geocache.

Saving Routes

There are at least five ways to save routes:

- **Entered while traveling.** One of the easiest ways to create a route is by saving waypoints along the way.

- **Manually selected.** You can select previously saved waypoints from the receiver's database in the order they are to appear in the route.

- **Loaded from a computer.** Load previously recorded routes into a receiver through the use of mapping software and a data cable.

- **From a saved track log.** Using the map pointer arrow, select key locations to save as waypoints along a track log.

- **Automatic routing.** Most newer receivers can automatically create a route to a selected location within the unit's software database. Some can even provide turn-by-turn driving directions.

When a route is saved, data is displayed on the active route page. It includes the distance between each waypoint and the total distance of the route. Detailed information is available for each leg of the trip, including the distance between waypoints, compass bearing, and ETA. Routes can also be easily edited by adding or deleting waypoints.

When a route is saved, the default name is the date it was created. You can rename the route at any time. One of the main benefits of using routes is that they are reversible. After the last waypoint destination is reached, you can reverse the route by an Invert command to backtrack to the starting point.

Auto Routing

As GPS receivers have become more advanced, standard features include the capability to search for addresses, intersections, and businesses from a preloaded software database. Automatic routing refers to the ability of the receiver to automatically create a route to a selected location within its database.

Using a Find feature creates these automatic routes. The receiver searches for the location and then establishes a route based on user-defined criteria such as reaching the location in the fastest time, in the shortest distance, or in a direct line in an off-road mode.

The screen shows an active route on the Magellan Explorist 710.
(Image used courtesy of Magellan Navigation, Inc. or its affiliates. Copyright © Magellan Navigation, Inc. or its affiliates.)

Navigation gets even easier with new guidance features that provide pop-up screens, audible alarms for next-turn, or even spoken turn-by-turn directions.

This latest technology is ideal for business travelers, emergency vehicle drivers, and anyone who needs to find unfamiliar addresses fast. These types of routing features are only as accurate as the maps in the unit, but they do work reasonably well. The main problem is that software is not always updated fast enough to reflect street changes. Auto routing will only improve as mapping software and database points of interest continue to be updated and improved.

The Least You Need to Know

- Take the time to learn the receiver buttons and screens on your GPS. It is important to be confident when using your device for outdoor navigational use.

- Carefully go through the setup options to ensure your receiver is programmed properly.

- Learn how to enter waypoint coordinates manually. Be able to find, recall, and navigate to waypoints confidently.
- Understand track logs and routes and how they may be helpful in your outdoor use.

Smartphones: The Next Step in Geocaching

Chapter 12

In This Chapter

- How smartphones are changing the game
- Apps to make geocaching more fun
- Geocaching in your pocket—anytime, anyplace
- The extra options smartphones offer you

Geocaching has enjoyed tremendous growth in the last few years—thanks in large part to increased access to technology. With today's GPS-enabled phones you can find yourself geocaching without ever having to break out your trusty old GPS device. In fact, you don't even need to log on to your home computer to download the geocache locations or log your finds afterwards. All these steps can be accomplished through the use of your GPS-enabled phone. It really is easier to go mobile with a mobile phone.

Geocaching itself is free, but previously you needed a specialized GPS unit, a computer, and Internet access. There was no problem if you already had the gear, but it took a pretty big commitment to trying the game out for a prospective player to purchase a GPS unit. Today, those barriers for entry are gone. Players can go on their first hunts using their existing smartphones and the Geocaching app.

The Official Geocaching App

As the anticipation built over the release of the GPS-enabled smart-phones, geocachers began wondering what would be in store for their favorite game. Groundspeak answered with an all-in-one application that puts the geocaching world in the palm of geocachers' hands. The application is available for many gadgets, including iPhone, Android, and Windows-compatible devices. There is even a free trial version you can try before you buy.

The Geocaching Application is available for iPhone, Windows, and Android platforms.
(Groundspeak)

So how exactly does the entire geocaching world fit in your pocket? Today's smartphones use a combination of GPS, Wi-Fi positioning, and cell towers to determine that device's approximate location. Groundspeak's Geocaching Application queries the Geocaching.com database in real time and provides a list of geocaches near that location. The application can also geocode addresses, search using a location from your address book, or look up a geocache by its GC code.

To hunt geocaches with your compatible smartphone, simply open the application, select a geocache you want to search for, hit the "navigate" button, and follow the arrow on the screen. You can also access the geocache details, such as recent logs and hints. You can even get the trackables pages to find out goals of Travel Bugs and Geocoins while out on the trail.

As the mobile computing world continues to grow, geocaching is determined to grow with it. New GPS-enabled devices simply mean that it's even easier for geocachers to get out and have fun.

iPhones and iPads

The popularity of Apple's iPhone made it a natural choice for the first version of the Geocaching App. There have been many updates and changes since it launched, but the official app remains the tool of choice for iPhone users in the Geocaching community. Manufacturers are always adding new features and improvements to the phones, but you don't have to worry about having the latest and greatest phone to use the app. The Geocaching App is best supported by the iPhone 3G or later, but it is also compatible with the iPod Touch and first-generation iPhones. Of course, you will need Wi-Fi access for the application to work on the iPod Touch. Also, since it does not have a GPS, compass navigation will not work on the first-generation iPhone. There are aftermarket accessories available for adding GPS functionality to first-generation iPhones, such as the Magellan ToughCase. Finally, the app is available in English, Dutch, French, German, and Japanese language versions.

Groundspeak's Geocaching iPhone App provides functionality similar to Geocaching.com, making it easy to navigate.
(Groundspeak)

Geocache search results page as shown using Groundspeak's Geocaching iPhone app.
(Groundspeak)

In addition to instant access to the Geocaching.com database of caches and trackables, you can use the app to:

- Search by current location, address, or GC code

- Filter your hides and finds from the Geocaching.com search results

- Access geocache details, including description, photo gallery, attributes, recent logs, hint, and inventory

- Look up trackable item details, including item goals, while on the trail

- Save geocache listings, including maps and photos, for quick retrieval and offline use

- Log geocache finds and post notes in the field

- Download active pocket queries for use while outside of network coverage

- Submit Trackable logs

- Upload photos when you log a geocache

- View geocache web pages on Geocaching.com without leaving the app by using the embedded web browser

- View nearby caches on the embedded map

- View cache size, terrain, and difficulty rating directly from the map screen

- Navigate to geocaches with a simulated compass arrow (iPhone 3G or later) or directly from the map screen

- Add custom waypoints when navigating to multi-caches

- Switch between street, topographic, and satellite maps (different map types may have different functionality)

- Rotate map to match your heading (iPhone 3GS or later)

Android Phones and Tablets

Groundspeak's Geocaching App is also available for devices running Android platforms 1.5 and higher, but the application works best with phones that have a built-in GPS system. If your phone does not support GPS, it will use the cellular network to determine your location. If the phone is unable to determine a location, you can still access cache information and view maps to use in coordination with another GPS device. You can also access previously downloaded Pocket Queries and caches saved for offline use.

Groundspeak's Geocaching App for Android.
(Groundspeak)

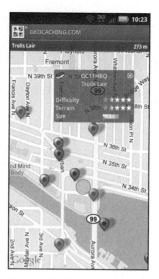

Geocaches can also be viewed on the built-in maps using Groundspeak's Geocaching App for Android.
(Groundspeak)

Once you select a geocache from the map, you can see the details right on the phone.
(Groundspeak)

When connected to the network you get instant, direct access to Geocaching.com's database of worldwide geocaches and you can:

- Search by current location, address, or GC code

- Sort by cache type, difficulty, terrain, size, and more using advanced search filters

- Access geocache details, including description, photo gallery, attributes, recent logs, hint, and inventory

- Look up Trackable details, including item goals, while on the trail

- Save geocaches, maps, and photos in custom lists for quick retrieval and offline use

- Log geocache finds and post notes in the field

- Download active pocket queries for use while outside of network coverage

- View geocache web pages on Geocaching.com without leaving the app by using the embedded web browser

- Get support for multiple users on a single Android device

- View nearby caches on the embedded map

- View cache size, terrain, and difficulty rating directly from the map screen

- Navigate to geocaches with a simulated compass arrow or directly from the map screen

- Add custom waypoints when navigating to multi-caches

- Switch between street and satellite maps

Windows Mobile

Windows Phone 7 and later use a combination of GPS, Wi-Fi positioning, and cell towers to determine the approximate location of the phone. The Geocaching App then queries the Geocaching.com database in real time and provides a list of geocaches near you.

Geocache search results page as shown using Groundspeak's Geocaching App for Windows 7 devices.

(Groundspeak)

With a smartphone running the Windows 7 or later operating system and the Groundspeak Geocaching App you may:

- Search by current location, address, or GC code

- Filter your hides and finds from the Geocaching.com search results

- Access geocache details, including description, photo gallery, attributes, recent logs, hint, and inventory

- Get full support for recording the movements of Trackables

- Log geocache finds and post notes in the field

- Keep personal notes on each geocache to help you remember important information

- Save geocache data and static bing map tiles to the device for use while outside of network coverage

- Get support for Geocaching.com Souvenirs

- Save and sort lists of geocaches

- View nearby caches on the embedded map

- View cache size, terrain, and difficulty rating on the map screen

- Navigate to geocaches directly from the map screen

- Switch between street and satellite maps

- Receive turn-by-turn walking and driving directions to geocache location

- Utilize a motion-based compass

- Mark and navigate to new waypoints from within the application

Once you have selected a geocache to search for, the application will even show you the way.

(Groundspeak)

Geocaching Challenges App

Geocaching Challenges is the first Groundspeak game designed to be played using a phone application. We will explore Geocaching Challenges and what they mean to the evolution of the game more completely in Chapter 18. In fact, many of the things that make Geocaching Challenges such an exciting new addition to the game were made possible by advances in smartphone technology that make it easier to interact with the world around you.

The free Geocaching Challenges app opens up a whole new world of exploration and adventure.

(Groundspeak)

Imagine exploring your neighborhood, using your smartphone to find great locations, and when you arrive you use this application to help you to "discover" a secret about that spot. Using the application you can seek out nearby Local Challenges or Worldwide Challenges that can be completed from nearly any location. You can then take a picture right from the application in order to complete the challenge.

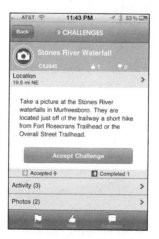

A sample Geocaching Challenge along a Middle Tennessee Greenway.

(Groundspeak)

Once you find a challenge that looks interesting, you can look up the details, accept it, and even post pictures and complete the challenge, all from inside the application right on your phone. This great free application opens an entire new world of adventure for geocachers and gives you a chance to get outside and play even when you might not be able to seek a traditional geocache.

Third-Party Geocaching Apps

The official applications are a great way to access the world of geocaching, but they aren't your only options when it comes to geocaching with your phone. By partnering with Geocaching.com, many other companies now offer applications that provide additional functionality or serve niche markets. In addition to these applications there are even hardware options to improve GPS accuracy for your phone and enable you to use it for navigation in your vehicle while it charges. Here are just a few of the many third-party geocaching applications on the market today, with many more germinating in the "app gardens" of software developers worldwide.

Trimble Geocache Navigator

The Trimble Geocache Navigator is a fully featured geocaching application for mobile phones. The software combines the GPS that is built into your phone with your phone's wireless data network to allow you to search for caches near your current location, address, coordinates, or waypoint.

You can then navigate to the geocache by following the arrow on your phone's screen, just as you would with your GPS. Once you find the cache, you can log your find right from your phone. Learn more at www.trimbleoutdoors.com.

CacheSense

CacheSense is a paperless (and PC-less) geocaching application for BlackBerry and Android smartphones, and was the first third-party application licensed to use the new Geocaching Live API. With secure online access to your Geocaching.com account you can search for nearby caches, download Pocket Queries, log your cache and Trackable finds, and upload photos—all from your BlackBerry smartphone. Find out more at www.cachesense.com.

CacheBox

CacheBox is a paperless mobile geocaching software for Android and Windows Mobile operating systems with online and offline maps support and Geocaching.com Live API capability. Manage and find mystery caches with intelligent handling of Final Waypoints and the Mystery-Solver module. Features include multi-database support, image and spoiler view, Field Notes upload, track recording, and viewing. Cachebox is a free open-source application. Check it out online at www.cacheboxstore.com.

NeonGeo

NeonGeo is a complete Android-compatible mobile geocaching suite for both online and offline usage, using the Geocaching Live API. You can search for geocaches on the go, import GPX files, log Trackables and geocaches online, keep field notes, set up custom map servers, and much more. You can learn more at www.neongeo.com.

GCBuddy

GCBuddy uses the Geocaching Live API to allow you to conveniently prepare your multi-cache visit at home, and enter all discovered clues into the app while in the field to reveal new waypoints to navigate to. This application makes managing multi-caches in the field a snap. Visit www.btstsoft.nl/apps/gcbuddy for more information.

In addition to applications, several companies offer accessories to make navigating with your smartphone better, like this Premium Car Kit from Magellan.
(Image used courtesy of Magellan Navigation, Inc. or its affiliates. Copyright © Magellan Navigation, Inc. or its affiliates.)

The Least You Need to Know

- Geocaching continues to embrace expanding technologies.
- The Official Geocaching App for iPhone, Android, and Windows 7 gives you access to everything you need to be a geocacher in the palm of your hand.
- Geocaching Challenges are best played using the free official application.
- There are several third-party applications that expand the possibilities of your Geocaching adventures.

Geocaching with Computers and Software

In This Chapter

- Explore how you can use computers to save, transfer, and organize your data
- Get the hang of tracking your current location on computer mapping software
- Learn how to make GPS receivers and computers work together
- Find out about the latest programs available to enhance your geocaching experience

Used along with mapping software programs and GPS devices, computers can be very useful navigational tools for your geocaching adventures. Whether at home or in the field, you can use a computer to help plan your trip by studying where you're going and how to get there. When you get back home, you can save a log of your travels and even share it with your friends and the online community.

This chapter explains how to utilize desktop and mobile computers in GPS and navigation, including how to manage, transfer, and save data for your geocaching adventures.

GPS with Computers

GPS and computers go together as naturally as geocaching and adventure. There are many applications for using computers in navigation, with or without a GPS device. Computers can run highly detailed mapping software and can even be transformed into GPS receivers. Desktop computers work great for trip planning, whereas laptops, tablets, and handheld PDAs are more easily taken into the field for more versatility.

EUREKA!

Some geocachers who do not have GPS units capable of paperless geo-caching use inexpensive PDAs to bridge the gap. These units can be used to display details for each geocache and for writing information about the cache in the field. Although they are not usually waterproof, their relatively low cost of replacement makes them a viable choice for keeping your geocaching adventure organized.

You can use a computer as a tool for navigation in four ways: as a receiver, as a map database, for data transfer and management, and for real-time tracking.

EUREKA!

To use a GPS receiver with other electronic devices, purchase one with a data port compatible with National Marine Electronics Association (NMEA) protocols. The NMEA has established a universal electronic standard to allow compatibility between GPS receivers and other electronic gear.

Computers as GPS Receivers

Laptop and handheld computers are easily converted into GPS receivers through kits that include software and a remote antenna. Laptops with built-in *Bluetooth* support can also use Bluetooth-enabled GPS devices. The advantage of doing so includes the ability to use computer equipment you already own and carry it with you. Computers have large color screens and virtually unlimited memory compared to GPS receivers. In addition, a greater number of high-quality map programs are available for computers as opposed to GPS devices.

GEO-LINGO!

Bluetooth is a wireless technology standard that allows devices to communicate easily and securely over short distances. There are lots of Bluetooth-enabled devices on the market that make it easy to mount your wireless GPS in a location where it will get the best signal while using your laptop in a comfortable and safe position.

It might be possible to save a little money by not duplicating gear and using your computer and PDA instead of a dedicated GPS unit. Keep in mind, however, that laptop and PDA setups do not have nearly the durability of a standard GPS receiver. Moisture and vibration can quickly disable the electronics. Computer-based setups are best for vehicle-based applications due to high power consumption and limited durability.

EUREKA!

Protective case manufacturers such as Pelican and Otterbox make special water- and shockproof cases to protect cell phones, tablets, and other electronic gear.

Map Databases

One of the benefits of bringing your computer along is that any one CD, DVD, or SD card can store more map data than your glove box could ever dream. Any of these resources can include highly detailed data on a favorite region or general highway map information for a whole country. The convenience of having highway, regional, and topographic maps in such a compact format is great. Plus, you don't have to fold them!

Despite the convenience of computer maps, they will not altogether replace paper maps, especially when hiking outdoors. Paper maps have a time and place for use and can be easier to read while bouncing down the road or identifying your location while out on the trail.

Data Transfer and Management

For geocaching, mobile computers work great for storing downloaded geocache data. Besides creating and storing information, data can be transferred between computers and GPS receivers. Transferring waypoints and route data created by trip-planning software directly to your receiver is incredibly helpful. Not only does it save considerable time but it also reduces the risk of error from manually entering coordinates or other information in the field. Upon your return, you can quickly and easily transfer waypoints, tracks, and route data to your computer to help document your travels. If your GPS unit supports paperless geocaching, you can transfer "field notes" from your GPS to your computer for upload to Geocaching.com. This great feature makes logging your finds much quicker and reduces the opportunity for error.

Another benefit of this feature is the ability to share GPS data with a friend. Waypoints for your favorite geocaches and outdoor areas can be easily saved and transferred. Plug a friend's GPS receiver into your computer and he can follow in your footsteps.

Real-Time Tracking

Real-time tracking is a fascinating way to use your receiver and computer together. An icon of your location displays your movements on the center of a digital map on your computer screen. Your position normally remains in the center of the screen while the map moves as you travel.

Displaying your location and direction of travel on a larger computer screen, rather than a small-screen receiver, is helpful if you are using a receiver without a basemap. It also provides two different screens of data—the driver can monitor the GPS receiver for information like speed and compass bearing, while the passenger watches your position on the computer.

GPS track logs are helpful when logging your geocaching adventures. They also help ensure your safe return.
(Carleen Pruess)

To set up this feature, plug your GPS receiver's data cable into an open port on your laptop or tablet. Most modern map software programs will connect to your GPS unit automatically, but you may need to make some adjustments or even set up the connection manually.

Setup menu options in both the GPS receivers and map software programs provide various interface options. The primary interface for real-time tracking and other receiver/computer functions is NMEA mode. As previously mentioned, the NMEA established this mode for electronic and navigation product compatibility. In the map software program, be sure to select the correct data port used for the data transfer. The next setup option is the baud rate. This is the rate at which electronic data is sent. The primary baud rate for real-time tracking is 4800. An incorrect baud rate is one of the primary reasons for interface failure. It may take a little experimenting to get the right settings, but it's worth the effort when you see your location appear on the computer screen.

DEAD BATTERIES

When driving, computers, cell phones, and GPS receivers can grow beyond distractions to serious hazards. Don't let the use of this gear get you into an accident. Let your passenger manage the electronics while you keep your eyes on the road.

Mapping Software

Mapping software is available in a variety of applications from many sources. It is a very practical application that provides tools and resources many geocachers consider invaluable.

The following are examples of standard features found in most mapping software applications:

- **Creating waypoints and routes.** Moving a cursor on a map program instantly provides coordinate information based on the cursor's location on the map. You can create waypoints with a simple click of a mouse, and then easily create routes along those waypoints. You can also customize waypoints on the map with names, colors, and symbols.

- **Real-time tracking.** You can use a GPS receiver to transfer a live track log into computer mapping software.

- **Recording travel history.** You can transfer track logs recorded in the field back to your computer to save them as recorded history of your travels. Computers provide virtually unlimited storage compared to the limited memory available in most receivers.

- **Search feature.** Most map programs provide a search feature that enables you to find parks, towns, and other landmarks instantly.

- **Terrain analysis.** Moving a cursor over a map instantly provides elevation information. By connecting two points on a map you can quickly see an elevation profile, distance, or bearing.

- **Transferring waypoints, routes, and track logs.** Through the use of a data cable, you can transfer data back and forth between a GPS receiver and a computer.

The following sections provide explanations of some of the types of map software available.

GPS Company Software

GPS manufacturers provide proprietary mapping software that works exclusively with their brands of GPS receivers. Additional map detail can be purchased on CD, DVD, or SD card to enhance a device's own basemap. For example, more detailed topographic, city, or nautical information can be purchased to improve navigation and enhance your receiver use. Imagine trying to navigate to a geocache without street names or trail data! Map software is typically available for major cities, regional areas, various countries, and other parts of the world.

Besides upgrading a receiver's basemap, the latest software programs include the most recent versions of commercial metro or travel information such as the location of restaurants, hotels, gas stations, and other helpful points of interest.

Aftermarket Software

Traditional map manufacturers like DeLorme and National Geographic also provide electronic maps for use with computers, tablets, and PDA devices. These programs work great for planning trips as well as for creating, transferring, and saving travel data. They include a number of great features, such as the ability to convert trails and roads into routes, and can provide a 3-D display of your map data. They cannot, however, be used to enhance a GPS receiver's existing basemap.

The U.S. Geological Survey offers digital maps known as digital raster graphics (DRG). DRGs are standard topographic maps scanned and made available in an electronic TIFF file. A 7.5-minute DRG averages 8 megabytes. These maps can be combined with other digital media, such as photographic or satellite data, for a unique perspective.

Map companies offer large topographic maps with your favorite location in the center. This is helpful in avoiding the problem of hiking into a map's corner, or having to bring multiple maps because the subject area is on the boundary. These maps can include any coordinate grid lines desired, and most are printed on waterproof paper. Map kiosk centers are becoming popular in outdoor stores. These centers are capable of instantly printing topographic maps of your favorite areas.

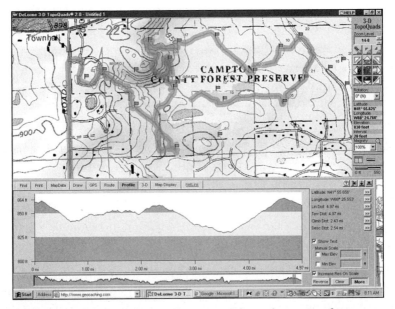

Using DeLorme software, the map shows a track log and waypoints from an event in St. Charles, Illinois.

(DeLorme)

Online Map Services

Online map services like Google Maps enable you to instantly conduct an Internet search to obtain a map of any area of interest. Depending on your preferred map site, you can enter coordinates to locations and then create and print a route or map with the location clearly marked. Most of these sites also allow you to view street, terrain, or aerial views of the area you are planning to visit, which can be very helpful in planning your trip. For even more detail you can use Google Earth to explore the area, and in many parts of the country you can even see a "street level" view that allows you to explore an area virtually.

When preparing to go geocaching, remember that many of these map services are available on the Geocaching.com cache details page. It's easy to select and view a map of the geocache online. On Geocaching.com, you can also use Geocaching Maps to filter geocache types in real time as you view and drag the map online.

Most online mapping services are free and can be very helpful in providing quick and accurate mapping information.

EUREKA!

You can use aerial photography similar to what intelligence agencies have been using for years. Geocache information pages on Geocaching. com include links to a variety of maps, including those featuring aerial photography.

Terrain Analysis

One of the primary benefits of using digital maps is the ability to study terrain. Regardless of software type, most applications provide features to allow you to study the ground before you get there. Knowing such factors as elevation and slope will make it easier to plan your trip. Determining how steep trails and roads are may make a difference in whether you can hike or drive there, or even help you determine whether you can bring children along for the hike.

Selecting two points with a click of a mouse can immediately provide distance bearing or elevation profiling. Maptech's Terrain Navigator software provides a unique 3-D perspective of any selected area. In 3-D mode, the area map can be rotated, tilted, and viewed from any bearing or elevation. A selected area can also be viewed in a topo map or aerial photo view format.

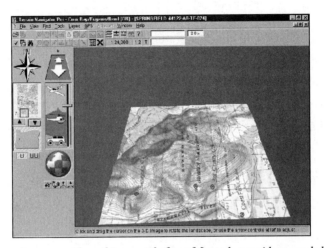

Electronic maps, such as this example from Maptech, provide many helpful features, including three-dimensional viewing.
(Maptech)

In the example shown in the previous figure, a group of caches are profiled in the Mount Pisgah area. The cache locations were entered and then Maptech's 3-D mode was activated to analyze the surrounding terrain. These high-tech tools are excellent for making flat maps come alive and making them much easier to interpret. Studying this information is as interesting as it is practical. Knowing what to expect can help avoid errors in calculating travel time and difficulty.

EUREKA!

Check your GPS receiver's manufacturer's website to determine the latest version of operating software or firmware that is available for your receiver. Manufacturers often update this software to fix bugs and make other improvements. Most receivers can be easily upgraded through an online download. There is typically no cost, and it usually takes only a few minutes.

Thousands of Geocaches at Your Fingertips!

Once you decide on the area in which you want to go geocaching, Premium Members at Geocaching.com can request a Pocket Query. A Pocket Query provides the ability to create custom searches so that you can receive information on only the caches you want to hunt. At any time, you may have several thousand geocaches stored on your computer with waypoints and details for each geocache that is waiting to be found.

The information included in a Pocket Query can be imported into a mapping software program for easy viewing of the geocaches. The cache locations are shown on detailed maps, making it easy to see the locations of geocaches in relationship to each other. Most newer models of GPS receivers allow you to import GPX files directly using a data cable.

Ready to head outdoors? Simply use a GPS data-transfer program to download the waypoint data from your computer into your GPS receiver, or drag and drop the GPX file, if your unit supports that, and you are set. It may sound like a complicated process, but once you've done this a few times you will feel like a pro.

Geocaching Software to Enhance Your Game

Because geocaching was adopted early on by computer and gadget geeks, those players began developing applications to improve their game from the start. Many of the programs that geocachers use today can be traced to the pioneers of the activity who contributed their time and know-how to their favorite activity. Other tools began as programs to enhance GPS usage and developed geocaching-specific functions as players adopted them for their own use.

It is difficult to say which programs are essential to geocaching. What *is* essential is finding something that works for you and gets you outside a little faster. The following sections discuss a few of the programs commonly used by geocachers.

Geocaching Swiss Army Knife (GSAK)

This all-in-one geocaching and waypoint management tool was one of the first to adopt the Geocaching API for greater integration with the main site at Geocaching.com. In addition to managing multiple waypoint databases with search and customization features, the macro language allows creative "remixes" of your geocaching data that make playing with the data a game of its own. GSAK also enables you to load Geocaching.com Pocket Queries onto your computer and export them directly to your GPS. GSAK works only on computers running Windows operating systems, and is available at www.gsak.net.

GEO-LINGO

API stands for "application programming interface," which, in its simplest form, is a way for different software components to talk to each other, providing a seamless experience for the end user.

GPSBabel

This extremely popular program has been helping geocachers convert waypoints, tracks, and routes between GPS receivers and mapping programs for over 10 years. GPSBabel enables users to freely move their waypoint data between the programs and hardware they choose to use. It also contains extensive data manipulation abilities, making it a convenient tool for processing large amounts of data offline. It has a graphic user interface (GUI) that allows for easy dragging and dropping of geocache data. It also has a command line version, which is used as the workhorse of conversions and transfers for many related tools including GSAK, MacCaching, GPSVisualizer, and Google Earth. GPSBabel runs on Windows, Mac OS/X, Linux, Solaris, FreeBSD, and OpenBSD. It's available at www.GPSBabel.org.

EasyGPS

EasyGPS works with many popular handheld GPS devices and can transfer waypoints, track logs, and routes from your computer to GPS and vice versa. Use it to back up and organize your GPS data, print maps, or load new waypoints onto your GPS for your next hike. EasyGPS runs on Windows operating systems and is available at www.EasyGPS.com.

Google Earth

Google Earth's interactive features make exploring maps fun. The detailed images available make it a much more personal experience than simply staring at a map. Pocket Query data can be loaded into Google Earth for viewing geocache locations. Plus, you can use the street view feature to virtually explore many locations including streets, bike paths, and even some trails. The unique 3-D view enables you to see the elevation profile of the hike for your geocaching expedition. You can then decide from your desk whether it's better to walk over that incline or around it. Google Earth is available for Windows, Mac OS/X, or Linux at www.google.com/earth.

CacheMate

CacheMate is a program for viewing Pocket Query information on a handheld PDA. In addition, notes can be taken through CacheMate and used later to write online logs. CacheMate was initially available only for Palm devices but has expanded for Pocket PC, and Windows and Google Android smartphones. It's available at www.smittyware.com.

Groundspeak Pocket Query as displayed using Google Earth.
(Groundspeak)

Geocaching Live Products and the Official API

As the hardware used to enhance geocaching and the software it runs becomes more advanced, Geocaching.com is evolving to make the game better. A big step into the future has come with the announcement of the Geocaching API. The next generation of Geocaching Live–enabled tools will use the Geocaching API to greatly enhance and extend your geocaching adventure.

So what does the API mean for geocachers? It means that there is an array of new tools available and several exciting opportunities on the horizon. Geocaching.com is now allowing some approved third-party developers to have direct access to data on the site. The API is a great way to crowdsource innovation by allowing developers to create new applications to better serve the entire community. From the Official Geocaching smartphone applications we discussed in Chapter 12 to the full array of third-party applications, live access to the Geocaching.com database by the community of developers is changing the game in important ways.

Since the project's launch, we have already seen developers create products that make it easier to manage multi-caches in the field, solve puzzles and confirm their solutions online, and provide geocaching solutions for platforms not supported by the official applications. The Geocaching API is made available at no charge and developers are able to profit from the Geocaching Live-enabled applications they create, encouraging more innovation across more platforms and a better game for all segments of the community.

Some Final Computer Bytes

With all this technology and the trip-planning features of mapping software, there is no doubt that bringing along a computer will allow you to get around much faster and more efficiently. It will also enable you to find more geocaches than you could have ever done before.

Remember that electronics do not hold up well to abuse, though. Vibration and moisture can easily send your expensive gear on a one-way ticket to the service shop. Also remember that thieves often target computer and electronic gear, so be sure to secure them and keep them out of sight when out on the trail.

> **EUREKA!**
>
> Some computer manufacturers make gear for extreme outdoor use, like the military-grade Panasonic Toughbook.

You must remember to use caution and not allow these electronics to become a dangerous distraction. Regardless of how you're traveling, taking your eyes off the road for a second to watch a screen can result in a serious accident. Allow a passenger to run the GPS and other gear so you can concentrate on driving, or pull over to do it yourself.

The Least You Need to Know

- If needed, you can easily convert your portable computer into a GPS receiver.
- The NMEA electronic format enables you to use your receiver with other gear including computers, PDAs, and tablets, so make sure to look for NMEA compatibility with any equipment you buy.
- Using computer mapping software will allow you to easily manage waypoints, routes, and track logs.
- There is a wide variety of geocaching software available to help you better organize your geocaching trips.

Going Old School— Using Analog Maps

In This Chapter

- Understand the basics of map reading
- Discover why detailed topographic maps are ideal for geocaching
- Learn how to interpret the terrain through contour lines, determine distance, and navigate like a professional
- Learn the navigation tricks and tips of the pros

At its most basic, geocaching is a matter of simply following an arrow to a destination. In the early days, this was the approach of the majority of geocachers. However, as GPS receivers have become more advanced, new tools and features, including map integration, are becoming readily available resources.

GPS users today often have at their disposal a collection of maps to help them find their way. While most geocachers do not get into the activity as skilled map readers, many learn that understanding the basics of reading and interpreting a map can ensure that you are able to navigate with confidence.

This chapter explains map basics. You'll find out why detailed topographic (topo) maps are great for geocaching, and then you'll learn how to read them. This chapter also shows you how to determine distance in the field and how to use topo maps to enhance your geocaching experience. Finally, this chapter provides some navigation tips that will keep you navigating like a pro.

Map Basics

From highway to topographic, from paper to electronic formats, maps come in a number of different scales and sizes. Many GPS receivers include electronic basemaps and the ability to add maps with greater detail. It is important to have an understanding of the map options available to help ensure that you use the correct map for the job.

When viewing a paper map, check out the information along the bottom before trying to find your position in the middle. This "collar" area is full of reference information that will provide aid in reading the map. This information includes the scale, legend, distance indicators, color codes, magnetic declination, map datum, and the year the map was published. The gridlines and tick marks around the edges determine what coordinates are provided. Reviewing this information will help ensure the selection of a map in the scale and detail appropriate for your application.

Map Scales

The map *scale* is the ratio between the distance displayed on a map relative to the actual distance on the ground. The state road map kept in a glove box might be a 1:500,000 scale. Used as a highway reference, an entire state fits on one side, where 1 inch equals approximately 8 miles. When you're performing detailed ground navigation, such as when geocaching, the greater the detail the map provides, the easier it will be for you to navigate the terrain.

GEO-LINGO

Maps are referred to as small- or large-**scale.** Small-scale maps cover a limited area in great detail. Small-scale maps range from 1:24,000 to 1:65,500. Large-scale maps are like state or highway maps that show a larger area in less detail.

The primary map used for short-range detail is the 1:24,000 scale 7.5-minute topographic. In this highly detailed scale, 1 inch equals 2,000 feet. The key to choosing the right map is to choose a map that covers enough area with adequate detail to prevent you from traveling outside of its boundary.

Map Name Series	Scale	1 inch represents	1 centimeter represents	Map area (approximate square miles)
Puerto Rico 7.5 minute	1:20,000	1,667 feet	200 meters	71
7.5-minute	1:24,000	2,000 feet	240 meters	40 to 70
7.5- by 15-minute	1:25,000	2,083 feet	250 meters (about)	98 to 140
Alaska	1:63,360	1 mile	634 meters (about)	207 to 281
Intermediate	1:50,000	0.8 mile	500 meters (about)	County
Intermediate	1:100,000	1.6 mile	1 kilometer (about)	1,568 to 2,240
United States	1:250,000	4 miles	2. 5 kilometers (about)	4,580 to 8,669

U.S. Geological Survey map scale chart.
(U.S. Geological Survey)

Topographic Maps

In the United States, the most detailed standard map used in the backcountry is the U.S. Geological Survey (USGS) 7.5-minute topographic map. These maps can be purchased at outdoor stores or from the United States Geological Survey (USGS). They are called 7.5-minute maps because they cover 7.5 minutes of latitude and longitude. That's an area approximately 6.5 miles wide, 8.5 miles long, and 55 square miles. These maps, often referred to as *topo maps* or *topos*, provide a three-dimensional perspective of the ground. This perspective is provided using *contour lines*, which indicate terrain shape and elevation. Topographic maps also include the primary geographic coordinate systems of latitude/longitude; Universal Transverse Mercator (UTM); and township, range, and section.

GEO-LINGO

Contour lines are the curvy brown lines on a topographic map that indicate the shape of the terrain. Every fifth darker brown line is the elevation index line. This line indicates the elevation in feet or meters.

Map Reading

Map-reading skills are universally applicable, regardless of the map's scale or type. Map reading is essentially the interpretation of lines, features, landmarks, and symbols on a map. It helps to think about the map in a three-dimensional way, instead of just a flat sheet of paper. This is done by focusing on major landmarks and high and low elevation features. Contour lines on topo maps make this easier, because the lines profile the terrain.

It is helpful to maintain the "big picture" of the area in which you are traveling by keeping major landmarks in perspective. Prominent features, being man-made or natural, include all major landmarks such as mountains, highways, waterways, and bridges. Prominent features are good to use as a reference in conjunction with a map to determine your general location. Baseline features are linear reference points such as roads, rivers, and power lines. These natural boundaries are ideal to follow or use as a return point.

 NAVIGATIONAL NUGGETS

When geocaching in the wilds, it is wise to bring a paper map and compass in addition to your GPS receiver. In this way, you can get to the geocache by the most appropriate means, while ensuring your safe return in the case that your GPS receiver fails.

In the field, maps are easier to read if they are set to the terrain, matching the prominent and baseline features on the map with those on the ground. This is known as *terrain association*. This helps reference landmarks and gives the user a better understanding of what lies ahead. This is done with the assistance of a compass by rotating the map until the top faces true north.

Understanding how to read topographic maps is important when tackling tough terrain outdoors.

(Brad Simmons)

Reading Topographic Maps

Our example is a 7.5-minute topo map of the Bohemia mining district, south of Cottage Grove, Oregon. This map was located by reviewing a state of Oregon USGS map coverage index to find the map of our exact area of interest. The state index map is divided into titled 7.5-minute sections. Our map is titled Fairview Peak Quadrangle-Oregon. The bottom section of the map gives details that include the following:

- **Map date.** Produced in 1986, revised in 1997. Topographic information is from 1980.

- **Datum.** North American Datum of 1927 (NAD 27). The datum is the global survey system used to create the map. This is important because GPS receivers need to be programmed to the same datum used to create the map.

- **Declination diagram.** The scale indicating the degree a compass is adjusted to correct magnetic north to true north. This map's declination is 17.5° as of 1999.

- **Map scale.** 1:24,000; 1 inch equals 24,000 inches on the ground.

- **Mileage scale.** One mile equals about 2⅝ inches.

- **Contour interval.** The elevation lines are 40 feet apart; every fifth darker brown line indicates the elevation in feet.

- **Other information.** This includes where this map is located in relation to the state, map names surrounding this map, and a list of symbols for highways and roads.

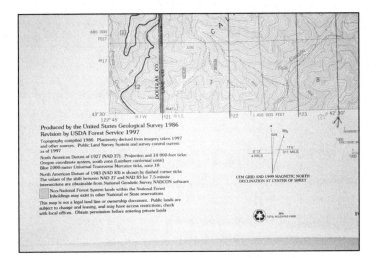

The collar area of a topographic map provides the information you need to read the map accurately.

(Jack W. Peters)

Check the Datum

When using GPS with any map, be sure to program the GPS receiver to the correct datum used on the map. Many U.S. topo maps use North American Datum 1927 (NAD 27 CONUS), or possibly the datum used in geocaching, World Geodetic System 1984 (WGS 84).

In Europe, it is the Ordnance Survey Great Britain (OSGB). The receiver is set to a default datum: check the Setup menu to ensure it is the correct one for your application. Failing to make this adjustment can cause errors of as much as 1,000 meters.

Grid Lock

Notice from the corner of this topo map that there are tick marks, lines, and numbers everywhere. Besides latitude/longitude and UTM coordinates, there are grids to indicate township, range, and section. To confuse matters further, there are also six-digit numbers with "FEET" behind them. This is a State Plane Coordinate (SPC) system, which is similar to UTM but uses feet rather than meters. When referencing numbers and tick marks, be sure you are referencing the correct markings before taking any readings.

Map Colors and Symbols

Topo maps are color-coded and are covered with symbols and markings. Fortunately, most are relatively self-explanatory. For example, on the color codes, black is used to designate roads, buildings, and other man-made objects. Blue is used to designate waterways, and brown is used for the contour lines. For a complete list of map symbols, check with the U.S. Geological Survey or whoever produces your favorite paper maps.

Contour Lines

Contour lines show the map's topography by indicating the shape of the terrain and its elevation. These lines make it possible to determine the height of the terrain and the depths of bodies of water. These lines do not cross each other because they join points of equal elevation. Every fifth line is darker and is known as an index line. The index lines provide the specific elevation listed in feet or meters above sea level. On our example topo, the elevation is listed in feet. There is a distance of 40 feet between each line, equaling 200 feet between each index line. The amount of distance between each line is known as the contour interval.

DEAD BATTERIES

Be aware that maps—even detailed topos—can be inaccurate. The data can be outdated and errors are sometimes made during the interpretation of the aerial photographs. Not surprisingly, locations on the ground often look entirely different from what you might think they would look like from a map.

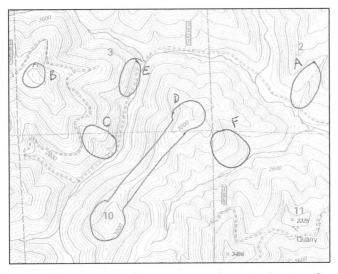

Each topographic map contour line represents a change in elevation. On most 7.5-minute maps this elevation measurement is 40 feet. Remember that contour lines may not indicate cliffs or crevasses that will make travel difficult.
(Jack W. Peters)

Contour lines provide a low-tech way for a map to come alive by providing a three-dimensional view of the terrain. Reading these lines is simple: the closer the lines are together, the steeper the terrain. Open-spaced contoured areas are flat; heavily lined areas are steep or cliff walls. With V-shaped contours, the tip of the V points uphill, as seen with creeks and rivers. U-shaped contours typically point downhill. The following are typical terrain features (marked by letters on the previous figure):

A.   V-shaped lines point to upriver. In this example, a creek is flowing down into a larger river.

B.   Mountain peak, indicated by the way the interval between circular contour lines becomes narrower toward the top.

C. Spurs, most likely caused by an ancient creek.

D. Saddle, where a plateau joins two mountain peaks.

E. Cliff wall, as indicated by a concentration of contour lines.

F. U-shaped lines point downhill.

Pacing

Some geocaches and GPS challenges require the ability to measure distance in the field. Pacing is a reasonably accurate way to do so by knowing the distance of your stride. A "stride" is two steps, the distance between where the same foot hits the ground twice. Tally strides by counting every time the same foot hits the ground.

To use this system, you have to know the distance of your stride. To determine the distance of your stride, measure off a predetermined distance, such as 100 feet, or 50 meters, and count the number of strides it takes to cover that distance.

Here are some points to consider while pacing:

- One stride (two steps) equals approximately 60 inches or 5 feet.

- Know how many of your strides are in 100 feet or 50 meters, whichever system is used.

- Each person's stride varies with their height and the terrain.

- Compensate for travel conditions that shorten strides (for instance, inclement weather, mud, snow, wind, visibility, and backpacks).

NAVIGATIONAL NUGGETS

Keeping track of pacing distances is easier with the aid of "pace beads" or handheld punch counters. Pace beads are used by sliding a bead over a string after a set number of paces. These aids reduce the chance for error and allow you to concentrate on counting paces instead of trying to remember distances.

Navigation Tips

Combining the traditional map and compass skills with a few tips will have you navigating like a professional. Understanding these skills also enables you to use your GPS receiver to its fullest potential. Here's a list of useful navigational skills to help keep you on track.

- **Aiming off.** This is traveling on a compass bearing in an indirect path to your target. This is done to bypass an obstacle, or to help find a target on a linear feature. For example, you believe your truck is parked on a roadway straight ahead at about 5°. You cannot see the vehicle because of dense vegetation, so you aim off slightly to the right at 15° knowing that when you reach the roadway, the truck will be to your left.

- **Calculate map distances.** Keep a small piece of wire in your navigation kit for measuring distances on a map. Bend the wire to follow a road or trail, and then straighten it out to find the distance using the map scale.

- **Catch features.** These are features that indicate you have missed a turn or have traveled too far. If circumstances make a destination difficult to find, know what roads or features are beyond the location. That way you will know whether you have traveled too far when you reach the catch feature you have chosen.

NAVIGATIONAL NUGGETS

Be sure to write down any coordinates that are being plotted. Check and double-check your work to avoid any errors. Remember, one wrong number could take you more than 100 miles off track.

- **Confirm location by elevation.** Altimeters are a useful way to help confirm your location on a map. Compare altimeter elevation readings with map markings. Remember, a GPS receiver's altimeter may not be as accurate as a manual barometric altimeter.

- **Dead reckoning.** This is used to confirm your location by recording your travels from a last known position. It requires keeping track of every distance and bearing traveled. Starting from a known position, record your route on a map or in a journal. This is an ideal way to back up a GPS receiver when traveling in unknown territory.

- **Directions from nature.** Remember the basics: the sun rises in the east, moves to the south, and then sets in the west. At night, find the North Star; also, the points on a crest moon point south.

- **Night navigation.** When traveling in darkness, remember that our natural night vision takes about 30 minutes to fully develop. Red LED lights or flashlight filters work great for producing adequate light without losing night vision. Besides using GPS, keep track of time and use pacing to maintain your position. Remember, pacing steps will be considerably shorter at night, and be sure that your compass glows in the dark.

- **Reverse perspective.** While traveling, remember to turn around and look for the reverse perspective. This is what the road or trail will look like when you return. Every few minutes, take a 360-degree scan. Notice the scenery and landmarks in every direction, paying special attention to what it looks like behind you.

- **Trail markers.** Manually back up your track log the old-fashioned way with the use of trail markers. Use natural resources, such as placing rocks or drawing arrows in the dirt with a stick.

- **Triangulation.** You learned how to use triangulation to confirm the location of a geocache. In this application, your location can be confirmed by taking a bearing to at least two or more different surrounding landmarks. A current location is determined by plotting the intersection of the bearings on a map.

The Least You Need to Know

- Various map options are available to ensure that you use the correct map when geocaching.
- Pay attention to important collar information and the coordinate system used on your topographic map.
- On most 7.5-minute topographic maps, each contour line indicates a change in elevation by 40 feet.
- Pacing is a remarkably accurate way to measure distances in the field by counting your stride. A stride is two complete and normal steps.
- When geocaching or hiking, traditional map and compass navigational skills enhance the use of a GPS receiver, and will be critical if your electronic gear fails.

Beyond Basic Geocaching

By now you're out there finding geocaches with the best of them. Each Travel Bug you release goes on journeys more epic than a Cecil B. DeMille movie, and you can read a map better than you can read your own handwriting. So what's left? If you're ready to advance to the next level, Part 4 is for you.

Get acquainted with the fun-loving, family-friendly geocaching community. Geocachers get together and find geocaches in nearly every country in the world. Discover how you can set up your own geocaching group and learn about attending or even hosting your own geocaching event.

We also talk about the exciting developments in the world of GeoTourism. How can you use geocaching as a virtual tour guide on vacation? Learn how both travelers and regional tourism agencies can take advantage of cohesive sets of geocaches with a common theme.

Developments in GPS-enabled devices make it easier than ever to find geocaches, but geocaching is just the beginning in a new world of location-based mobile entertainment. As the game evolves, new activities are born. In this part, we introduce you to the closely related worlds of Geocaching Challenges, Waymarking, and Wherigo.

Getting Involved in Geocaching Communities

Chapter 15

In This Chapter

- Online interactions and community building
- Local geocaching clubs and organizations
- National groups incorporate geocaching
- Geocaching and education

When you think of geocaching, an image might come to mind of one or two people out by themselves on a trail. In certain cases, that is true. Geocaching is a great way to get away from it all and simply enjoy nature. Yet, as the activity has evolved, geocaching has become driven by social interaction. For many people, geocaching is not only a way to spend quality time with family and friends but also a way to share similar experiences and meet new people.

Chances are, when you started geocaching you didn't know any other players. As you became more involved, you slowly got to know other geocachers through their logs, the geocaches they placed, forum posts, and the occasional e-mail exchange. What often develops out of those first geocaching interactions are friendships that run deeper than the game itself. You can find people who share a lot of the same interests and create relationships that feel like family—complete with that crazy uncle that no one quite seems to understand.

Geocachers are an international group of fun-loving people made up of every age, sex, race, and background. Most geocachers will agree that the next best thing to finding a well-hidden geocache is sharing the adventure with other geocachers.

It's great fun to meet other geocachers, whether online, on the trail, or at one of the many geocaching events. It is especially enjoyable the first time you get to associate a face and personality to the geocaching username of someone you've met online. You will probably find that many geocachers are not too different from you. Many geocachers have busy lives with family, children, and careers. But in all of life's chaos, they take the time to seek out a geocache or two, and they also take time to get together with each other to share the many experiences of geocaching.

Since the inception of the activity, geocachers have established friendships, teams, groups, and organizations; these enable them to get even more enjoyment from geocaching. Some have even found love through geocaching—proposing marriage using a specially placed geocache and sealing the deal with a published geocaching event that was also their wedding! Geocachers spend hours online and off discussing all aspects of geocaching, from rules and policy to adventures and experiences.

In this chapter, you'll learn how geocachers use online forums, local organizations, and events to cultivate an active social community.

A milestone geocache for ThePipers.
(Brad Simmons)

Online Interactions

The Internet was a key element in the development of geocaching and has been equally responsible for its rapid growth. The web is used in a number of ways, ranging from informing new players about the activity and listing the available geocaches to allowing geocachers to keep in contact and discuss their favorite hobby. The following sections discuss some of these online groups and forums.

Latitude 47: The Official Geocaching Blog

In 2010, as part of the tenth anniversary of Geocaching and a year's worth of Lost & Found Celebrations, Groundspeak launched the Latitude 47 Official Geocaching Blog. The name is a tip of the hat to Groundspeak since the home office (also known as "The Lily Pad") is located in Seattle, Washington, at 47° North Latitude, 122° West Longitude.

This engaging site is dedicated to telling the stories of geocachers around the world through articles, photos, and videos. Whether they are discussing the importance of rating handicapped-accessible caches properly, sharing best practices, celebrating milestones, or showing off really cool caches, there is always something exciting to learn. You can check it out yourself at blog.geocaching.com

Learn more about the Geocaching Community with the official blog.

(Geocaching.com)

Online Sharing for the Masses

Just as geocaching has evolved, so too have the number of ways in which people can share their beloved activity. There are hosted podcasts from around the world in addition to thousands of personal blogs, photos, and videos dedicated to geocaching adventures. A simple online search of "geocaching" can return many hours of enjoyment, reading about and learning of adventures from around the world!

Podcasts and Blogs Unite the International Community

A quick online search reveals thousands of personal weblogs from around the globe dedicated to both the game and the geocaching community. These blogs run the gamut from simple stories of families who like to hunt together and record their adventures for family and friends, to full blown sites with weekly updates, regular columns, and guest writers. The same is true of geocaching podcasts, which can range from occasional discussions on the sport to fully produced regular episodes.

For example, every week Sonny and Sandy from PodCacher produce a new episode that addresses issues within the geocaching community, and features listener milestone call-ins, and great on-location reports from geocaching events through www.podcacher.com. Another great way to learn about geocaching and members of the community is by listening to the Cache-a-Maniacs podcast at www.cacheamaniacs.com. Each episode features a prominent member of the geocaching culture. It is a great way to get insight not only on that person, but also on the history of the sport.

Geocaching.com Discussion Forums

Groundspeak's online forum has been a key element in the development of geocaching. The online discussion forums provide a setting where any geocacher can ask questions or search for answers. These discussion forums start off with someone asking a question or making an announcement or comment. Then, others respond and the conversation continues in the form of a *discussion thread*.

GEO-LINGO

A **discussion thread** is the topic that ties a string of conversations together in a discussion forum.

The Geocaching Forums
(Geocaching.com)

The forum has dedicated areas of topic discussion that range from "Getting Started," an area for newbies, to technical forums like "GPS and Technology," where geocachers can seek product reviews and information. There are also unique content areas, including Benchmark Hunting, which is about monument recovery efforts for the National Geodetic Survey. Here is a quick breakdown of the areas of discussion you can use every day on the Geocaching Forums:

- **Notices from Groundspeak:** Check here for the latest official Geocaching announcements and regular software release notes.

- **General Geocaching Discussions:** This is the most popular section of the forums including Getting Started, Geocaching Topics, and Featured Discussions and Suggestions.

- **Trackables:** There is always lively debate when geocachers get together to discuss Trackables in the Travel Bug and Geocoin subforums.

- **Bug Reports:** A necessary evil for a game based on rapidly changing technology and constant innovation.

- **Related Topics:** Include discussions on Technology, Ham Radio, Cache In Trash Out, EarthCaches, and even a GPS Garage Sale for bargain hunters. You'll find a very helpful Hiking and Backpacking section and a link to ClayJar's IRC chat. The forum also includes sections on Benchmarking, the National Geodetic Survey, and Map Corps. Premium members can also connect with other members of the community through the popular Off Topic section.

- **Geocaching and Education:** It has specific areas dedicated to using GPS and geocaching in the classroom from K-7 and 8-12, College Curriculum, Outdoor Camps, Youth Organizations, and even Adult Team Building and Seminar exercises. This is your destination for great ideas for educators of all types.

- **Regional, National, and Multilingual Forums:** No matter where you live around the globe, there is a forum section dedicated to discussing the local issues important to you, in your language. These forums are a great way to meet fellow cachers and get advice before traveling abroad.

Additionally, there are forums dedicated to each Mega-Event around the world where you can discuss travel plans, make arrangements to meet up with your fellow cachers, or discuss the event with its hosts. If that were not enough, there are more forums for the Geocaching-related games like Waymarking, Geocaching Challenges, and Wherigo. We'll talk more about the game-specific forums in Chapter 18.

These forums are filled with geocaching's colorful characters, many of whom are the pioneers of the activity and who helped it evolve into what it is today. Geocaching continues to evolve because of participants like you who test the latest GPS gear or Geocaching.com site changes and who consistently contribute new ideas. But we warn you, it's easy to get lost for hours in the ongoing discussions, learning and chatting about everything you ever wondered about geocaching!

After a little while in the forums, you will begin to become familiar with the personalities of many of the geocachers who post and participate frequently. If you have a question and post it in the discussion forums, you will likely receive your answer within minutes, or you might get *markwelled*.

GEO-LINGO

Often in the Geocaching.com discussion forums, you may be **markwelled** when you ask a question. "Markwelling" is a geocaching term that refers to when someone points you to a discussion in the past that answers your current question. Markwelling originates from geocacher Markwell, who would often direct new geocachers to existing topics.

The Geocaching.com forums are a great place to learn about the latest developments in the GPS-based gaming circles, such as new product releases, fixes, contests, and a variety of other topics related to geocaching. With millions of posts and a searchable format, the geocaching forums are a great place to start for those with a lot of questions or a hunger to expand their knowledge of geocaching.

And the community certainly really enjoys it if you simply want to tell your adventures from today's outing!

Regional and Local Forums and Websites

Within the Groundspeak forums you will find a host of regional forums that cover just about every area around the globe. These forums are great places to discuss geocaching in the local environment, focusing on specific issues and details that would not be as pertinent to a broader forum. These are also great places to get to know some of the geocachers in your home area. Some of the regional forum discussions take place in that specific region's native language.

Discussions about geocaching on a local level often take on some very important topics. Issues of how to promote geocaching in a specific area or working with local park boards are best discussed in these types of forums. Aside from the Groundspeak regional forums you can also find a wide variety of local geocaching clubs and organizations that have their own websites and discussion groups for just these purposes.

Local Clubs and Geocaching Organizations

Ready to get more involved? Want to meet local geocachers on a more frequent basis, or do you have a strong desire to give back to your local community? Then you may be interested in joining or even creating a local geocaching club or organization.

You can often find links to local geocaching organizations within the Groundspeak regional forums. If not, you can ask some of the more established geocachers in the area. Chances are they're familiar with the different websites, e-mail groups, or forums that exist in the area.

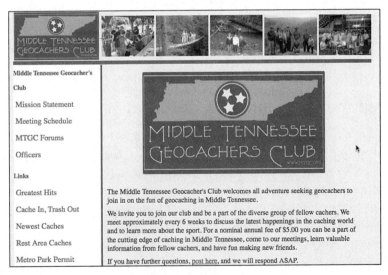

Local Clubs provide a great way to get involved in the Geocaching community.
(Middle Tennessee Geocachers Club)

Many of the more established geocaching organizations have developed their own websites and resources, and represent regional or metro areas, so they're helpful in keeping members informed about the latest news and events in their areas. These organizations help new geocachers by providing the basic information to get started, building a local geocaching identity, hosting and promoting events, and helping to facilitate relationships with local land managers.

So there are active geocachers in your area but no established club or organization? This might be the ideal time to start your own organization. Being part of a local group is a great way to meet fellow geocachers as well as get out more often by planning events and outings. An organization also enables you to promote the activity and provide a positive public image through projects such as trail maintenance or Cache In Trash Out (CITO) events. The first step is to get the locals together. An easy way to do this is by hosting an event cache. This is a cache where participants find a social event instead of a cache container. Find a family-friendly park or pizza parlor, record the coordinates, and post the event on Geocaching.com. Event caches are also covered in more detail later in the next chapter.

Publicize the event by posting notices in local, regional, and Geocaching.com discussion forums, and send invitations to people finding geocaches in the area. At the event, provide name tags to help people start to get to know each other. Have fun, eat, and do a little geocaching. Afterward, make sure you have everyone's name and contact information so that you can organize the group and plan the next event.

When you have a group of people interested, start a website or use a group forum (for instance, a Facebook Group). Use your new web home to post membership information, photos, resources, and details of the next event. Group message boards allow members to post information and keep in touch. Be creative with your events and the member list will continue to grow. There are a lot of fun and interesting things for a group to do: hide a group geocache, have a barbecue, camp out, invite special guests, host training seminars, visit historical or interesting outdoor places, and organize community projects. Involve members by asking them to come up with ideas and help plan the next events.

As your group grows, give it some organization. Its structure could be very informal, as long as projects are assigned to members who will follow through to keep things going. At some point, you'll need a leader, a treasurer, and someone organized enough to keep track of everything. The group can raise a little money to pay for web fees or T-shirts.

The main thing is for everyone to have fun. Don't bog the group down with meetings, politics, or business. People go geocaching to get away from those things. Use the get-togethers as opportunities to meet fellow geocachers and get outdoors more often.

National Groups Get in the Game

As the popularity of geocaching has grown, it has garnered the attention of some pretty impressive partners. Many groups recognize the educational benefits of a sport that combines playing with technology and problem solving with the great outdoors.

For their 100th Anniversary Celebration, the Boy Scouts of America (BSA) created their "Get in the Game!" initiative that includes:

- the new Geocaching Merit Badge

- the "Pillars of Scouting" Travel Bugs that go from cache to cache around the nation to highlight core Scouting values

- "Cache to Eagle" geocaches that are hidden by BSA districts across the country to showcase Eagle Scout service project sites

- "Treasures of Scouting" geocaches that showcase Scouting people and their respective programs: Cub Scouts, Boy Scouts, Venturing, Scouting Alumni, and Volunteers

Here are just a few of the many Geocaching Partnership projects out there today:

- **PBS/Dinosaur Train:** Special Dinosaur Train themed geocaches featuring fun dinosaur facts were hidden by PBS stations throughout the United States with support from the Jim Henson Company. This program encourages children to explore their surroundings, use observational skills, and have an adventure right in their own neighborhood.

- **Geocache with Rails to Trails Conservancy:** A partner-ship to encourage the mapping of the national rails-trails system in an effort to protect our irreplaceable rail corridors by transforming them into multiuse trails. Geocachers help this process by using their GPS units to record waypoints along the trails so that accurate trail maps can be created and registered.

- **Ranger Rick's Geocache Trails:** This partnership with the National Wildlife Federation encourages parks departments and the public to create trails with a series of branded caches and a fun passport to stamp along the way.

Geocaching in Education

As seen in the previous partnerships, GPS and geocaching are naturally integrated into many educational subjects, including mathematics, sciences, geography, English, social studies, history, art, health, and even physical education. Around the world, educators of all ages and experiences are integrating interactive, multimedia educational experiences around these technologies.

In the classroom, teachers utilize the experiential nature of a GPS device to get kids outdoors exploring their world. Students not only learn the curriculum in a way that can be easily remembered, they also learn important skills such as problem solving, and how to effec-tively communicate and collaborate as teams.

Classrooms are also supplying students with Travel Bug tags to attach to items to release into the world. In doing so, students learn about the richness of the world around them. With the ability to have stories and photos uploaded to a Travel Bug page, students learn that they can make an impact in the world, sharing and learn-ing from people from all walks of life. Placing a geocache as a class project is also a great way to teach environmental education and stewardship as well as community ownership and responsibility.

Outside the classroom, organizations and civic groups are using GPS and geocaching as tools to not only teach but to also cultivate lasting community relationships. Schools and other civic groups, including the Boy Scouts, Girls Scouts, 4H, and more, integrate GPS usage into community projects that impact a great number of people.

A recent example of such collaborative educational programming is Bellevue, Washington's Sculptural Travel Bug Project. Teens from Bellevue's Boys and Girls Club and students from four Bellevue high schools created more than 200 small-scale sculptures out of recycled and renewable materials. Each sculpture was attached to a Travel Bug tag and released into the geocaching world. The sculptures had the goal of traveling and returning to City Hall while sharing art with the public along the way! You can find more information regarding this program at www.sculpturaltravelbugs.com.

As another example of geocaching in education, in 2006, Groundspeak partnered with Minotaur Mazes to create the GPS Adventures Maze, an educational traveling exhibit that introduces GPS technology—its history, current uses, and future possibilities.

Participants move through the GPS Adventures Maze and encounter a variety of environmental differences as well as obstacles on their search for geocaches, just like in real life!
(Groundspeak)

Through the interactive displays and informative maze wall panels, participants are led through a variety of environments to simulate the experience of searching for a geocache, while learning about diverse subjects, including the basics of traditional and current navigation, outdoor ethics, and how to prepare for heading outdoors. In the short time the exhibit has been available, it has become a much sought-after educational resource for museums and science centers. From children to adults, visitors love the colorful displays and interactive educational activities. As a geocacher, you will be amazed at how well the GPS Adventures Maze captures the experience and spirit of geocaching in the great outdoors.

EUREKA!

The GPS Adventures Maze is also a unique geocache type on Geocaching.com. After a geocacher has visited the exhibit, he or she can log a "find" and share his or her experience with other geocachers.

The GPS Adventures Maze is always on the move. Visit www. gpsmaze.com to find out when it will be in your area. While the use of geocaching and GPS technology in education is in its infancy, the positive impacts are already being experienced.

The Least You Need to Know

- Participation in a geocaching group is a great way to keep in contact with fellow geocachers and be a positive influence in your community.

- Use the Geocaching.com and/or regional discussion forums to keep up on the latest GPS news and geocaching activity developments.

- Geocachers love to share their personal stories and experiences while geocaching. From online forum posts to podcasts and blogs, geocachers have a great number of opportunities to learn from one another.

- Geocaching events are a great way to meet new geocachers and to celebrate geocaching.

Geocaching Goes Social

Chapter 16

In This Chapter

- Joining the community through geocaching events
- Bringing the world together through Mega-Events
- Giving back through CITO events
- Setting up your own geocaching event
- Incorporating geocaching games into other events

Geocaching Events

From the early beginnings of geocaching, people wanted to share information, ideas, and locations; it was only natural for this online sharing to move offline. Event caches get geocachers to discuss and share their common bond—geocaching. Events are held in a wide variety of locations, from meeting halls to local parks, but are always created for and by geocachers.

You can find a list of upcoming geocaching events on the front page of Geocaching.com under the "Community" tab. Click on the link to view the full Event Calendar. On the Event Calendar you will find state, region, and country listings of events happening on any given day. If you see one that appears to be in your area, simply click on the link for that day and follow it to the detailed event page.

Geocaching events are also promoted through the Groundspeak Weekly Notification e-mail that is available to any registered geocacher on an opt-in basis. Any event that is occurring within your local area will be listed in the weekly e-mail along with links to Mega-Events around the world.

You never know who might show up when you plan an event.
(Brad Simmons)

EUREKA!

Organizing an event can be a lot of fun. Events are submitted to Geocaching.com much like other geocaches. However, make sure you post the event at least two weeks prior to the date so that potential attendees have sufficient notice to make plans.

As with the traditional geocache type, the event cache type has also evolved over time with community contribution and now includes the original Event Cache, Mega-Event Cache, and CITO Event. More permutations will arise over time as we continue to combine this game of solitary hiking with some technological gadget with the social needs of its gregarious community.

Meet and Greet Fellow Cachers

There are many different types of geocaching events, and different regions develop events that take on their own styles. One of the most common types of events is the simple Meet 'n' Greet. These are relaxed, informal meetings that normally take place in parks or at restaurants in reserved meeting areas. Meet 'n' Greets are great opportunities to sit down and get to know the other geocachers in the area.

Sometimes, these events take on more of a competitive flavor with special games and competitions set up by the event organizers. In this setting, geocachers get to know each other even better by working together to complete the tasks in the games. Often this style of event takes place in large parks where temporary geocaches might be hidden specifically to be found at the event. Prizes are often awarded and usually there is a large picnic or potluck meal that everyone enjoys.

Geocaching 101—Educational Events

Some of the most popular events are those set up to teach novice geocachers more about the game. Many local clubs or organizations come together regularly to host Geocaching 101 educational events. These events are great community outreach opportunities and are often conducted in collaboration with local parks, land managers, museums, and even schools. They usually consist of a short introductory program explaining the general tenets of the game followed by group hunts of existing geocaches or of temporary geocaches placed specifically for the event.

> **EUREKA!**
>
> When setting up an educational geocaching event, it is important to teach not only the fun aspects of the game, but to also educate new or prospective players on the accepted standards of the game and how we strive to give back to the communities we play in. One of the best ways to do this is to lead by example. After explaining the CITO (Cache In, Trash Out) program, hand out trash bags and encourage your new students to take part.

Even though Geocaching 101 events are created to help new players learn about the game, they are also a great way for more experienced players to give back to the community. Often these players not only help with running the event and by answering questions, but they also provide a great learning opportunity by lending their experience to prospective cachers and leading the group hunts. Having several seasoned geocachers on hand allows you to have smaller groups go out to hunt together, which provides a better experience for everyone. Plus, there is someone in each group who can answer questions and your prospective cachers gain the benefit of seeing different perspectives on the game.

Camping with Cachers—Multi-Day Events

Geocachers are, by their nature, people who enjoy the outdoors. Even those who don't think of themselves as "outdoorsy types" in the beginning soon learn to love and respect the outside world, which has suddenly become their playground. With this in mind, it is only natural that many events have come to incorporate a camping aspect. Camping with geocachers can be great fun. Whether group camping at a large park within feet of the parking lot or hiking with friends into the backcountry for a more rugged event, sitting around the campfire sharing geocaching stories is a great way to make new friends and learn more about geocaching.

Geocaching camping events are often spread over a couple of days, so more people can attend. For example, while most would choose to camp out and enjoy all the festivities, some cachers might attend just the dinner Saturday night and some time around the campfire, while others might pop in Sunday morning for breakfast to visit with their fellow cachers. No matter how you choose to enjoy the event, one thing is sure: camping is more fun when shared with friends.

Mega-Events

In the early days of the sport some regional events began to have much larger attendance figures than your everyday events. As the sport grew, a few get-togethers became truly special events where geocachers would travel from around the country or even the world to attend.

In response, Groundspeak created a new event cache type: the Mega-Event. This is a special designation reserved for event caches where, among other requirements, there are at least 500 attendees. A Mega-Event Cache may be published up to one year prior to the event date and typically attracts geocachers from all over the world. By attending a Mega-Event, you are awarded a distinctive icon on your profile. Many Mega-Events also have their own digital souvenir that is awarded for attendance, so not only do you get to attend a great event, your online profile will reflect that as well. Many Mega-Events offer geocoins and t-shirts or other souvenirs as part of an optional paid registration, but like regular geocaching events, attendance is usually free or at a very low cost. These are not meant to be profit-making ventures, after all; these are simply for the community to gather.

GeoWoodstock, Where It All Started

In 2003, a Tennessee geocacher named JoGPS had a vision. His dream was to host a geocaching event that would bring together the top cachers of the time from all over the country in one place. After consulting with friends and choosing Louisville, Kentucky, as a central location he hosted the first "GeoWoodstock." Although it was originally conceived as a national event, it quickly gained international status as cachers travelled from around the world to attend the "world's largest gathering of geocachers." Since then the event has enjoyed many "firsts," including being the first event to attain Mega-Event status, the first *event Geocoin*, the first event with over 1,000 and 5,000 attendees, and the first Mega-Event to feature social media with integrated Tweet-ups and Facebook functionality.

GEO-LINGO

Event Geocoins are a special type of Geocoin created to commemorate a specific geocaching event. They often come in multiple finishes, with one sold to help fund the event and another given as a special thank you to volunteers who work at the event. These coins are often highly sought-after souvenirs of the event. The very first event coin was made available in Jacksonville, Florida, at GeoWoodstock III.

Thousands of geocachers came together for GeoWoodstock VII in Bell Buckle, Tennessee.

(Daniel Johnson)

Unlike many regional events, GeoWoodstock is hosted all over the United States. The GeoWoodstock organizing committee (composed of past hosts) takes bids from local groups who then host the event according to a set of guidelines set by the committee. The Olympics-style setup allows for a consistent event experience and management while supporting the city's own local flair. GeoWoodstock is always held on either Memorial Day weekend or the weekend nearest Independence Day (July 4th) in order to assure the best weather possible.

Past events have been held all over the United States:

- GeoWoodstock I (2003)—Louisville, Kentucky
- GeoWoodstock II (2004)—Nashville, Tennessee
- GeoWoodstock III (2005)—Jacksonville, Florida
- GeoWoodstock IV (2006)—Dallas, Texas
- GeoWoodstock V (2007)—Raleigh, North Carolina
- GeoWoodstock VI (2008)—Wheatland, California
- GeoWoodstock VII (2009)—Bell Buckle, Tennessee
- GeoWoodstock VIII (2010)—Seattle, Washington
- GeoWoodstock IX (2011)—Warren, Pennsylvania
- GeoWoodstock X (2012)—Sellersburg, Indiana

From its humble roots in a small park, GeoWoodstock has become an annually celebrated event that continues to grow in global attendance and excitement. As with the original Mega Event, GeoWoodstock attendance is a feather in any geocacher's cap. In fact, many geocachers schedule their summer vacations around attending this famous event.

Here is a group photo of GeoWoodstock attendees who have attended the annual event every year since its inception! Bottom row: WCNUT, JoGPS, koneko, mtn-man. Top row: Show Me the Cache, Turtle3863, robertlipe, Southpaw.
(Photo by Alan Freed/Freedmultimedia.com)

Mega-Events Grow and Go Global

Of course, GeoWoodstock is not the only Mega-Event; as the game continued to grow, Mega-Events began to appear around the country. Many of these are now well-loved annual events with attendance in the thousands. From the Midwest Geobash to MOGA to Geocoinfest, several groups put together great events for geocachers to look forward to.

In June 2007, Mega-Events went global with a full weekend of fun in Bochum, Germany, with the MegaPott GeOlympics. Since that time there have been Mega-Events all over continental Europe, Scandinavia, the United Kingdom, Canada, Australia and New Zealand, and elsewhere. With the incredible growth of geocaching in Europe it is not surprising that one of the largest Mega-Events ever held was the Geocoinfest Europa 2011 in Cologne, Germany, with well over 6,000 attendees.

CITO Events—Giving Back and Having Fun

It should be clear by now that geocachers will use any excuse to get together, and one of their favorites is a Cache In Trash Out (CITO) event. As discussed in Chapter 2, CITO is an ongoing environmental initiative supported by the geocaching community. Since 2002, geocachers have been dedicated to cleaning up parks and other cache-friendly places around the world, as well as helping in the removal of invasive species, revegetation efforts, and building trails.

The term Cache In Trash Out comes from geocachers carrying a small plastic bag with them to pick up trash on their way back out of the trail from a geocache. It is one of the ways in which geocachers help preserve the natural beauty of our outdoor resources.

A CITO Event is held for the specific purpose of getting geocachers together to improve a cache-friendly area. CITO Events are often held in cooperation with local park departments or community organizations. They're a great way to emphasize geocachers' interest and support of the environment.

Although practiced regularly as an ongoing effort, Groundspeak celebrates an Annual International CITO Weekend where geocachers have an opportunity to participate in coordinated worldwide clean-up efforts. Geocachers host CITO events in their local areas on the same day or weekend as other geocachers around the world. Events can focus simply on trash removal or can take on massive park improvement projects. CITO events are not only a fun way to get geocachers together but also make positive social and environmental impacts in our communities.

Organizing Your Own Geocaching Event

Are you thinking of hosting your own geocaching event? Great! Of course, you will need to do a little bit of planning in order to ensure a successful gathering. Following is a list of topics to consider when organizing your event.

- **Communicate event goals.** What is the purpose of the event? Is this a Meet 'n' Greet at a local pub or a potluck where attendees should bring a dish to share? Perhaps you intend to gather folks for trail maintenance where gloves and resources would be beneficial? Clearly state the event expectations on the cache page so that geocachers know what to anticipate. Also remember that geocaching events should be free to participants.

- **Location, location, location.** The success of your event will be highly dependent on the location you choose.

  For an outdoor event, find a large park or outdoor area where you can get permission to hold the event. Reserve the location and secure whatever permits you may need far in advance. Find an area that is interesting for geocaching and that includes basic amenities such as parking, shelter, and bathrooms.

  For an indoor event, try to find a location where there are no entry or rental room fees. Ask in advance about large parties and potential payment options if you anticipate a large number of attendees ordering food and beverages. Make sure to also consider the ages of potential attendees, especially children. If you choose a particular location, will children be able to attend? Clearly communicate this information in advance. Finally, in metro areas, consider available transportation and parking needs.

- **Organization is key.** Before the event, post as many details as possible. For the event, put together a program or information board explaining event details. It is always a good idea to decide in advance what to do if it rains.

- **Plan in advance.** Post your event details at least two weeks before the event date to allow people time to make plans to attend. In fact, posting at least a month in advance is even better. This gives participants the opportunity to take the time off to attend. Also, campgrounds and lodging may be booked long in advance. Make sure lodging and camping is available if you are planning a weekend-long event.

To also ensure good attendance, do not forget to check the online event calendar on Geocaching.com to review potential event conflicts in the area.

- **Make sure everyone has fun!** Keep things simple and the mood light. Even if you are hoping to have some competitive games, don't let the atmosphere become so intense that it overrides the ability of people to simply enjoy themselves.

EUREKA!

Many people add educational opportunities to their geocaching events by providing seminars on various topics relating to navigation, GPS, and geocaching.

A variety of games helps keep an event interesting and fun. You can offer a number of game variations to keep players engaged. Here are some commonly used basics:

- **Traditional timed cache events.** Participants attempt to find as many caches as possible within a specified time limit. Each cache contains tickets or envelopes taken by the finders to verify they were there. Some form of handicap system could be used to allow older and younger teams to compete with the highly experienced or athletic ones.

- **Hide and seek.** Participants provide their own cache containers and hide them for the officials to find. Players are judged by their creativity in creating and hiding the caches. Some players have become very innovative and have made custom cache containers out of hollowed logs and pinecones.

- **Puzzle caches.** Use your imagination to come up with games to keep players guessing and using their creativity. One example is to place items in caches that, when found, require participants to make something with the contents. Another idea might be to have players find envelopes containing trivia questions. Players receive points for questions answered correctly.

With creativity and good organization skills, your event will undoubtedly be a great success.

Adding Geocaching Games to Your Events

The possibilities for adding geocaching-style games to outdoor events are as endless as there are geocaches to find. Families, clubs, companies, and all kinds of organizations can use geocaching to liven up their picnics and events. This is being done now by a wide variety of organizations, ranging from Boy Scout troops to search-and-rescue teams to church groups. Outdoor skills trainers are also recognizing the benefit of these games as a practical and fun way to teach GPS and navigation.

Adding geocaching-style games to your next event is a great idea for a number of reasons:

- It's fun. Remember that? In our busy lives, especially in a corporate or organizational setting, how often do we get the opportunity to enjoy ourselves? It gives everyone something to do other than sit around and eat. It will intrigue your guests, leaving them with a positive experience they will be talking about later.

- It exposes people to GPS, navigation, and outdoor skills. Geocaching provides an introduction to these skills, allowing guests to determine whether they want to pursue the activity further.

Adding geocaching games to your events might be easier than you think. Do a search for geocaches in the area of your event and bring the information along with you. Most parks, picnic areas, and camp locations have caches hidden in and around them. The other option is to hide a few of your own. Geocaches could be filled with prizes or gift certificates that would have special meaning to the group. Be creative: a day-off pass would be popular at a company picnic, for instance.

Corporate team-building company PlayTime Inc. uses geocaching for its GeoTeaming program. After a brief classroom-style training session covering GPS, geocaching, and navigation basics, the group breaks up into teams that head out to compete for points by finding geocaches of various difficulties and distances in a certain amount of time. These programs are fun and educational, and help groups learn how to work better together to accomplish goals.

The Least You Need to Know

- Geocaching Events help build community and are a great way to get to know your fellow cachers.
- Event details should be posted at least two weeks in advance, to allow people time to make plans to attend.
- When more than 500 geocachers attend an event it can become a Mega-Event.
- CITO Events help geocachers give back to the environment by focusing the efforts of a large crowd on improving a cache-friendly area.
- Adding geocaching games to corporate or civic events and retreats is a great way to introduce people to the sport and encourages team-building.

Hitting the Road: GeoTourism

Chapter 17

In This Chapter

- Working geocaching into your vacation plans
- Exploring with GeoTours
- Choosing geocaches to hunt on your trip
- Packing for a geocaching vacation

As much fun as geocaching can be in your own community, it's also a great way to explore the world as you travel, whether for work or on vacation. So if you are heading off on a trip, don't forget to bring along your GPS receiver! Traveling with your device is not only a good way to minimize the stress of navigating an unfamiliar area, but it is also an excellent way to explore unique locations.

While most people may be inclined to use their devices to search only for hotels, restaurants, and other points of interest, geocachers learn to take advantage of the more unknown tourist destinations— the local geocaches placed in the area!

By now you may have found a few geocaches and have probably realized that people place geocaches in areas that they consider to be special. When you travel, seeking out the local geocaches is a great way to find some exceptional places and adventures that might not show up in traditional guidebooks. In this chapter, we discuss how to easily go geocaching when you travel, including what items to bring, and how to identify the must-do geocaches in the area.

Exploring Your World with GeoTourism

Geocaching has long been a great way to explore a new area. In most spots you will find geocaches hidden near the popular "tourist" destinations, but you will also find those off-the-beaten-path destinations that only the locals know about.

One way to seek out really interesting locations is through the use of geocaching "Favorites." When on the Geocaching.com website searching for geocaches to hunt on your trip, you can reorder any search result to show the most "favorited" caches as we discussed in Chapter 2. By focusing your efforts on these highly recommended geocaches, you are likely to find some really great locations and hiding styles. Many experienced geocachers use this method to create their itineraries when hunting in a new location or while on vacation.

Take a Tour with the Locals

In addition to creating your own route through the caches on your itinerary, you also have the option of hunting along an organized GeoTour that you can find at Geocaching.com. A GeoTour consists of a cohesive collection of geocaches placed within a specific area or along a specific route, often becoming a draw for tourism and boosting economic development.

Many times a GeoTour organizer creates a special passport that functions as a logbook for visitors to track their progress as they proceed through the tour. Some GeoTours include special rewards for completion, such as custom Geocoins or other Trackables. GeoTours can be a simple series of caches highlighting parks and local attractions in a town. Some take the form of a guided trail through artistic installations while others are an elaborate tour of notable sites that teach the history of an area by marrying the events of the past with their physical locations. When it comes to GeoTours, the only limitations are the Geocaching.com guidelines and the imaginations of the people who organize them.

Many organizations come together to create these GeoTours not only to encourage tourists to visit their locations, but to provide a "virtual tour guide" through the geocaches and their webpages. Not only is a well-organized GeoTour an enticing reason for travelers to visit a destination, but it can also provide measurable impact. By tracking the number of passports and Geocoins deployed, and the number of geocaching "logs" entered by visitors on Geocaching.com, groups can monitor the ongoing impact of their GeoTour.

GeoTours Help Explore History

GeoTours, sometimes also called GeoTrails, are a series of geocaches engagingly tied together by a common theme, such as the history of a given area or region. There is not necessarily a fixed itinerary, like on a traditional trail, but rather a series of points of interest in a sort of self-guided, goal-oriented plan. For example, the Allegheny GeoTrail encompasses 10 counties throughout northwestern Pennsylvania, with 10 to 20 designated geocaches in each county making up the GeoTour. By finding these caches, geocachers can earn Geocoins while exploring a beautiful area of the country that they might have otherwise missed.

Geocachers record their progress along the Captain John Smith GeoTrail in their passports, which can be exchanged for a collectible Geocoin upon completion.
(Geocaching.com)

Here are a few other historically themed GeoTours/GeoTrails you may want to explore:

- **Star-Spangled Banner GeoTrail:** A unique journey through American history and across the landscapes of the Chesapeake Bay region. It commemorates the dramatic chain of events, people, and places that led to the birth of our National Anthem during the War of 1812. Participants can explore more than 30 forts, museums, battlefields, ships, parks, and preserves, each with its own story to tell about the War of 1812. In 2012, for the 200th anniversary of the War of 1812, the Star-Spangled Banner GeoTrail is expanding into even more locations. This first-of-its-kind, multi-state initiative is sponsored by Friends of Chesapeake Gateways, the Maryland Geocaching Society, the National Park Service, and partner sites across the region. There are also dozens of volunteer geocachers who donated their time and expertise placing the caches that make up the tour. Geocachers who visit and collect a code word from at least 20 of these locations are eligible to receive a collectible Star-Spangled Banner GeoTour Geocoin.

- **Captain John Smith GeoTrail:** This adventure was designed and created by volunteer geocachers from the Maryland Geocaching Society, working with the Chesapeake Conservancy and the National Park Service. Geocaches were placed at nearly 40 sites on five rivers representing particular stories or scenes from John Smith's adventures on Chesapeake Bay 400 years ago. When cachers visit 15 of these sites, and record a code word from each in their CJS Geotrail Passport, they become eligible to receive a distinctive and collectible Captain John Smith Geocoin.

- **Camino de Santiago GeoTrail:** The Camino de Santiago, or the "Way of Saint James," which spans roughly 500 miles of northern Spain, is the oldest, most travelled, and most famous route in Europe. In 1987, the trail was declared the first European Cultural Route and in 1993 a World Heritage Site by UNESCO. The "geoPelegrins" is a project to help guide pilgrims and geocachers along as they explore the

Catalan Way of Saint James. This series of GeoTrails cross-
ing along the Way of Saint James consists of 16 sections. In
each section geocachers find a different stamp to record their
journey in a special passport.

E.T. Phone Home: It's All About the Experience

In the previous examples, GeoTours were created to showcase existing historical sites and off-the-beaten-trail tourist destinations. But
would it be possible to create a GeoTour where the caches themselves
would become the destination? The answer is a resounding *yes* and
that is exactly what has happened a couple of hours north of Las
Vegas, Nevada, along what is known as the Extraterrestrial Highway
given the area's mythology surrounding UFOs. Since these 1,500-
plus caches were placed by the pair called Clay4&whtwolfden in
2010, geocachers from around the world have been travelling to the
desert to hunt them in droves—all in the pursuit of logging a large
number of geocaches in a short amount of time. Be sure to get a
power nap in before attempting this one.

A view of the E.T. Highway just north of Rachel, Nevada.
(Geocaching.com)

In fact, the allure of the E.T. Highway has had far-ranging effects. Connie West, who runs one of the highlight stops along the trail, the Little A'Le'Inn in Rachel, Nevada, explains the impact that geocachers have had on the local economy. "Those are people that otherwise wouldn't have come here," West said. "They're putting money into our community. They are buying fuel, rooms, food, groceries." She goes on to add that since they opened in 1990, "For the first time in the history of our business, our rooms were booked all winter long, and we did not lay off any staff."

Destination Caches

While many people choose to geocache while on vacation, there are many geocaches that have become geocaching destinations in their own right. Sometimes it is a great hide or scenic vista a short drive or hike from home and sometimes it requires serious planning and flying halfway around the world. One sure thing is that some caches get a reputation for being worth going out of your way to hunt. There are many reasons why caches become destinations worthy of great travel and planning; let's take a look at a couple of the more famous examples:

- **Mingo-GC30:** The world's oldest active geocache is located just off the interstate near Mingo, Kansas. Many cachers go out of their way to hunt the oldest active cache in each state and Mingo is the crown jewel of elder caches. Some say that it is just a simple roadside stop in a non-descript area, but it means much more than that to the 2,000-plus cachers who have made a special trip to log this cache since it was created in May 2000.

The oldest active geocache, near Mingo, Kansas.
(Brad Simmons)

- **Original Stash Tribute Plaque-GCGV0P:** One of the most visited caches in the world can be found near Beaver Creek, Oregon, where the first geocache was hidden in May 2000. This cache has had more than 5,500 finds since a commemorative plaque was placed there in September 2003. This great location "where it all started" and its accompanying tribute cache have become a mecca of sorts for geocachers from around the world.

The Original Stash Tribute Plaque at the location of the very first geocache.
(Brad Simmons)

- **Groundspeak HQ-GCK25B:** No geocacher's trip to Seattle would be complete without a visit to "the Lily Pad" to seek out the cache in the lobby of Groundspeak, the company that runs Geocaching.com. With nearly 4,000 finds since July 2004, it is clearly a popular destination. This location offers not just an interesting container (an antique treasure chest), but it is usually filled with cool trade items and Trackables from well-travelled geocachers. As a bonus, visitors get to meet at least one of the Groundspeak Lackeys.

- **View Carre'-GCE02C:** New Orleans is home to one of the most talked about and visited geocaches in the Eastern United States. Located atop one of the city's tallest buildings, this great destination cache has provided geocaching fun and great views of the French Quarter to nearly 2,000 finders since March 2003.

The view of the French Quarter from this exceptional View Carre' cache location.
(Brad Simmons)

- **Project A.P.E.-GCC67:** Not every destination cache has lots of finds. In fact, one of the most elusive and desirable geocaches on the planet has been logged only 32 times since June 2001. Located in the jungles of Intervales State Park a few hours southwest of Sao Paolo, Brazil, the last remaining Project A.P.E. cache is a dream geocaching trip for people around the world. It is visited relatively rarely since it costs a pretty penny for most geocachers to fly to Brazil, and then you have to be willing to brave the flora and fauna of a South American rainforest.

Kerstin76 traveled from Germany to Brazil to find this holy grail of geocaches.
(Geocaching.com)

Planning Your Trip

Before you hit the road, you will want to load your GPS unit with geocaches to hunt along the way. The best method is to create a Pocket Query on Geocaching.com and have this e-mailed to you for download into your device. Among other things, a Pocket Query allows you to filter by geocache type, distance from a known point, and cache attributes so that you can get the best list of geocaches possible for where you are traveling and what you will have time to search for. Depending on the amount of free time you'll have, you may want to consider filtering out multi-caches and mystery caches, as these normally take longer to complete. Depending on your level of geocaching expertise, you also might want to limit your Pocket Query to caches with lower terrain and difficulty ratings for the same reason.

On the other hand, if you have time to explore, take a closer look at what the area has to offer. You might find some interesting EarthCaches that will be not only fun but educational. You also might discover one or two caches that are considered must-dos in the area. Check for highly favorite caches in your searches and look closely at any bookmark lists you find on local geocache detail pages. Geocachers often create lists of their favorite geocaches in an area. You can glean a lot from the experiences of others.

Geocaching while on a family vacation can be memorable.
(Alan Torrigino)

If you are really looking for some of the special, not-to-miss geocaches in your travels, be sure to search the regional forums on Geocaching.com or consider posting a request for suggestions. Traveling geocachers post notes asking for cache suggestions or links to the local geocaching groups where local geocachers can provide resources and advice. Chances are good that you can even find a geocaching buddy and tour guide for all the geocache-finding and sightseeing you can handle. If not, you will at least be equipped with local knowledge of the must-do geocaches in the area.

Finding Caches Along Your Route

There is a special type of pocket query you may want to download if you are driving to your destination. On the Pocket Query page is a tab titled "Find Caches Along a Route," which will lead you to www. geocaching.com/my/userroutes.aspx. From this page you can search for routes created by your fellow geocachers or create a custom route to your destination. Once you have created your route, you have the option to create pocket queries based on that route.

Of course, you can customize that pocket query to show up to 1,000 of the types of caches you wish to hunt. Even better, this special type of pocket query returns only those caches within an up to 10km wide corridor that follows your route. Not only does this allow your query to cover more distance, but it keeps you moving from cache to cache along your way.

Geocaching Vacations

Many geocachers actually plan their vacations around well-known destinations for geocaching. For example, some geocachers pride themselves on having found a geocache in every U.S. state, while others would like to find one of every unique geocache type. Whatever the motivation, this desire to travel has not escaped the notice of the travel and tourism industry. Recently, more and more geocaching packages are being offered as enticements to travelers.

Many hotels and bed-and-breakfasts are beginning to offer geocaching adventure packages for their guests. These hotels will often loan you a GPS device, provide instructions and coordinates for use, and even pack a picnic lunch for you to enjoy on your outing.

Visitor centers and tourist bureaus are also creating interpretive programs using GPS, geocaching, and self-guided GeoTours. These programs promise tourists scenic vistas, historic settings, education, and plenty of geocaches to find along the way.

If you are looking for an adventure on water, don't dismiss a cruise. Geocaching on cruises is becoming more popular as a shore excursion. With over 1.75 million geocaches hidden around the world, you can geocache while sailing to Alaska, the Caribbean and the Mediterranean, or just about anywhere else.

Local Treasures

Much of the enjoyment of travel is to visit places of special meaning, like historical sites, awesome vistas, or places that represent our families' roots. These places inspire us and help us appreciate our ancestors who contributed so much to what our lives are today. Through geocaching, travelers have a reason to see and experience these locations they would probably never see otherwise.

These out-of-the-way waterfalls in rural Tennessee are not in the tour guidebooks.
(Brad Simmons)

When traveling, it is tempting to place a geocache in a location that you found exceptionally beautiful or that has special meaning to you. However, placing geocaches outside your home area is discouraged. Caches need to be maintained and that is difficult to do if you live far away. If the geocache gets wet or damaged you need to be able to easily repair or replace it in a timely manner. If you are unable to do so, you shouldn't place a geocache in the area. Generally, vacation caches will not be published on Geocaching.com due to the ongoing maintenance requirement.

Packing for Vacation Geocaching

Self-described nerd Markus explains a dilemma that many of us have. "Let's see, swimsuit, sunblock, sunglasses, …. When you're a technology-obsessed nerd, it's not quite so simple." Markus assembled all the electronic gear needed for a geocaching trip across the desert southwest of the United States. Obviously, most of us do not require this many electronics, but it's a fun example of techno-travel accessorizing. Besides, even this much gear is still lighter than a bag of golf clubs!

Imagine how much fun it is trying to get this stuff through airport security!
(Markus Wandal)

Approximately bottom right to top left, we have:

- Laptop computer for storing digital pictures, GPS data, and GPS mapping software
- Power supply and line cord for the laptop
- Power inverter, to use line-powered gadgets in the car
- Cigarette-lighter plug expander
- Compact flash adapter, for reading digital camera memory cards
- GPS receiver case (a cell phone case)
- Digital camera and case
- Spare digital camera batteries
- Charger for digital camera batteries
- Spare batteries for headlamp
- LED headlamp
- Spare batteries for GPS receiver
- GPS receiver
- Cigarette-lighter extension cord
- AC extension cord (for use with power inverter)
- AC multiplug
- Charging base for FRS (two-way) radios
- Belt clips for FRS radios
- FRS radios
- Auto power/data cable for GPS

Ah, the modern convenience of it all.

International Considerations

When traveling internationally to geocache, it makes sense to pack some additional resources to help you find your way around and adjust to the local customs and requirements. Some of these items may include guidebooks, language translators, international power adapters, and international maps (both electronic and traditional printed maps).

You may also want to post a topic to the International section of the Geocaching.com discussion forums for the country to which you are traveling. You can ask locals for cool cache recommendations or even tips on local travel, restaurants, and other accommodations. It's possible that your visit will coincide with an event already on the geocaching calendar. With some luck, the locals might even host a geocaching event in your honor.

Flying with GPS

As great as the temptation might seem, don't turn your receiver on while flying on a commercial plane without first asking the flight attendants. Although seeing where you are as you fly over a country may sound like fun, this is often frowned upon by airline crews. Their common response is that receivers and other electronic devices could interfere with the plane's own navigation system. In these days of heightened security there is no reason to cause concern or draw unnecessary attention to yourself.

If flying with GPS receivers, computers, and cameras, it is often best to pack them in a sturdy case and carry them onto the plane. This helps prevent the gear from becoming lost or stolen.

Use Some Discretion

Before turning on your receiver, be aware of your surroundings. It is wise not to use a GPS receiver around any areas where you might be perceived to be suspicious. For example, you may wish to avoid using your GPS or other electronics in close proximity to embassies, military bases, and other prominent government build-ings. Obviously, some parts of the world are more sensitive to this than others. The last thing you want to do is extend your trip with lengthy interrogations by authorities. Be forewarned: it is not uncommon for "officials" to determine that your gear is better than theirs, so that they will let you off with a warning and relieve you of that unnecessary travel baggage.

DEAD BATTERIES

Use a GPS receiver in the wrong place at the wrong time and you could be considered a spy. In 1997, a Qualcomm wireless communication engineer was charged with espionage by Russian authorities. Richard L. Bliss was using a GPS receiver while installing a cellular phone system in the city of Rostov-on-Don. The Russian agents that arrested him insisted he was spying on secret sites. Bliss was detained for more than a month and, despite being released to return to America, the charges of espionage have still not been dropped.

The Least You Need to Know

- Geocaching is a great way to explore unique locations while traveling.
- The travel and tourism industry is beginning to use geocaching as an activity to encourage visitation.
- GeoTours are a great way to explore and learn more about an area.
- Use caution when using your GPS device while traveling abroad to avoid security problems. Do not use it around sensitive areas such as embassies and government buildings.

Geocaching Evolves: The Variations

In This Chapter

- Learn all about Geocaching Challenges
- Find out what Waymarking is
- Get the facts on Wherigo
- Explore the world of benchmark hunting

Finding a geocache is fun and rewarding, but there have always been limitations when it comes to traditional geocaching. As a physical object, some places are inappropriate for placing a cache. They can't be hidden close to each other (to reduce confusion), many locations have to be regulated by land managers, and some locations just can't support a hidden container. But there are lots of cool and interesting locations that people like to visit in the world. So how can people turn visiting these sites into an adventure without hunting an actual geocache?

In this chapter, we'll talk about Waymarking, Wherigo, and other cool ways geocachers are expanding the game beyond environmental limitations.

Geocaching Challenges— The Newest Addition to the Game

Geocaching's earliest attempt at sharing these locations was to support virtual caches, which weren't geocaches at all but unique locations in the world for people to discover. The best of those virtuals still exist today as grandfathered listings, but there was a time when virtuals were hard to qualify. The biggest reason was that the same guidelines for physical geocaches were applied to virtuals, which required a reviewer to publish them. No one could determine the subjective threshold for what was a virtual and what wasn't, so the constant angst resulted in the retiring of virtuals. For years Geocaching.com focused on the core game of geocaching, but with an eye toward finding a way to share these great locations.

In 2011, Geocaching.com decided to bring virtuals back into the game with the creation of Geocaching Challenges, for people to "go somewhere and do something." This new setup resolved the difficulties with some of the original virtual caches, and welcomed a whole new crop of enthusiastic participants.

Geocaching Challenges open a new world of adventure. You can find them on your Geocaching profile by looking for this icon.
(Groundspeak)

Adding Challenges to Your Geocaching Adventure

Most Geocaching Challenges are location specific based challenges created by members of the geocaching community. These are known as "Local Challenges." You might be challenged to take a picture of yourself walking across the Abbey Road crosswalk or tasked to take a picture from the top of the Empire State Building. These are fun outdoor adventures that can happen even in locations that do not support physical caches.

In addition to Local Challenges, there are a limited number of "Worldwide Challenges" created by Geocaching.com based on community suggestions. For old timers, these challenges have a lot in common with the former locationless cache type. For example, a worldwide challenge might be something you could do anywhere, like taking a picture of yourself on a boat, kissing a frog, or dressed like a pirate.

But don't get the idea that these challenges are all just for fun. There are many worldwide and local challenges that are all about giving back to the community. For example, the "10,000 Fewer Pieces of Litter" instructs geocachers to go to a local park or other location and pick up 10 pieces of trash. At the time of this writing, the challenge has been completed by more than 5,000 Geocaching Challenges aficionados. That means that this simple challenge is directly responsible for the removal of over 50,000 pieces of litter, with more being picked up every day. Now that is a challenge that makes a difference we can all get behind.

The 10,000 Fewer Pieces of Litter Worldwide Challenge encourages fun, while helping the environment.
(Groundspeak)

Photo Challenges

At their core, photo challenges are a pretty simple concept: Follow instructions to take a photo or discover something unique to a specific location. Of course, the real fun starts when you get creative. Rather than just taking a basic "vacation photo," do something exciting—take a picture of yourself holding up the Tower of Pisa or pull Lenin's statue's finger in Seattle. You might be challenged to hike the Inca Trail to Machu Picchu, sing a song in the middle of Times Square, or take a picture of yourself walking through the Brandenburg Gate in Berlin.

Photo Challenges require a picture in order to be completed. This icon will help you identify Photo Challenges on the site.
(Groundspeak)

Challenges are not limited in the way traditional geocaching has been in the past, so you can invite people to locations where they would not normally be able to geocache.

You can also work with an organization to use Geocaching Challenges to help create awareness of an issue, location, or event. For instance, through Geocaching.com, the Seattle Symphony's Sonic Evolution Challenge created a series of branded challenges to support their upcoming schedule while sharing the fun and even opportunities to win tickets with the geocaching community.

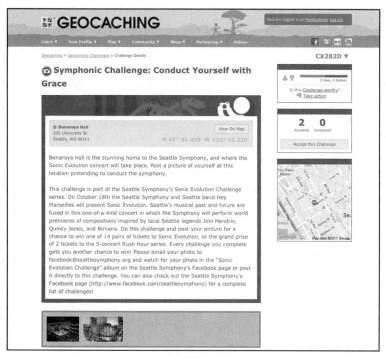

Challenges are a great way to increase awareness.
(Groundspeak)

Discover Challenges

Discover Challenges really embrace the spirit of "virtual" caches of old. A Discover Challenge is when you visit a location to uncover information at the coordinates. What you are discovering remains a surprise until you arrive at the destination. Once there, you must answer a question to complete the Discover Challenge. For example, the "World's Fair Fun Fact" says "Finding this Seattle, Washington, landmark from the 1962 World's Fair isn't all that hard, but this discovery requires math, a keen eye, and some patience" and instructs seekers to proceed to the coordinates. Upon arrival, it is hard to miss Seattle's most famous landmark, the Space Needle. You must answer the question, "How many windows are on one of the Space Needle Elevators?" to complete the challenge. After answering correctly, the challenge can be logged and shared online. Of course, the possibilities for this kind of challenge are limited only by the imagination of the creator. Discover Challenges create a great new way for geocachers to share those great secret spots around their community while providing a little excitement and mystery for their fellow seekers.

The Discover Challenge icon will help you identify challenges that will show you surprises hidden around every corner.

(Groundspeak)

Creating Your Own Challenges

Geocaching.com has created a set of mobile applications for Challenges on the iPhone, Android, and Windows Phone 7 and higher. The expectation is that this new activity will be primarily accessed through these free applications. There have been several updates as the applications evolve to better serve this quickly growing game. Now you can not only hunt challenges anywhere in the world with your smartphone and the free application, but you can even create your own challenge right on the spot to share the fun with the rest of the Geocaching world.

The Geocaching Application is free and makes it easy to seek out adventure,
wherever you are.
(Groundspeak)

So what are the guidelines for issuing a challenge? Unlike caches, there aren't any official guidelines. Instead, you can rate challenges with thumbs up or thumbs down, and there are reporting tools available in the case that a challenge is inappropriate or unavailable. These tools help to ensure that the community can collectively decide what is appropriate and what isn't. For example, the 528-foot separation guideline for geocaches does not apply to Challenges, and Challenges won't be blocked from being issued at Disney World, or even a local pub. Geocaching Challenges are truly community driven, so do your part by issuing some challenges of your own.

Waymarking—A New Way to Hunt

Waymarking is a way to share unique locations around the world, provide related information for those locations, and categorize them for easy reference and sharing. GPS technology enables users to pinpoint any location on the planet, mark the location, and share it with others; waymarking is the toolset for categorizing and adding unique information for those locations.

WAYMARKING

Waymarking makes seeking and sharing unique locations fun and easy.
(Groundspeak)

The website at Waymarking.com contains over 1,042 unique location categories, such as fishing holes, historical markers, covered bridges, and abstract public sculptures. Each category is managed by a group called *waymarkers*, who define categories and then review and accept all qualified waymark submissions for those categories.

> **GEO-LINGO**
>
> A **waymarker** is a casual term used to describe a waymarking enthusiast, someone who actively participates in the waymarking community.

A New Game with Deep Roots

In the early days of geocaching, as the game was still developing, the creativity of the players led to the development of new geocache types. One of the early geocache variations was the virtual cache. At the same time, another type of geocache known as a location-less cache was beginning to present its own set of difficulties. Locationless caches, or reverse geocaches, were a type of cache where the job of the geocacher was to find a location that matched the category set up by the owner. For example, if the cache owner's category was "Natural Land Bridges," the geocacher would have to find a place that matched that category and record the coordinates for that location (often accompanied by a picture).

While the idea of locationless caches was enjoyed by many playing the game, the results were difficult to manage. Geocaching.com had not been created to support the type of content that was being logged. For instance, a single locationless cache page could contain thousands of "finds" from all over the world.

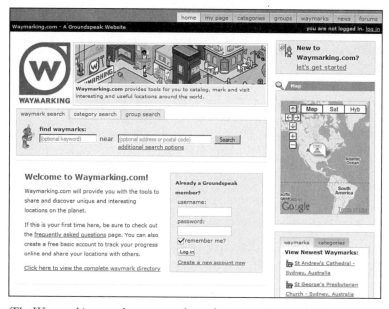

The Waymarking.com homepage, where almost any spot on the planet can be catalogued and searched for.
(Waymarking.com)

Rather than fundamentally modify the Geocaching.com site to address virtual and locationless caches, Groundspeak developed a new, dedicated site. Waymarking.com was designed to handle locationless caches more appropriately, by providing people the opportunity to organize and search for these unique locations by category. This change organized places in a way that made them both searchable and fun to find.

Person, Place, or Thing?

In geocaching there are those who enjoy seeking caches and others who enjoy hiding. Similarly, in waymarking there are those who enjoy searching for objects and locations that match a specific category and others who enjoy the challenge of creating and managing a waymarking category.

The waymark category directory works in a hierarchical format, moving from general categories to specific categories and then to the individual waymarks. One top-level category might begin with "Art/Music," then contain a subcategory of "Statues," and be followed by yet another subcategory of "Insect Sculptures." From here you will find individual waymarks that have been located and cataloged by individual players. The waymark might be a 10-foot tall praying mantis in North Carolina or the Boll Weevil Monument in Enterprise, Alabama. The key is that each individual waymark fits within the specified parameters of the categories containing the waymark.

Searching for a Waymark

On the Waymarking.com site, you can search for waymarks using postal code, keyword, coordinates, or address. Once your search is complete, you can view all of the search results to find a location or object that interests you. You can view waymark details, see photos, and read logs from others who have visited that waymark.

Once you've found one that you'd like to visit, you can enter the coordinates into your GPS receiver to take you there, just like finding a geocache! Location coordinates are prominently displayed on each waymark detail page and can be either entered by hand or downloaded in a file format for use in a number of applications.

As with geocaching, be sure to read the waymark detail page before heading outdoors. There you will find information about the location you are visiting as well as instructions on how to log your visit to the waymark. Oftentimes the waymark owner will request a picture or some other information as valid proof that you actually visited the site.

After you've visited a particular waymark location and met the waymark requirements, you can return to the waymark detail page on Waymarking.com and log your visit online. Waymark visits are recorded much like geocache visits, complete with the ability to add your comments and photographs.

> **EUREKA!**
>
> Some waymarking categories have the potential to be useful for people doing research. Because waymarks are often found by people who are simply searching for information online, waymark owners have been known to be contacted by people seeking permission to use their information and photos!

Wherigo—Redefining Location

What if you could bring your favorite adventure video game into the outdoor world using GPS technology? Can you imagine an experience where participants have to physically move around in the real world to accomplish tasks, interact with characters, and complete goals? Back in 2001, when Geocaching.com was first created, the founders of Groundspeak began to research and develop ideas that would do just that. Passionate about location, they created what was to be called Wherigo, a platform for creating location-based games in the real world.

Wherigo brings virtual elements into the real world. Look for this icon to explore this exciting game.

(Groundspeak)

What Is Wherigo?

If you are familiar with adventure games like Zork, Myst, or the Secret of Monkey Island, you can think of Wherigo as an adventure game construction set for the real world. Unlike these traditional video games, however, with Wherigo you don't type "north" or click your mouse to move your character around on a computer screen. Instead, participants literally move themselves in the real world and interact with objects and characters using a handheld GPS-enabled device.

The Wherigo.com homepage where you can search for cartridges and download the Wherigo Builder and Player Applications.
(Wherigo.com)

The Wherigo platform includes a Wherigo Player Application and a Wherigo Builder Application, both available for free online at Wherigo.com. To play, one must search for and download an experience, called a *cartridge*, and load this into a compatible GPS device.

GEO-LINGO

A **cartridge** describes the experience created by a Wherigo Builder. It is not a physical object but a self-contained file that is downloaded from Wherigo.com and then run using the Wherigo Player Application and a compatible GPS device.

Get in Gear—Equipment for Playing

If you're interested in playing a Wherigo experience outdoors, you have to look to a whole new generation of GPS devices. Due to the advanced feature set of Wherigo, these devices have more in common with your computer than with your compass. Currently, you can participate in Wherigo using most GPS-enabled Pocket PC's, also known as Windows Mobile Classic devices, and some handheld GPS units. Groundspeak is also currently working to bring the Wherigo platform to other GPS-enabled devices, including mobile phones.

If you're a Pocket PC user, you may already have the equipment needed. Many of these units have built-in GPS receivers, while many others can connect either by wire or wirelessly to GPS receivers.

If you are using either a Garmin Colorado, Nuvi 500/550, or Oregon GPS, you likely have the Wherigo Player Application preloaded onto your device. However, it is always wise to check Wherigo.com to ensure that you have the latest Wherigo Player installed. If you intend to play with a Pocket PC, you need to download the free Wherigo Player Application from Wherigo.com and install it on your device.

If you do not have access to a compatible GPS device, you can still experience Wherigo! Download the free Wherigo Builder program and use it to "emulate" a cartridge on your computer. While not the intended use, the emulator allows you to drag a character from location to location online, simulating what you would have experienced in real time outdoors. Many Wherigo builders use this as a tool of inspiration and innovation, reviewing unique cartridges from around the world so that they can build experiences of their own.

Wherigo: Getting into the Game

Now that you have downloaded a cartridge and loaded it into your GPS-enabled device, you are ready to head outdoors. But wait, let's discuss what you can expect.

Wherigo cartridges are created by people who want to share a unique experience with you. A cartridge will likely direct you to a number of locations, similar to a multistage geocache, asking you to speak to characters or complete tasks along the way.

The basic building block of a Wherigo experience is called a *zone*. A zone is essentially a predefined shape. For instance, if you were to draw a shape on a paper map, say outlining a city block, this defined area would be called a zone. Zones can be big or small, and round, square, or any other shape as defined by an author. In other words, a zone is a predefined area marked by several waypoints.

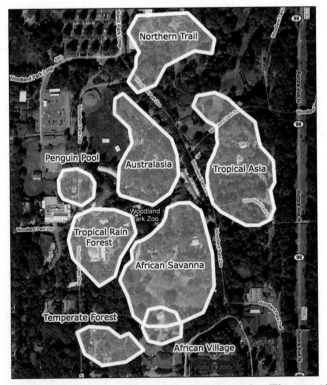

A map of the zones shown in the "Penguin Escape" Cartridge. This cartridge takes players on a fun and interactive adventure through Seattle's Woodland Park Zoo.

(Groundspeak)

How does Wherigo work? When your GPS device detects that you have entered a zone, the Wherigo software responds with an event that the author has programmed into the game. As a player moves in and out of different zones within a Wherigo cartridge, he might encounter a virtual character on his screen who will give him information he needs to continue the game. Or he might be given a virtual object (such as a key) to place in his inventory to use later in the game.

EUREKA!

Several different types of media can be incorporated in a Wherigo cartridge. Some include sound effects when entering different zones or completing certain tasks. However, note that not all devices are designed to play sound files.

How to Play

Now that you understand how to navigate to a zone or location, let's learn about the other components of play.

Within the Wherigo playing experience, there are potentially four main areas of focus: "Locations," "You See," "Inventory," and "Tasks."

- **Locations.** The zones within a cartridge. A location can contain characters and items (both real and imaginary) that a player can interact with. Players mostly interact with locations by entering and exiting the predefined areas.

- **You See.** A list of items (can be characters or objects) that the player's character can see from the current location of the character. You can often click on items you see to investigate them further.

- **Inventory.** A collection of items that belong to a player. It is helpful to think of it as a virtual backpack for storing items obtained during the game. For instance, if an author created a murder mystery cartridge, she might make you collect virtual clues that will enable you to catch the killer as part of the experience. If it's a science fiction adventure, you might collect alien artifacts or fuel cells to refuel your rocket.

- **Tasks.** Typically used by an author to help direct the playing experience. This is simply a list of all tasks that need to be completed in the cartridge. Some tasks do not show up on the list until you receive them in the game or accomplish other tasks. Since Wherigo cartridges can be linear or nonlinear, it helps to check the "Tasks" every now and then just to make sure you are on the right path to completing the cartridge.

As the Wherigo adventure progresses, you might find yourself needing to complete certain tasks set up by the author of the game. You may need to unlock a virtual door with a virtual key that you picked up earlier. If the game is taking you on a tour of a city, you might be asked to walk to a certain landmark and enter another zone to continue the game. In an adventure cartridge, the task might require you to complete mini-quests before continuing the main adventure.

To add to the challenge, the game author may also include a question to be answered of the player (called an *input*) or integrate the use of a timer for completing tasks. So, for example, you may have to reach a particular destination within a certain time frame. The rest of the adventure can depend on whether you make it or not.

GEO-LINGO

An **input** is a way for a Wherigo author to ask a player a question. The question is displayed in a window on the device, where the user can then respond to it. There are three types of inputs: Text (where the player uses an onscreen keyboard to type in an answer), Multiple Choice (the player chooses one of several options via a list of buttons), and True/False.

More Than Just a Game

Wherigo is unique in that it is a platform that can be used to create diverse experiences. The Wherigo Builder and tools available are designed to be open-ended, so Wherigo cartridge builders can create any number of interesting experiences for a player. Here are some examples of what can be created with the Wherigo Builder:

- A walking tour of city sights

- A neighborhood scavenger hunt

- An interactive fictional adventure

- A tour of historic sites or landmarks

- An alternate reality game

In addition to games that are location specific, it's also possible to play games designed to be played anywhere. These are called "Play Anywhere Cartridges." The zones for these cartridges are not predefined; they are generated based on where the player is when he starts the cartridge. Although they are a bit more complicated to create, these cartridges can be played by many more people all over the world. To play these cartridges, all that is normally needed is a wide-open space.

Wherigo Geocaches

While the Wherigo game grew out of the evolution of geocaching, it hasn't completely left that world. Wherigo geocaches are a unique geocache type that incorporates the fun and fantasy of a Wherigo cartridge with an actual physical geocache container at the end.

As with the Wherigo game, geocachers seeking a Wherigo geocache must download the cartridge and complete the tasks the author has laid out. Once completed, the geocacher can log her find/adventure on both Geocaching.com and Wherigo.com.

Benchmark Hunting

Benchmark hunting is searching for survey markers from a list maintained by the U.S. National Geodetic Survey (NGS). Benchmarks are geodetic control points that are permanently affixed objects at various locations throughout the United States. They are used for land surveying, civil engineering, and mapping. The NGS maintains a database of these locations, and each benchmark control point marker has a permanent identifier number (PID) and a datasheet of information about it. Many of these markers are old, and much of the descriptive data used to find them is outdated. There are, however, more than 700,000 of these markers within the United States, and they are still used today for the ongoing process of surveying our country.

There are two basic types of benchmark control points:

- **Vertical control points.** They establish the precise elevation at their placement point. They are typically small brass or aluminum discs, concrete posts, iron pins, or bolts permanently attached to a stable foundation.

- **Horizontal control points.** There are several names for these control points: triangulation stations, traverse stations, trilateration stations, GPS stations, and intersection stations. These, too, can be a small brass or aluminum disc, concrete post, iron pin, or bolt similar to the vertical control points. They can also be other features such as radio towers, water towers, church spires, mountaintops, or any other objects that can be identified from a distance.

EUREKA!

In the surveying profession, the term *benchmark* is applied only to the vertical control type; for benchmark hunting, however, we use the term for both vertical and horizontal control points.

Searching for Benchmarks

Searching for benchmarks to find is easy. On the Geocaching.com website, click on "Find a Benchmark" and search by postal code or point ID. A list of benchmarks will appear from the nearest to the farthest. A unique feature of benchmark hunting is that it does not require GPS. A receiver is helpful to get you in the right area, but then it's up to you to interpret the instructions on the benchmark's datasheet. Benchmark information pages from the Geocaching.com site do provide coordinates and directions.

A Bureau of Land Management marker found by a geocacher. Markers like this are used by land management agencies to mark locations and elevation.
(Bret Hammond)

Part of the challenge in searching for benchmarks is that the coordinates for the locations are usually not very accurate. Benchmarks were placed before the use of GPS, using coordinates plotted from a map, and may be more than a couple hundred feet away from the marker. Study the description and use the posted coordinates to determine the location.

If the benchmark page indicates that the location is "adjusted," you are looking for a horizontal control point that most likely has been plotted with highly accurate surveying-grade GPS equipment.

Finding a Benchmark

When you find a marker, do not tamper with it or take it. These markers are protected by law because they are public property and still actively used in surveying. Take pictures of the marker and the surrounding area, and then log your find at Geocaching.com. Don't forget to upload the photos to the website's gallery.

Some listings describe things like radio towers, church steeples, and smokestacks. These kinds of large-object station markers are known as *intersection stations.* They are usually landmarks taller than any surrounding objects, allowing them to be seen from many miles away in several directions. This makes them valuable points of reference for surveying.

When logging these benchmarks, keep in mind that in very unusual cases there is a benchmark disc, surveying nail, or other small object that can't be seen from the ground, the top of the tower, steeple, or smokestack. The datasheet will specify such a marker if this is the case. If not, simply log your find, and if you have a camera, take a picture of the structure from the ground. For safety and legal reasons, it is obviously best not to climb these structures.

Logging a Benchmark

When logging a benchmark, the choices are "Found it!", "Didn't find it!", "Post a Note", and "Mark Destroyed." When you find a marker, be sure to double-check the description and datasheet to confirm it's the right one.

It's not unusual to find benchmarks that are not in the NGS database. This is because there are survey markers everywhere and the NGS is not the only organization that creates and uses benchmarks. Other agencies include the U.S. Army Corps of Engineers (USACE), the Bureau of Land Management (BLM), and other federal agencies, along with highway departments, county and private surveyors, and engineers.

DEAD BATTERIES

Use caution when seeking benchmarks. Some are located on private property or in hazardous areas. Also, remember these markers are very important for surveyors, engineers, and others, so do not tamper with them or take them.

You may log an official report to the NGS if any of these three points are met:

- When the description of how to get to the station marker has significantly changed.

- When a station marker has not been visited in a long time: 30 years or longer. You can find this information on each benchmark page in the description area. See a sample at www.geocaching.com/mark/details.aspx?PID=CG1067.

- When the station marker is obviously destroyed. "Destroyed," to the NGS, means that you found the marker and that it is obviously out of its installed position. If you cannot find the marker for any reason, don't report it to the NGS as destroyed.

NAVIGATIONAL NUGGETS

The NGS website (www.ngs.noaa.gov) is an excellent resource for learning how to read datasheets. Review samples by clicking "Datasheets."

Make sure that the marker's history has not changed in the official database of the NGS before planning your report. Also, do not report benchmark coordinates to the NGS for any reason. The existing coordinates on the NGS datasheets cannot be changed, except through very rigorous mathematical procedures. Geocaching. com has additional instructions and information related to finding, logging, and submitting reports to the NGS. Learn more at www. geocaching.com/mark.

The Least You Need to Know

- Geocaching Challenges are an exciting way to share locations around the world where a traditional geocache might not be appropriate.
- Waymarking is a great way to share more information about special spots and to create lists of unique formations and locations around the world.
- Wherigo allows you to play virtual games in the physical world.
- Benchmarks are used for surveying around the United States and can be challenging and rewarding to find.

What the Future Holds for Geocaching

In This Chapter

- Changing technology and geocaching
- Technology + nature help us reconnect
- Some final thoughts for ongoing success

Geocaching as an activity has long since evolved beyond the concept of finding a box in the woods. Today, geocaching is a global community of outdoor enthusiasts who create and share location-based adventures with each other.

As GPS technology has continued to develop and become more feature rich, we too, have seen the changes and innovation within geocaching. But what will happen next?

In this final chapter, we look at technology today as well as the areas of continued development in geocaching. We also consider the future of geocaching and leave you with thoughts for its continued success and sustainability as an activity.

Geocaching Grows and Evolves

From May 2000 until today, geocaching has grown from a single geocache hidden in rural Oregon to 1.75 million geocaches being discovered in nearly every corner of the world. As GPS technology continues to evolve, there will be an increased opportunity for access. As dedicated GPS units become more economical and integrated into other technologies there is little doubt that locational awareness will become an integral part of people's lives.

Next Steps in Geocaching

Today, GPS and other location services are being integrated into mobile handheld devices, including cell phones, handheld gaming consoles, and dedicated recreational units. With the rise in popularity of social networking sites, people can also share messages in real time based on where they are and what they are doing. The next era of geocaching will most likely begin to integrate these technologies as geocachers themselves innovate the way we play and communicate with one another.

> **EUREKA!**
>
> Geocaching applications for smartphones are contributing to the growth of geocaching at levels never before imaginable. Using cell phone data services and these applications, geocachers can now obtain real-time geocache data, including recently submitted cache logs, while out on the trail.

Today many geocachers are geocaching with their mobile phones, sharing logs and photos with their families and friends in real time. Coordination of information related to who we are, where we are located, and what we are doing will continue to be explored as more location-based technologies are introduced.

We will also increasingly participate in activities for which GPS has been incorporated as a complementary activity. From bicycling to skiing, to horseback riding and car racing, GPS and geocaching are being used in a way that is entertaining and educational. This integration is limitless as more and more people infuse creativity in their use of GPS technology.

The Ever-Changing GPS Constellation

It's easy to forget that the recreational location system we use, GPS, is actually a tool for the military. The U.S. Air Force is tasked with the day-to-day upkeep of this system that allows anyone on or near the surface of the planet to establish their exact position.

While there are many threats to the accuracy of the current GPS system from bandwidth encroachment, natural conditions such as solar storms, and the possibility of equipment failure, the U.S. Department of Defense remains committed to keeping the system fully functional. According to the U.S. Air Force, there are currently 32 satellites in the GPS constellation. These GPS satellites orbit the earth actively broadcasting positioning, navigation, and timing messages to users 24 hours a day, 7 days a week, 365 days a year. To maintain current GPS standards there must be at least 24 active satellites in the constellation and the Air Force has "high confidence" that it will be able to sustain this service into the foreseeable future. In addition to the currently active satellites, the Air Force maintains five older satellites in orbit on residual status that can be made operational again, if needed.

Geocaching relies on the GPS constellation to guide adventurers to their goal.
(Groundspeak)

There are plans to modernize the constellation even more in the future, which should enhance the performance and capabilities of the system. The Air Force launched the first of 12 GPS Block IIF satellites in May 2010, and the next generation of satellites, GPS III, is currently in development and on schedule for a first launch in 2014. Advancements in technology will make the system more accurate while decreasing costs, which will mean better service for all GPS users.

Geocaching and Augmented Reality

What was once the realm of science fiction is our modern reality. Although the concept of *augmented reality* still seems like a future technology, it has begun to creep into our everyday lives. Check it out the next time you watch sports on TV. The yellow "first down" line seen in television broadcasts of American football games shows the line the offense must cross to receive a first down. The real-world elements are the football field and players, and the virtual element is the yellow line, which augments the image in real time. The same is true in ice hockey, where many broadcasts feature a colored augmented reality trail to help viewers keep up with the location and direction of the hockey puck.

NAVIGATIONAL NUGGET!

Augmented reality is about enhancing the real world environment with virtual information thereby improving people's senses and skills. Augmented reality uses virtual information and interactivity to help you understand and explore elements of the actual world.

This technology is also making its way from the military. The heads-up displays they've been using for years in planes and ships are now in the consumer world. Today you can purchase cars with heads-up displays that relay important information (such as speed and directions) by projecting this data onto the windshield, so the driver never has to look away from the road. Similarly, there are many new smartphone applications that project data over the images of the real world collected by the phone's camera. It is safe to say that augmented reality is here to stay, but what does that mean for geocaching?

One of the most exciting things about geocaching and its related games is the extension of digital data into the real world. In many ways, the entire concept of geocaching is based on the connection between the virtual world of the computer and the physical world. It is easy to forget that even when exploring the trails with a paper printout of a cache page and our GPS we are having our outdoor experience enhanced by our connections online. This is even more apparent when using our smartphones to navigate the world. As you make your way to the geocache location you can see your avatar moving along the map, mirroring your steps in the physical world. With information about your quest at your fingertips, there is little doubt that the online world is directing your offline adventure.

Geocaching Challenges, like this one in Berlin, bring virtual adventures into the physical world.
(Groundspeak)

The same can be said of geocaching related games such as Wherigo and Geocaching Challenges. This is especially true with Wherigo cartridges, since you are guided on a virtual adventure with each new choice triggered by entry into a "zone" in the physical world. Wherigo cartridges can even have virtual tour guides to help you in your adventure and to share information about the world around you along the way. As exciting as this is, Geocaching Challenges are moving even closer to a truly augmented reality experience. With their easy accessibility across many platforms that many people have in their pockets at this moment, challenges are just beginning to scratch the surface of things to come. With their online location-based questions, verifications, and "discoveries" in the physical world, Geocaching Challenges are the next step in exploring the physical world.

As technology continues to advance, it is easy to imagine a day when geocaching will not only guide us to a hidden treasure in the real world, but will also serve as a virtual tour guide sharing interesting history and points of interest along the way.

Reconnecting with Nature in the Digital Age

In our modern world, it is easy to become disconnected from the natural world around us. We can virtually explore the globe without ever leaving our desks or even our sofas. As we spend more and more time sitting behind our computer screens, interacting through email and text rather than conversations, we begin to feel the isolation of all our conveniences. That is why it is more important than ever to find new ways to get outside and enjoy the beauty of the world around us.

Groundspeak's mission is to inspire outdoor play using location-based technology. Their goal is for everyone to be able to walk out their door and find an adventure—or 100 adventures—nearby. That adventure might take the form of a geocache hidden at your local park, a Challenge to take a photo of yourself performing a task at a specific location, a "Ginormous Everyday Object" that you discover through Waymarking, or an interactive Wherigo experience. No matter what the inspiration, it is clear that the technology that drives these games is helping to get us back out into the real world.

Geocaching is a great vehicle to encourage exploration not only of the world around us as we hike along the trail to the next cache, but also to connect us to the wider community of geocachers. Whether through organized events or chance meetings at geocache locations, a shared love of the game helps to create connections and a sense of belonging. The opportunity to join friends and family for an afternoon of geocaching at a local park allows us a great way to reaffirm the ties that bind us to one another through shared experiences.

Geocaching gets you out of the office and back into nature.
(Brad Simmons)

Technology Brings Us Back to Our Roots

Geocaching is a nearly perfect marriage of technology and nature that inspires us to find new places to explore. It is true that we are born with a desire to see what lies just beyond the next ridge, to hike to the edge of the map and see new vistas, to embrace the *wanderlust* that drives many of us to explore. Perhaps geocaching appeals to the primordial hunter-gatherer in each of us, giving outlet to our natural instincts. Whatever the reason, it is at this place in time that the technology exists to guide our wanderings out of our offices and living rooms and get us back into nature, on the trail hiking, with a purpose.

GEO-LINGO

Wanderlust is a strong, innate desire to travel and explore. The term originates from the German words *wandern* (to hike) and *lust* (desire). Placing the two words together, you get "to enjoy hiking," although it is commonly described as an enjoyment of strolling, roaming, or exploring. This seems to be a pretty good match for the game, since geocaching is often called "hiking with a purpose."

Above and beyond this reconnection with the physical world around us, geocaching also helps us to rediscover the sense of wonder that we had as children, the innate desire to follow clues on a search for hidden treasure or solve a mystery. Many geocachers focus solely on hunting "Mystery or Unknown" geocaches, simply for the mental challenge. Solving these puzzles allows them to engage in mentally stimulating problem solving with the promise of an offline adventure as their reward.

As our society has changed and evolved through the use of technology, we have, in many cases, found ourselves spending more time indoors. Our work has moved from the fields into offices where we use computers. When we take time to play we often find ourselves inside exploring virtual worlds on video gaming systems, rather than out in the real world. The beauty of geocaching is that the same technology that took us out of nature in the first place is now leading us back out of doors and reintroducing us to the beauties of the natural world around us.

Remember not every trail can be hiked; sometimes you will need to learn new skills to find that elusive cache.

(Brad Simmons)

The Geocaching Community Goes Mainstream

In the early days of geocaching, it was unusual to run into a fellow enthusiast or even anyone who had heard of the game before, but times are changing. Today, geocachers are everywhere and the game has gone from a small subculture to a mainstream activity with millions of participants around the globe. Geocaching is featured regularly in news articles and magazines on every continent, with stories that range from an introduction to a great family-friendly outdoor activity to stories of geocachers giving back through CITO (Cache In Trash Out) activities.

Geocaching has also been featured prominently on television, in news and special interest items, and in many documentaries. These documentaries focus on geocaching from many angles. Some, such as *Treasure Trackers*, tell the story of geocaching, how it evolved, and how it affects the lives of the people who play it, while others look at more specific segments of the game. One recent documentary, *Brain Fitness: Peak Performance*, featured an entire segment focused on how geocaching helps with mental performance by training the brain to notice small details that many people overlook. Geocaching has also been featured prominently as a plot point in prime-time dramas, such as *Law and Order*, and on the reality television show, *Extreme Makeover*, where one of the families went on a geocaching adventure to discover a new car as their "treasure." That's a pretty good First To Find prize!

Geocaching's appeal in the entertainment world hasn't stopped on the small screen; there have been several independent films that feature geocaching as a major theme, including *G.P.S. The Movie, Tracker*, and *Find Me*. In 2009, Atlantic Pictures released *Splinterheads*, the first big-budget film to feature geocaching prominently. This film starring Rachael Taylor, Lea Thompson, and Dean Winters is a coming-of-age romantic comedy that features several scenes of the main characters getting to know each other better through geocaching.

The growth from an "outsider" underground game to the main-stream is greatly due to the widespread appeal of the game. No other hobby, game, or sport encourages you to share your outdoor adven-tures with the online community quite like geocaching does. Plus it is family friendly and accessible to all ages and skill levels. How many hobbies are just as much fun for a couple with young children, retirees with mobility impairments, middle-aged businesspeople, and adrenaline-seeking extreme sports types? Many geocachers attribute great personal growth to the sport, since it encourages you to develop many skills—physical, social, and mental—in order to find an elusive cache. From mental puzzle-solving abilities, to scuba diving, rock climbing, and rappelling, geocaching gives you the opportunity and a reward for pushing your own limits and learning new abilities. With new advances in technology and the ease of access geocaching will continue to grow in popularity as it moves further into the mainstream, and now you are here with us on the front edge of this great sport.

Geocaching is fun for all ages!
(Brad Simmons)

It Is a Brave New World: Go Outside and Play

Thank you for taking the time to learn about geocaching, the related games, tools for playing, and GPS technology. We are excited about the opportunity to offer this book, and appreciate having you along to learn and enjoy it. Regardless of what happens in geocaching, we hope to leave you with three final thoughts:

- Geocaching has grown rapidly and maintained a positive reputation because geocachers care about the activity and its impact in the world. Geocachers have a high level of personal ownership and accountability and go out of their way to make sure that the people are well informed about the activity and the community. This kind of affirmative impact will remain only as long as we continue to self-regulate the activity and each other. That means picking up after ourselves and, unfortunately, sometimes others, as well as leaving everyone we meet with a positive impression of the game and those who play it. It is an awesome responsibility, and you can rest assured that geocachers are up to the task.

- Geocaching is about having fun in the outdoors. With all the high-tech twists and turns that game variations may take, remember the basics. Recall the days when you were a little kid with an unlimited sense of wonder. Although it may be just a hidden container or a great location, each geocache presents the potential for new discovery and adventure. Don't forget the simple joy of playing in the outdoors. Getting out on the trail is truly good therapy and one of life's simple pleasures, especially when shared with family and friends.

- Remember that, like life, the enjoyment of the activity often lies in the journey as much as the destination. Geocaching can allow us to reflect about what is really important, while bringing us to see beautiful places, with the potential for meeting new people. Contribute to the geocaching community by sharing your journey, stories, and experiences along the way—we will all be richer for it.

Happy geocaching! We hope to meet you sometime, somewhere on the trail.

The Least You Need to Know

- Geocaching has evolved along with improvements and developments in GPS technology. It is a fun activity with a promising future.

- The success of geocaching will have much to do with the community's environmental stewardship, and our commitment to education.

- Geocaching is a way in which we can celebrate the outdoors.

- Positive sharing of your adventures contributes to the community and is key to the long-term success of geocaching.

Resource Directory

This appendix contains a list of contact and website information for many of the resources, manufacturers, and related programs mentioned throughout this book.

Compass Manufacturers

The Brunton Co.
2255 Brunton Ct.
Riverton, Wyoming 82501
Phone: 307-857-4700
Website: www.brunton.com

Suunto Finland
Phone: 1-855-258-0900
Website: www.suunto.com

Geocaching.com Resources

Geocaching 101
www.geocaching.com/guide

Benchmark Hunting
www.geocaching.com/mark

Cache In Trash Out
www.geocaching.com/CITO

Geocaching in the News
www.geocaching.com/press

Geocaching Challenges
www.geocaching.com/challenges

Geocaching Software
www.geocaching.com/waypoints

GPS Adventures Maze
www.gpsmaze.com

Groundspeak Forums
forums.groundspeak.com

Guide to Geocaching
www.geocaching.com/videos

GPS Manufacturers

The Brunton Co.
2255 Brunton Ct.
Riverton, Wyoming 82501
Phone: 307-857-4700
Website: www.brunton.com

Cobra Electronics
6500 West Cortland Street
Chicago, Illinois 60707
Phone: 773-889-3087
Website: www.cobra.com

DeLorme
Two DeLorme Drive
PO Box 298
Yarmouth, Maine 04096
Phone: 1-800-561-5105
Website: www.delorme.com

Garmin International
1200 E. 151st Street
Olathe, Kansas 66062
Phone: 1-800-800-1020
Website: www.garmin.com

Lowrance Electronics, Inc.
12000 E. Skelly Drive
Tulsa, Oklahoma 74128
Phone: 1-800-324-1354
Website: www.lowrance.com

Magellan Navigation Inc.
960 Overland Court
San Dimas, California 91773
Phone: 909-394-5000
Website: www.magellangps.com

Trimble Navigational Ltd.
935 Stewart Drive
Sunnyvale, California 94085
Phone: 1-800-874-6253
Website: www.trimble.com

Geocaching Software

A list of software applications that support GPX and LOC file formats.
www.geocaching.com/waypoints

ClayJar Watcher (GPX): Geocaching-specific freeware application that helps you manage your Pocket Query GPX files.
www.clayjar.com/gc/watcher

EasyGPS for Groundspeak (GPX/LOC): A great (free) application for managing both LOC and GPX file types.
www.easygps.com

Geocaching Swiss Army Knife (GPX/LOC): A powerful and useful application that allows you to edit and combine GPX files and load them to your GPS and PDA.
www.gsak.net

Google Earth(GPX/KML): In addition to viewing caches via Network KML, Google Earth can overlay the travels of trackable items on geocaching.com. Google Earth also uses GPS Babel to allow Premium Members the ability to drag a Pocket Query GPX file onto the application to overlay geocaches.
www.googleearth.com

GPS Connect for Mac OS X (GPX): Garmin-specific application that works with GPX.
www.chimoosoft.com/products/gpsconnect

GPSBabel (GPX/LOC/KML): A free console-based application for converting LOC and GPX to various other formats. Source code is available.
www.gpsbabel.org

GPX Spinner (GPX): Geocaching-specific shareware application that can convert GPX files to iSilo and Plucker format.
www.gpxspinner.com

Groundspeak's Geocaching Apps for smartphones: Real-time access to Geocaching.com data with full geocaching capability.
www.geocaching.com/iphone
www.geocaching.com/android
www.geocaching.com/wp7

MacCaching Geocache Manager (GPX/LOC): A geocache manager for Mac OS X.
www.maccaching.com

Trimble's Geocache Navigator: Fully featured geocaching application for mobile phones.
www.geocachenavigator.com

GPS Software

DeLorme
PO Box 298
Yarmouth, Maine 04096
Phone: 1-800-561-5105
Website: www.delorme.com

Fugawi
60 St. Clair Avenue East, Suite 902
Toronto, Ontario M4T 1N5 Canada
Website: www.fugawi.com

Maptech
10 Industrial Way
Amesbury, Maine 01913
Phone: 1-888-839-5551
Website: www.maptech.com

National Geographic Maps
375 Alabama Street, Suite 400
San Francisco, California 94110
Phone: 415-558-8700
Website: www.topo.com

OziExplorer
www.oziexplorer.com

TopoGrafix
PO Box 783
Medford, Maine 02155
Website: www.topografix.com

Map Resources

Google Maps
maps.google.com

Microsoft Live Search
maps.live.com

Open Street Map
www.openstreetmap.org

Trackmaker
www.gpstm.com

Yahoo Maps
maps.yahoo.com

Newsgroups, Podcasts, and Zines

With how easy it is these days to create and publish a Podcast and other web-based resources, this list may not include the newest and most cutting-edge newsgroups, Podcasts, or ezines, but here are a few that are worth checking out.

Cache-A-Maniacs—United States
www.cacheamaniacs.com

Centennial State Geocaching—Colorado, United States
centennialstategeocaching.com

Dosen Fischer—Germany
www.dosenfischer.de
(German language)

Geocaching Podcast—United States
www.geocachingpodcast.info

Geotalk—Australia
geotalk.libsyn.com

GPSInformation.net
gpsinformation.netGPS Magazine
www.gpsmagazine.com

Icenrye's Geocaching Videozine
www.icenrye.com/new

Ontario Geocaching Podcast—Canada
ontariogeocaching.podomatic.com

PodCacher—United States
www.podcacher.com

sci.geo.satellite-nav
www.gpsy.com/gpsinfo/gps-faq.html

Twin Cities GeoCaching Podcast—Minnesota, United States
www.tcgcpc.com

Paper Map Resources

Canada Map Office
Department of Energy, Mines, and Resources
615 Booth Street
Ottawa, Ontario K1A0E9 Canada
Phone: 1-800-465-6277

The Earth Science Information Center Headquarters
Phone: 1-800-USA-MAPS

Getty Thesaurus of Geographic Names
www.getty.edu/research/conducting_research/vocabularies/tgn

National Ocean Survey Map and Chart Information
Distribution Branch N/CG33
Riverdale, Maryland 20737
Phone: 303-436-6990

National Oceanic and Atmospheric Administration
1401 Constitution Avenue, NW
Room 5128
Washington, DC 20230
www.noaa.gov

U.S. Census Bureau
www.census.gov/cgi-bin/gazetteer

U.S. Geological Survey
507 National Center
Reston, Virgina 22092
Website: www.usgs.gov

Related Activities

Armchair Treasure Hunt Club
www.treasureclub.net

Bookcrossing.com
www.bookcrossing.com

Canadian Money Tracker
www.cdn-money.ca

The Degree Confluence Project
www.confluence.org

EarthCaching
earthcache.org

EuroBillTracker
en.eurobilltracker.com

International Orienteering Organization
www.orienteering.org

Letterboxing North America
www.letterboxing.org

Waymarking
www.waymarking.com

Where's George?
www.wheresgeorge.com

Where's Willy?
www.whereswilly.com

Wherigo
www.wherigo.com

User-Generated Geocaching Tools

Geocacher University
www.geocacher-u.com

Geochecker
www.geochecker.com

Prime Suspect's Greasemonkey Scripts
gmscripts.locusprime.net

Team Markwell's GPS Adventures
www.markwell.us/geo.htm

Weather

National Weather Service
www.nws.noaa.gov

The Weather Channel
www.weather.com

Glossary

almanac data   The information broadcast from GPS satellites used by the GPS receiver for computing its location.

altimeter   A gauge for measuring elevation.

archive   A cache that has been removed from the listings of Geocaching.com. The cache page is still available for administrative review, but will not show up when the public searches for caches. Geocaches are generally archived when they are missing, destroyed, or removed by the owner. Caches that simply need attention or repair are "temporarily disabled" rather than archived.

attributes   These are small graphics on a cache detail intended to provide filterable information to geocachers who wish to find specific features in caches. These graphics represent cache characteristics to explain what to expect at a cache location, like kid-friendliness, 24-hour-a–day availability, swimming requirements, camping conveniences, and more. Attributes are also a tool to help you filter the types of caches you would like to search for when building a Pocket Query.

autorouting   A GPS function that provides turn-by-turn directions to a waypoint. Directions may be in the form of arrows or automated voice commands.

back bearing   Reversing a bearing for a return trip. It is 180 degrees in the opposite direction.

baseline navigation   Baseline or handrail terrain features are linear reference points, such as roads, rivers, and power lines.

bearing (BRG)   A direction measured by a compass degree needed to travel to stay on a course. Also known as an azimuth.

benchmark hunting   The search for National Geodetic Survey (NGS) navigational survey markers. These markers document elevation or latitude/longitude points. Survey markers can be found with GPS or by following written instructions provided by the NGS.

Bison tube   A small, rust-proof cylindrical container with a watertight o-ring. These containers are often used for micro caches due to their size and durability.

Bookmark List   A feature for Premium account members of Geocaching.com. Allows users to organize geocaches based on their own criteria.

Bureau of Land Management (BLM)   A U.S. government agency within the Department of the Interior. It manages 262 million acres of America's public lands, located primarily in 12 western states.

BYOP   Bring Your Own Pen/Pencil. An acronym often used by cache owners to communicate to other geocachers that you need to bring your writing instrument in order to sign the cache logbook.

cache   A shortened version of the word geocache. A hidden container that includes, at a minimum, a logbook for geocachers to sign.

Caches Along a Route   A Premium Member feature that allows you to identify caches along a specific itinerary for quick and easy geocaching. You can choose from routes already created by other geocachers or use Google Earth to build your own unique trip.

cardinal points   The primary compass points: N, E, S, and W. The intercardinal points are NE, SE, SW, and NW.

Charter Member   During the very early years of Geocaching.com when Premium Memberships were first offered, they were called Charter Memberships. Be sure to thank the Charter Members you meet on the trail since the site would not be here today without them.

CITO (Cache In Trash Out)   An ongoing environmental initiative supported by the worldwide geocaching community. As simple as geocachers who clean up the trails by removing the trash that they find while geocaching, and as elaborate as organized efforts. to remove invasive species, encourage revegetation, and build trails.

course   A direction traveled between two points, or to reach a destination.

datum   A global survey system used to create maps. They are titled from the year they were created. Latitude and longitude are calculated differently for each datum. Geocaching uses the WGS 84 datum for all caches.

decimal minutes   Geocaching uses this format of the latitude/longitude system, in which seconds are not shown. This is represented in the GPS receiver as HDDD° MM.MMM. HDDD stands for "hemisphere" and "degrees." MM.MMM stands for "minutes" in the decimal format.

declination   The deference in degrees between magnetic north and true north.

DGPS (differential correction)   A system to improve GPS accuracy through ground-based radio transmitters to correct existing GPS signals for accuracy averaging 5 meters.

DNF (Did not find)   An acronym used by geocachers to state that they did not find a cache. This is also a type of online log on Geocaching.com and is useful for alerting cache owners of potential issues. A cache owner who repeatedly receives DNF logs should check to see that her cache has not been removed.

D/T (Difficulty/Terrain)   Difficulty relates to the mental challenge of finding a cache and terrain describes the physical environment. Geocaches are rated in two categories, each designated on a 5-point scale. A 1/1 difficulty/terrain rating would be the easiest cache to find, while a 5/5 difficulty/terrain rating would be the most difficult.

EarthCache   A special place that people can visit to learn about a unique geoscience feature of our Earth. EarthCache pages include a set of educational notes along with cache coordinates.

estimated time en route (ETE)   The amount of time needed to reach the destination based on current speed and course.

estimated time of arrival (ETA)   The time scheduled to arrive based on current speed and course.

Event Cache   A geocacher's term for a party. It's a gathering of geocachers to discuss geocaching, sometimes sponsored by geocaching organizations. The Event Cache page specifies a time for the event and provides coordinates to its location.

FTF (first to find)   An acronym written by geocachers in physical cache logbooks or online when logging cache finds to denote being the first to find a geocache.

GC Code   A unique identifier associated with every geocache listing. The GC Code starts with the letters "GC" and is followed by other alphanumeric characters.

geocache   A hidden container that includes, at a minimum, a logbook for geocachers to sign.

geocaching   A worldwide game of hiding and seeking playful treasure. A geocacher can place a geocache in the world, pinpoint its location using GPS technology, and then share the geocache's existence and location online.

Geocoin   A custom-minted item, often metal, that is used as a signature item for geocaching. Most Geocoins are trackable at Geocaching.com, just like Travel Bug tags.

GeoSense   The uncanny ability to know instinctively where a cache is hidden when you get within a certain proximity.

Global Positioning System (GPS)   The global, satellite-based navigation system operated by the U.S. government. With the use of a GPS receiver, you can find your position anywhere in the world, and it is the basis for the game of geocaching.

GPS Adventures Maze Exhibit   A museum exhibit built to travel and to teach students of all ages about geocaching, GPS technology, and the science of location through interactive experiences.

GPSr   A GPS receiver.

GPSr food   A slang term for batteries.

ground zero (GZ)   The point when your GPS says you have arrived at the cache. At Ground Zero, you are zero feet (or zero meters) away from your destination.

heading   A marine term to describe a desired direction of travel.

hitchhiker   An item that is placed in a cache with instructions to relocate it to other caches. Sometimes they have logbooks attached so you can log their travels. Travel Bugs and Geocoins are examples of hitchhikers.

KB   Abbreviation for the Knowledge Books, a free resource provided by Groundspeak to further explain the finer points of geocaching as well as other location-based activities. They can be found at support. groundspeak.com.

latitude   The angular distance north or south from the earth's equator measured through 90 degrees. Think of latitude as rungs on a ladder.

letterbox(ing)   Another form of treasure hunting that uses clues instead of coordinates. In some cases, the letterbox owner has made their container both a letterbox and a geocache and posted its coordinates on Geocaching.com. If there is a stamp inside a Letterbox Hybrid, it is not an item intended for trade; the stamp is meant to remain in the box so that visitors can use it to record their visit.

LOC   The original download format for the search results page on Geocaching.com.

locationless (reverse) cache   A former cache type that could be considered the opposite of a traditional cache. Instead of finding a hidden container, you locate a specific object and log its coordinates. Locationless caches evolved into Waymarking and Worldwide Geocaching Challenges.

longitude system   The angular distance measured on a great circle of reference from the intersection of the adopted zero meridian with this reference circle to the similar intersection of the meridian passing through the object. Think of the long lines running north and south.

magnetic   Direction of a compass needle as it points to magnetic north.

man overboard (MOB)   A GPS receiver function allowing a waypoint to be quickly saved in an emergency situation. This is typically done by holding down the GoTo or Enter button.

markwelled   When a response to a new post in the forums points you to a similar topic in the past. Based on the user Markwell.

match safe   A small waterproof container designed to hold matches. They also make great micro cache containers.

Mega-Event Cache   An Event Cache that is attended by 500+ people. Mega-Events offer geocachers elaborate planned activities. There are often several days of additional activities surrounding a Mega-Event. These large events attract geocachers from all over the world and are often held annually.

muggle   A non-geocacher. Based on "Muggle" from the Harry Potter series, which is a non-magical person. Usually this term is used after a non-geocacher looks puzzled after befriending a geocacher searching for a cache, or when a non-geocacher accidentally finds a cache.

multi-cache (offset cache)   A multi-cache ("multiple") involves two or more locations. The final location is a physical container. There are many variations, but most multi-caches have a hint to find the second cache, and the second cache has a hint to the third, and so on. An offset cache (where you go to a location and get hints to the actual cache) is considered a multi-cache.

mystery or puzzle caches   The "catch-all" of cache types, this form of geocache may involve complicated puzzles that you will first need to solve to determine the coordinates. Mystery/puzzle caches often become the staging ground for new and unique geocaches that do not fit in another category.

National Marine Electronics Association (NMEA)   A universal electronic standard established to allow GPS, radios, and computers to exchange navigational data.

nautical mile   6,080 feet, or 1.152 of a statute mile.

pacing   A method of tracking distances by counting footsteps. A pace is one step. A stride is two steps, typically about 5 feet.

Pocket Query (PQ)   A Premium Member feature, a Pocket Query is a custom geocache search that you can have emailed to you on a daily or weekly basis. Pocket Queries give you the ability to filter your searches so you only receive information on the caches you want to search for in either a GPX of LOC format. This feature lets you download up to 1,000 caches at one time.

Project A.P.E. Cache   In 2001, 14 geocaches were placed in conjunction with 20th Century Fox to support the movie *Planet of the Apes*. Each cache represented a fictional story in which scientists revealed an Alternative Primate Evolution. These caches were made using specially marked ammo containers. Each cache had an original prop from the movie. Only one Project A.P.E. cache, located in the jungles of Brazil, exists today.

real-time tracking   A GPS receiver is connected to a computer loaded with mapping software. The user's current location is displayed on a computer screen as an icon centered on the digital-moving map.

reviewers   Highly experienced volunteers from all over the world who confirm compliance with the guidelines and publish the cache listings on Geocaching.com.

ROT-13   The encryption method utilized by the encrypted hints or logs on Geocaching.com.

route   A series of waypoints listed in sequence from start to finish.

selective availability (SA)   A degree of inaccuracy programmed by the U.S. government, causing civilian receivers to be off as much as 100 meters. SA was discontinued in May 2000.

signature item   An item unique to a specific geocacher that is left behind in caches to signify that they visited that cache. These often include personalized Geocoins, tokens, pins, craft items, or calling cards.

spoiler   Text or photo that gives away too many details of a cache location, spoiling the experience for the next cachers who want to find it. Also used to describe a person who gives away details to other geocachers.

statute mile   A standard ground mile with the distance of 5,280 feet.

SWAG   An acronym often referred to as standing for "Stuff We All Get." It includes the trade items left in caches by geocachers.

terrain association   A way to orient a map to actual terrain by matching up prominent features and baseline features.

TFTC (Thanks for the cache)   An acronym written by geocachers in physical cache logbooks or online when logging cache finds.

TNLN (Took nothing, left nothing)   Usually written in cache logbooks by geocachers who do not trade for material contents in a cache.

TNLNSL   Took nothing, left nothing, signed logbook.

TNSL   Took nothing, signed logbook.

topographic or topo map   A detailed small-scale map showing elevation with contour lines.

track log   An electronic breadcrumb trail that is stored and displayed by a GPS receiver, indicating a path traveled.

trade items   The most commonly used term (after treasure) for items found in a cache.

traditional cache   The original geocache type consisting of, at minimum, a container and a logbook or logsheet. Larger containers generally include items for trade. "Nano" or "micro" caches are tiny containers that only hold a logsheet. The coordinates listed on the traditional cache page provide the geocache's exact location.

Travel Bug   A trackable tag that you attach to an item. This allows you to track your item on Geocaching.com. The item becomes a hitch-hiker that is carried from cache to cache (or person to person) in the real world and you can follow its progress online.

triangulation   Confirms a location by taking a bearing to more than one surrounding landmark. Effective in the field or on a map.

true   Direction to the actual North Pole.

universal time coordinated (UTC)   A universal time standard based on some point in the world. Many GPS receivers use the UTC at Greenwich, England.

Universal Transverse Mercator (UTM) system   The world's second primary navigation coordinate system. Often considered an easier system to use because it uses metric meters and kilometers instead of degrees, minutes, and seconds.

U.S. Forest Service (USFS)   An agency within the Department of Agriculture administering 191 million acres (77.3 million hectares) of National Forests, Grasslands, and Prairies. These public lands are generally geocaching-friendly, with exceptions of designated Wilderness Areas, and other specially designated botanical, wildlife, and archaeological sites.

variation   Another term for magnetic declination.

Virtual (cache)   This former cache type involved discovering a location rather than a container. The requirements for logging a Virtual Cache vary—you may be required to answer a question about the location, take a picture, complete a task, etc. In any case, you must visit the coordinates before you can post your log. Virtual Caches evolved into Geocaching Challenges.

watchlist   A list of users on Geocaching.com who are subscribed to a particular hitchhiker or cache. When a listing is logged, users on the watchlist are notified by email.

waypoint   A reference point for a physical location on Earth. Waypoints are defined by a set of coordinates that typically include longitude, latitude, and sometimes altitude. Every geocache listed on Geocaching.com is a waypoint. The website generates a unique "GC Code" associated with every geocache listing.

webcam cache   These are grandfathered caches that use existing web cameras placed by individuals or agencies that monitor various areas like parks or business complexes. The idea is to get yourself in front of the camera to log your visit. Webcam caches evolved into a Waymarking category.

WGS84   The most current geodetic datum used for GPS is the World Geodetic System of 1984 (WGS84). The significance of WGS84 comes about because GPS receivers rely on WGS84.

Wherigo cache   A cache type that allows geocachers to interact with physical and virtual elements such as objects or characters while still finding a physical geocache container. A Wherigo-enabled GPS device is required to play a cartridge.

wide-area augmentation system (WAAS)   A system of satellites and ground stations that provide GPS signal corrections, improving position accuracy in the United States.

Navigation and Map References

Distance

1 inch	25.4 millimeters	2.54 centimeters	
1 foot	12 inches	30.48 centimeters	
1 yard	3 feet	.914 meter	
1 mile (statute)	5,280 feet	1,760 yards	1.609 kilometers
1 nautical mile	6,080 feet	1,853 kilometers	1.15 of a mile
1 millimeter	.039 inch	.1 centimeter	
1 centimeter	.394 inch	10 millimeters	
1 meter	39.37 inches	3.28 feet	
1 kilometer	3,280.8 feet	.62 mile	1,000 meters
1 acre	43,560 sq. feet	approx. 208.7 feet	

Map Scales

1:500,000	1 inch = 8 miles
1:250,000	1 inch = 4 miles
1:150,000	1 inch = 2.4 miles
1:62,000 (15 minute)	1 inch = 1 mile
1:24,000 (7.5 minute)	1 inch = 2,000 feet (topo size)

UTM

Each grid is 1,000 meters (1 kilometer) square.

Latitude/Longitude

- Latitude lines run horizontally and measure north-south coordinates. Think of these as a "ladder" going up and down the globe.

- Longitude lines run vertically, intersecting the poles to measure east-west coordinates. Think of them as the "Long" lines that cross the poles.

- 1° (degree) = 60' (minutes), 1' (minute) = 60" (seconds).

- 1° (degree) = 69.05 statute miles = 111 kilometers.

- 1 minute = 1 nautical mile or 1.15 statute miles = 1.85 kilometers.

- 1 second = 100 feet = 30.83 meters.

  Distances apply to latitude, but only to longitude at the equator.

Township, Range, Section

- A township equals 36 square miles.

- Each square mile is a section. Each section is numbered from 1 to 36. Section 1 begins in the northeast corner as the numbers proceed west, then east, alternately down each row, ending with 36 in the southeast corner.

- Each township has a township and range designation to define its 36-square-mile area.

- The horizontal rows are the township designation.

- The vertical rows are the range designation.

Sections are divided into quarters, which are further quartered to describe a property location: for example, SE 1/4, NW 1/4, Section 23, T.1 S., R.1 E., of the Salt Lake Base Line.

Geocaching Sample Log Sheet

When you are ready to hide your own geocache you will need a log for geocachers who find your cache to sign. This sample logsheet will help you get started if you choose to create your own or can be photocopied and used in your geocache.

Geocaching Cache Log

GEOCACHING.COM®

Geocache Name: _____

Placed by: _____

Contact Info: _____

Take something, leave something, sign the log.

Found by: _____   Date: _____
Notes:_____
_____
_____
_____

Found by: _____   Date: _____
Notes:_____
_____
_____
_____

Found by: _____   Date: _____
Notes:_____
_____
_____
_____

Found by: _____   Date: _____
Notes:_____
_____
_____
_____

Found by: _____   Date: _____
Notes:_____
_____
_____
_____

Found by: _____   Date: _____
Notes:_____
_____
_____
_____

Geocache Notification Sheet

When hiding a geocache you should always include a note to welcome the cache finder. Groundspeak provides this standard note that explains the activity in case someone accidentally finds your cache. You can download the note, which has been translated into several languages, at www.geocaching.com/seek/default.aspx#cachenote.

The English language version of this note has been included on the next page to be photocopied and used in your geocache.

GEOCACHE SITE—PLEASE READ

Congratulations: You've found it! Intentionally or not!

What is this hidden container sitting here for? What the heck is this thing doing here with all these things in it?

It is part of a worldwide game dedicated to GPS (Global Positioning System) users, called geocaching. The game basically involves a GPS user hiding "treasure" (this container and its contents), and publishing the exact coordinates so other GPS users can come on a "treasure hunt" to find it. The only rules are: if you take something from the cache, you must leave something for the cache, and you must write about your visit in the logbook. Hopefully, the person that hid this container found a good spot that is not easily found by uninterested parties. Sometimes, though, a good spot turns out to be a bad spot.

IF YOU FOUND THIS CONTAINER BY ACCIDENT:

Great! You are welcome to join us! We ask only that you:

- Please do not move or vandalize the container. The real treasure is just finding the container and sharing your thoughts with everyone else who finds it.

- If you wish, go ahead and take something. Please also leave something of your own for others to find, and write about it in the logbook.

- If possible, let us know that you found it by visiting the website listed below.

Geocaching is open to everyone with a GPS and a sense of adventure. There are similar sites all over the world. The organization has its home on the Internet. Visit our website if you want to learn more, or have any comments:

www.geocaching.com

If this container needs to be removed for any reason, please let us know. We apologize, and will be happy to move it.

Travel Itinerary

Critical Information to Leave Behind

Start Date & Time: _____

Planned Return Date & Time: _____

Destination: _____

Geocache Name(s): _____

Coordinates: _____

Location Description: _____

Planned Route: _____

_____

Motels/Campgrounds: _____

Comm. Ham: Frequencies _____ Cell ( ) _____

Sat. Ph. ( ) _____ CB: Ch. 1 _____ Ch. 2 _____ FM: _____

Person(s):

Name _____ Contact Phone _____

_____

_____

Vehicle(s):

Make _____ Model _____

Color _____ License Plate _____

Photocopy this page courtesy of Alpha Books.

Index

Numbers

10 Years! Event Cache, 95

A

accuracy (GPS receivers), 137
  EGNOS (European
    Geostationary Navigation
    Overlay Service), 138
  features, 146
  initialization process, 141
  ionospheric interference, 139
  limitations, 142-143
  MSAS (Multi-functional
    Satellite Augmentation
    System), 138
  multipath interference, 139
  WAAS (Wide-Area
    Augmentation System), 138
Active Route page (GPS
  receivers), 166
address finders (GPS receivers),
  146
aftermarket mapping software,
  203-204
aiming off (navigation tip), 222
alarms, GPS setup options, 147,
  169
altimeters (GPS receivers), 147
Androids, Groundspeak's
  Geocaching Application,
  188-190

animals, safety precautions, 79-81
antenna jacks (GPS receivers),
  147
API (application programming
  interface), 208
application programming
  interface. See API
applications (GPS-enabled
  smartphones)
  Geocaching Challenges
    Application, 192-194
  Groundspeak's Geocaching
    Application, 184-192
    Androids, 188-190
    iPhones, 185-187
    Windows Phone 7, 190-192
  third-party geocaching
    applications, 194-196
    CacheBox, 195
    CacheSense, 195
    GCBuddy, 195-196
    NeonGeo, 195
    Trimble Geocache
      Navigator, 194
archived caches (Geocaching.
  com), 53
augmented reality concept,
  298-300
auto routing (GPS receivers), 147,
  180-181

B

backlight timers, GPS setup
options, 169
basemaps (GPS receivers), 147,
160
batteries (GPS receivers),
158-159
  battery life, 147
  conserve battery modes, 172
  setup options, 170
bearings, 20
benchmark hunting, 289
  control points, 290
  finding benchmarks, 291-292
  logging benchmarks, 292-293
  search tips, 290-291
blogs
  Latitude 47 Official
    Geocaching Blog, 229
  personal weblogs, 230
Bluetooth-enabled devices, 199
BYOP (bring your own pen/
pencil), 23

C

Cache In Trash Out Event. *See*
CITO Event
CacheBox application, 195
CacheMate, 209
caches, 86
  destination caches, 260-264
  EarthCache, 16, 90-91
  event caches, 93, 241
    10 Years! Event Cache, 95
    Cache In Trash Out Events,
      93
    camping, 244-245
    CITO (Cache In Trash
      Out) Event, 249

educational events, 243-244
Event Cache page, 93
geocaching-style games,
  252-253
geocoins, 246
Groundspeak Block Party,
  94
Meet 'n' Greets, 243
Mega-Events, 94, 245-248
organizational tips, 249-251
finding, 55
  clues, 58-59
  entering GPS coordinates,
    56-58
  environmental ethics and
    stewardship, 83-84
  Geocaching.com, 24-25
  ground searches, 59-60
  guidelines, 62-65
  interacting with non-
    geocachers, 81-82
  navigational tips, 60-63
  safety precautions, 76-81
  search techniques, 72-76
  souvenir awards, 65-66
game guidelines, 19-23
  choosing items, 20-21
  CITO (Cache In Trash
    Out), 21-22
  online logs, 22-23
  photo posts, 22-23
  replacing items, 21
  signing logbooks, 21
gear essentials, 29-35
  clothing, 34
  communication options,
    34-35
  long hunts, 31-32
  overnight trips, 32-33
Geocacher's Creed, 17-18
geocaching communities, 17

GPS Adventures Maze
  Exhibit, 92
Groundspeak Headquarters
  Cache, 92
hiding
  care and maintenance, 105
  container considerations,
    99-101
  guidelines, 97-98
  locations, 27-29
  obtaining permission, 101
  placing and saving
    coordinates, 102-103
  posting to Geocaching.
    com, 103-104
  review process, 104-105
  rules and guidelines,
    105-107
letterbox hybrids, 16, 89-90
locationless caches, 95,
  280-281
multi-caches, 16, 87-88
mystery and puzzles, 16,
  88-89
Project A.P.E., 92
searches (Geocaching.com)
  creating accounts, 39-40
  difficulty/terrain ratings,
    47-48
  disabled and archived
    caches, 53
  nearby listings, 40-42
  paperless geocaching, 42-45
  selection criteria, 46-47
  using maps and clues, 49-52
  watch lists, 52-53
terms, 23-24
tips and tricks, 67-84
  environmental ethics and
    stewardship, 83-84
  familiarizing self with
    surroundings, 70

interacting with non-
  geocachers, 81-82
map considerations, 70-71
planning and preparations,
  68-69
safety precautions, 76-81
search techniques, 72-76
Trackables, 109
  Geocoins, 120-123
  promotions, 123-124
  Travel Bugs, 110-119,
    125-127
traditional caches, 15, 86-87
treasures
  prohibited items, 26-27
  signature items, 25-26
virtual caches, 16, 94
webcam caches, 95
Wherigo, 91
CacheSense application, 195
Camino de Santiago GeoTrail,
  258
camping events, 244-245
Captain John Smith GeoTrail,
  258
cartridges (Wherigo), 285
catch feature (navigation tip), 222
Chain Chomp, 118
challenges (Geocaching
  Challenges)
  creating, 278-279
  Discover Challenges, 277-278
  Local Challenges, 274
  Photo Challenges, 276-277
  Worldwide Challenges, 275
Cindy (the Cinder Block), 118
cities, hiding caches, 29
CITO (Cache In Trash Out),
  21-22, 249
climate, safety concerns, 78
clothing, essential gear, 34
cloverleaf search technique, 73-74

clubs and organizations, 234-236

clues
finding caches, 58-59
search tips (Geocaching.com),
49-52

colors, reading maps, 219

communication options
radio frequencies, 34-35
satellites, 34-35

communities
local clubs and organizations,
234-236
national groups, 236-237
online groups
discussion forums, 230-233
Latitude 47 Official
Geocaching Blog, 229
podcasts and blogs, 230
regional and local forums,
233-234
overview, 17

Compass page (GPS receivers),
166

computer interface (GPS
receivers), 148

computers
GPS receivers, 198-202
data transfer and
management, 200
map databases, 199
real-time tracking, 200-202
mapping software, 202-205
aftermarket, 203-204
manufacturers, 203
online map services, 205
Pocket Queries, 207
software programs, 207-209
CacheMate, 209
EasyGPS, 208
Google Earth, 209

GPSBabel, 208
GSAK (Geocaching Swiss
Army Knife), 208
terrain analysis, 205-206

conserve battery modes (GPS
setup options), 172

containers, hiding considerations,
99-101

contour lines
reading maps, 219-221
topographic maps, 215

control points (benchmark
hunting), 290

coordinates
downloading, 43-45
entering, 56-58
GPS setup options, 170
saving, 102-103

creating
Geocaching Challenges,
278-279
Geocaching.com accounts,
39-40
Travel Bugs, 116-117

D

Darth Vader TB1 Travel Bug,
125-126

data transfer (GPS receivers), 200

datum (maps), 57, 218

dead reckoning (navigation tip),
223

DeLorme PN-60 GPS receiver,
154

destination caches, 260-264

Didn't Find It log, 64

difficulty/terrain ratings, 47-48

disabled caches (Geocaching.
com), 53

Discover Challenges, 277-278

discussion forums, 230-233

discussion threads, 231
distance measurements (GPS setup options), 170
durability (GPS receivers), 148

E

EarthCache, 16, 90-91
EasyGPS, 208
educational events, 243-244
educational experiences, 237-239
EGNOS (European Geostationary Navigation Overlay Service), 138
electronic compass (GPS receivers), 148
Enter button (GPS receivers), 165
environmental ethics, 83-84
environmental safety concerns, 77-78
ethics, environmental ethics, 83-84
European Geostationary Navigation Overlay Service. *See* EGNOS
event caches, 241
  10 Years! Event Cache, 95
  Cache In Trash Out Events, 93
  camping events, 244-245
  CITO (Cache In Trash Out) Event, 249
  educational events, 243-244
  Event Cache page, 93
  geocaching-style games, 252-253
  Geocoins, 246
  Groundspeak Block Party, 94
  Meet 'n' Greets, 243
  Mega-Events, 94, 245
    Geobash, 248
    Geocoinfest, 248
  GeoWoodstock, 246-248
  MegaPott GeOlympics, 248
  organizational tips, 249-251
evolution
  future expectations, 295-300
  GPS receivers, 132-135
  Travel Bugs, 119
external antenna jacks (GPS features), 160
Extraterrestrial Highway GeoTour, 259-260

F

Family Radio Service. *See* FRS
features (GPS receivers), 136-137
  accuracy, 146
  address finders, 146
  alarms, 146
  altimeters, 147
  antenna jacks, 147
  auto routing, 147
  basemaps, 147, 160
  battery life, 147
  computer interface, 148
  durability, 148
  electronic compass, 148
  external antenna jacks, 160
  interface capabilities, 160
  memory, 148, 160
  power sources, 160
  routes, 148
  screen sizes, 161
  sun and moon positions, 148
  tide page, 149
  track logs, 149
  water-resistant, 149
  waterproof, 161
  waypoint averaging, 149
  waypoints, 149

field notes, 64
finding
   benchmarks, 291-292
   caches, 55
      clues, 58-59
      entering GPS coordinates,
         56-58
      environmental ethics and
         stewardship, 83-84
      Geocaching.com, 24-25
      ground searches, 59-60
      guidelines, 62-65
      interacting with non-
         geocachers, 81-82
      navigational tips, 60-63
      safety precautions, 76-81
      search techniques, 72-76
      souvenir awards, 65-66
   Travel Bugs, 112-115
first to find. *See* FTF
flying and GPS receivers, 270
forums
   discussion forums, 230-233
   regional and local forums,
      233-234
Found It log, 63
FRS (Family Radio Service), 34
FTF (first to find), 23
full-featured handheld GPS
   receivers, 153-155
future expectations, 306
   augmented reality concept,
      298-300
   GPS receivers, 296-297
   growth and evolution,
      295-300
   mainstream popularity,
      303-305
   reconnecting with nature, 300
   wanderlust, 301-302

G

gaiters, 78
game guidelines, 19
   choosing items, 20-21
   CITO (Cache In Trash Out),
      21-22
   geocaching-style games,
      252-253
   online logs, 22-23
   photo posts, 22-23
   replacing items, 21
   signing logbooks, 21
Garmin Etrex 10 GPS receiver,
   152
Garmin eTrex GPS receiver,
   150-151
Garmin Montana 650t GPS
   receiver, 154
GCBuddy application, 195-196
gear
   essential equipment, 29-35
      clothing, 34
      communication options,
         34-35
      long hunts, 31-32
      overnight trips, 32-33
   Wherigo, 285
Geico's Find the Gecko Travel
   Tags promotion, 123
geo-senses, 72
Geobash, 248
Geocacher's Creed, 17-18
geocaching
   communities, 17
   EarthCache, 16
   Geocacher's Creed, 17-18
   Geocaching.com website,
      11-13
   letterbox hybrid caches, 16

multi-caches, 16
mystery and puzzle caches, 16
origins, 8-11
overview, 4-8
popularity and growth, 13-15
traditional caches, 15
virtual caches, 16
Geocaching API, 210
Geocaching Challenges
    creating, 278-279
    Discover Challenges, 277-278
    Local Challenges, 274
    Photo Challenges, 276-277
    Worldwide Challenges, 275
Geocaching Challenges
  Application, 192-194
Geocaching.com
    discussion forums, 230-233
    finding caches, 24-25
    posting caches, 103-104
    review process, 104-105
    searches
        creating accounts, 39-40
        difficulty/terrain ratings,
          47-48
        disabled and archived
          caches, 53
        nearby cache listings,
          40-42
        paperless geocaching, 42-45
        selection criteria, 46-47
        using maps and clues, 49-52
        watch lists, 52-53
    souvenir awards, 65-66
    uploading photos, 65
Geocaching Live enabled tools,
  210
Geocaching Swiss Army Knife.
  See GSAK
Geocoinfest, 248

Geocoins
    defining characteristics, 24
    events, 246
    overview, 120-122
    tracking, 122-123
geotourism, 255
    destination caches, 260-264
    GeoTours
        Extraterrestrial Highway,
          259-260
        historically-themed,
          257-259
        local tours, 256-257
    international considerations,
      270-271
    trip-planning tips, 264-266
    vacations, 266-269
        local treasures, 267-268
        packing tips, 268-269
GeoWoodstock, 246-248
"Get in the Game!" initiative,
  236
Google Earth, 209
GoTo button (GPS receivers),
  165
GPS Adventures Maze Exhibit,
  92
GPS receivers
    accuracy, 137-138
        EGNOS (European
          Geostationary Navigation
          Overlay Service), 138
        ionospheric interference,
          139
        MSAS (Multi-functional
          Satellite Augmentation
          System), 138
        multipath interference, 139
        WAAS (Wide-Area
          Augmentation System),
          138

Active Route page, 166
batteries, 158-159
choosing, 146
Compass page, 166
computers, 198-209
    data transfer and
      management, 200
    map databases, 199
    mapping software, 202-205
    Pocket Queries, 207
    real-time tracking, 200-202
    software programs,
      207-209
    terrain analysis, 205-206
coordinates
    downloading, 43-45
    entering, 56-58
    saving, 102-103
DeLorme PN-60, 154
distance measurements, 60
Enter button, 165
evolution, 132-135
features, 136-137
    accuracy, 146
    address finders, 146
    alarms, 146
    altimeters, 147
    antenna jacks, 147
    auto routing, 147
    basemaps, 147, 160
    battery life, 147
    computer interface, 148
    durability, 148
    electronic compass, 148
    external antenna jacks, 160
    interface capabilities, 160
    memory, 148, 160
    power sources, 160
    routes, 148
    screen sizes, 161

    sun and moon positions,
      148
    tide page, 149
    track logs, 149
    water-resistant, 149
    waterproof, 161
    waypoint averaging, 149
    waypoints, 149
flying tips, 270
full-featured handhelds,
  153-155
future expectations, 296-297
Garmin eTrex 10, 152
Garmin eTrex H, 150-151
Garmin Montana 650t, 154
GoTo button, 165
ground searches, 59-60
handheld with basemap
  database, 151-152
handheld without basemap
  database, 150-151
Highway page, 167
Information page, 167
initialization process, 141
joysticks, 165
laptops and tablets, 156
limitations, 142-143
Magellan Explorist 710, 153
Magellan Explorist GC, 151
Map page, 167
Menu button, 165
navigational tips, 60-63
obtaining satellite fix, 139-141
Power button, 165
routes
    auto routing, 180-181
    savings, 179-180
SA (selective availability)
    defining characteristics, 8
    removal, 8-11
satellite signals, 135-136

Satellite Status page, 168
setup options
    alarms, 169
    backlight timers, 169
    battery types, 170
    conserve battery modes,
        172
    coordinates, 170
    distance measurements, 170
    map datums, 170
    map-page orientation, 171
    north, 171
    time, 171
    timers, 172
smartphones, 157-158
track logs
    programming options,
        177-178
    saving, 178
usage guidelines, 270-271
vehicle-based receivers, 155
waypoints, saving, 173-177
Zoom button, 165
GPS-enabled smartphones, 183
    Geocaching Challenges
        Application, 192-194
    Groundspeak's Geocaching
        Application, 184-192
        Androids, 188-190
        iPhones, 185-187
        Windows Phone 7, 190-192
    third-party geocaching
        applications, 194-196
        CacheBox, 195
        CacheSense, 195
        GCBuddy, 195-196
        NeonGeo, 195
        Trimble Geocache
            Navigator, 194
GPSBabel, 208

Great American GPS Stash
    Hunt, 9
grids, reading maps, 219
ground searches, 59-60
Groundspeak Block Party, 94
Groundspeak Headquarters
    Cache, 92
Groundspeak's Geocaching
    Application
    Androids, 188-190
    iPhones, 185-187
    Windows Phone 7, 190-192
groups
    local clubs and organizations,
        234-236
    national groups, 236-237
    online groups
        discussion forums, 230-233
        Latitude 47 Official
            Geocaching Blog, 229
        podcasts and blogs, 230
        regional and local forums,
            233-234
growth
    factors, 13-15
    future expectations, 295-300
GSAK (Geocaching Swiss Army
    Knife), 208
guidelines
    finding caches, 62-66
        field notes, 64
        logging caches, 63-64
        souvenir awards, 65-66
        uploading photos, 65
    hiding caches, 97-98, 105-107
    usage guidelines (GPS
        receivers), 270-271

H

handheld with basemap database GPS receivers, 151-152
handheld without basemap database GPS receivers, 150-151
heat exhaustion, 77
hiding geocaches
    care and maintenance, 105
    container considerations, 99-101
    guidelines, 97-98
    locations
        cities and suburbs, 29
        parks, 28
        wide-open spaces, 27
    obtaining permission, 101
    placing and saving coordinates, 102-103
    posting to Geocaching.com, 103-104
    review process, 104-105
    rules and guidelines, 105-107
Highway page (GPS receivers), 167
historically themed GeoTours, 257-259
hypothermia, 77

I

Information page (GPS receivers), 167
initialization process (GPS receivers), 141
insects, safety precautions, 78-79
interface capabilities (GPS features), 160
international travel considerations, 270-271

Internet (online groups)
    discussion forums, 230-233
    Latitude 47 Official Geocaching Blog, 229
    podcasts and blogs, 230
    regional and local forums, 233-234
ionospheric interference, 139
iPhones, Groundspeak's Geocaching Application, 185-187
Irish, Jeremy, 12

J-K

Jeep 4X4 Geocaching Challenge, 123-124
joysticks (GPS receivers), 165

L

laptops, GPS receivers, 156
Latitude 47 Official Geocaching Blog, 229
leaving no trace principle, 70
letterbox hybrid caches, 16, 89-90
limitations of GPS receivers, 142-143
Local Challenges, 274
locationless caches, 95, 280-281
locations
    confirming by elevation, 222
    hiding geocaches
        cities and suburbs, 29
        parks, 28
        wide-open spaces, 27
logging caches
    benchmarks, 292-293
    field notes, 64

log types, 63-64
online, 22-23
signing logbooks, 21
track logs (GPS receivers), 177-178
uploading photos, 65

M

Magellan Explorist 710 GPS receiver, 153
Magellan Explorist GC GPS receiver, 151
mainstream popularity, 303-305
maintaining caches, 105
manufacturers, mapping software, 203
Map page (GPS receivers), 167
mapping software, 202-205
    aftermarket, 203-204
    manufacturers, 203
    online map services, 205
maps
    considering factors, 70-71
    databases, 199
    datum, 57, 170
    navigation tips, 222-223
    overview, 214
    reading, 216-217
    scales, 214-215
    search tips (Geocaching.com), 49- 52
    topographic
        overview, 215
        pacing, 221
        reading, 217-221
markwelling, 233
Mary Proppins, 118
Meet 'n' Greet events, 243

Mega-Events, 94, 245
    Geobash, 248
    Geocoinfest, 248
    GeoWoodstock, 246-248
    MegaPott GeOlympics, 248
MegaPott GeOlympics, 248
memory features (GPS receivers), 148, 160
Menu button (GPS receivers), 165
Mingo-GC30 geocache, 260
MSAS (Multi-functional Satellite Augmentation System), 138
muggles, 24, 101
multi-caches, 16, 87-88
Multi-functional Satellite Augmentation System. *See* MSAS
multipath interference, 139
mystery caches, 16, 88-89

N

national groups, 236-237
nature connection, 300
navigation tips
    aiming off, 222
    catch features, 222
    confirming location by elevation, 222
    dead reckoning, 223
    finding caches, 60-63
    night navigation, 223
    reverse perspective, 223
    trail markers, 223
    triangulation, 223
Needs Archived log, 64
Needs Maintenance log, 64
NeonGeo application, 195

night navigation tips, 223
north, GPS setup options, 171

O

online groups
   discussion forums, 230-233
   Latitude 47 Official
      Geocaching Blog, 229
   podcasts and blogs, 230
   regional and local forums,
      233-234
online logs, 22-23
online map services, 205
organizations, 234-236
organizing events, 249-251
Original Stash Tribute Plaque
   geocache, 261
overnight trips, essential gear,
   32-33

P-Q

pacing distances, 221
packing tips
   essential gear, 29-35
      clothing, 34
      communication options,
         34-35
      long hunts, 31-32
      overnight trips, 32-33
   vacation geocaching, 268-269
paperless geocaching, 42-45
   downloading GPS
      coordinates, 43-45
   Pocket Queries, 45
parks, hiding caches, 28
permissions, obtaining, 101
Pet Rock, 118
Photo Challenges, 276-277

photos
   postings, 22-23
   uploading, 65
planning trips, 68-69
PMR (Private Mobile Radio), 34
Pocket Queries, 45, 207
podcasts, 230
popularity, 13-15
posting caches
   Geocaching.com, 103-104
   photos, 22-23
Power button (GPS receivers),
   165
power sources (GPS features),
   160
Private Mobile Radio. *See* PMR
prohibited cache items, 26-27
Project A.P.E., 92, 263
promotions (Trackables)
   Geico's Find the Gecko
      Travel Tags, 123
   Jeep 4X4 Geocaching
      Challenge, 123-124
   Unite for Diabetes Trackables,
      123
puzzle caches, 16, 88-89

R

radio frequencies, 34-35
ratings, difficulty/terrain ratings,
   47-48
reading maps, 216-221
   colors and symbols, 219
   contour lines, 219-221
   datum, 218
   grids, 219
real-time tracking (GPS
   receivers), 200-202
regional and local forums,
   233-234
relocating Travel Bugs, 115

reverse caches, 95

reverse perspective (navigation tip), 223

review process (Geocaching. com), 104-105

route features (GPS receivers), 148

  auto routing, 180-181

  saving, 179-180

S

SA (selective availability)

  defining characteristics, 8

  removal, 8-11

safety precautions, 76-81

  bites and stings, 78-79

  environmental, 77-78

  wildlife, 79-81

satellite signals (GPS receivers), 135-136

  communication options, 34-35

  obtaining fix, 139-141

Satellite Status page (GPS receivers), 168

saving

  coordinates, 102-103

  routes, 179-180

  track logs, 178

  waypoints, 173-177

scales (maps), 214-215

screen sizes (GPS features), 161

searches

  Geocaching.com

    creating accounts, 39-40

    difficulty/terrain ratings, 47-48

    disabled and archived caches, 53

    nearby cache listings, 40-42

    paperless geocaching, 42-45

    selection criteria, 46-47

    using maps and clues, 49-52

    watch lists, 52-53

  techniques, 72-76

    cloverleaf, 73-74

    triangulation, 74-76

  tips

    benchmarks, 290-291

    waymarking, 282-283

selective availability. *See* SA

senses (geo-senses), 72

setup options (GPS receivers)

  alarms, 169

  backlight timers, 169

  battery types, 170

  conserve battery modes, 172

  coordinates, 170

  distance measurements, 170

  map datum, 170

  map-page orientation, 171

  north, 171

  time, 171

  timers, 172

signature items, 25-26

signing logbooks, 21

smartphones, 183

  Geocaching Challenges Application, 192-194

  GPS receivers, 157-158

  Groundspeak's Geocaching Application, 184-192

    Androids, 188-190

    iPhones, 185-187

    Windows Phone 7, 190-192

  third-party geocaching application

    CacheBox, 195

    CacheSense, 195

    GCBuddy, 195-196

    NeonGeo, 195

    Trimble Geocache Navigator, 194

software
  mapping software, 202-205
    aftermarket, 203-204
    manufacturers, 203
    online map services, 205
  programs, 207-209
    CacheMate, 209
    EasyGPS, 208
    Google Earth, 209
    GPSBabel, 208
    GSAK (Geocaching Swiss
      Army Knife), 208
  terrain analysis, 205-206
souvenir awards, 65-66
spoilers, 24
Stanley, Jon, 120
Star-Spangled Banner GeoTrail,
  258
stewardship, 83-84
stings, safety precautions, 78-79
sun and moon positions (GPS
  receivers), 148
SWAG (stuff we all get), 21, 24
switchbacks, 60
symbols, reading maps, 219
Sysop Travel Bug, 126

T

terms, 23-24
terrain
  analysis, 205-206
  difficulty/terrain ratings,
    47-48
TFTC (thanks for the cache), 24
third-party geocaching
  applications
    CacheBox, 195
    CacheSense, 195
    GCBuddy, 195-196
      NeonGeo, 195
      Trimble Geocache Navigator,
        194
tide pages (GPS receivers), 149
Tigger Travel Bug, 126-127
time, GPS setup options, 171-172
tips
  cache adventures, 67
    environmental ethics and
      stewardship, 83-84
    familiarizing self with
      surroundings, 70
    interacting with non-
      geocachers, 81-82
    map considerations, 70-71
    planning and preparations,
      68-69
    safety precautions, 76-81
    search techniques, 72-76
  navigation tips
    aiming off, 222
    catch features, 222
    confirming location by
      elevation, 222
    dead reckoning, 223
    finding caches, 60-63
    night navigation, 223
    reverse perspective, 223
    trail markers, 223
    triangulation, 223
TNLN (took nothing left
  nothing), 24
topographic maps
  navigation tips, 222-223
  overview, 215
  pacing, 221
  reading, 217-219
    colors and symbols, 219
    contour lines, 219-221
    datum, 218
    grids, 219

track logs (GPS receivers), 149
  programming options,
    177-178
  saving, 178
Trackables, 109
  Geocoins
    overview, 120-122
    tracking, 122-123
  promotions
    Geico's Find the Gecko
      Travel Tags, 123
    Jeep 4X4 Geocaching
      Challenge, 123-124
    Unite for Diabetes
      Trackables, 123
  Travel Bugs, 110
    Chain Chomp, 118
    Cindy (the Cinder Block),
      118
    creating, 116-117
    Darth Vader TB1, 125-126
    evolution, 119
    finding, 112-115
    Mary Proppins, 118
    Pet Rock, 118
    relocating, 115
    Sysop, 126
    Tigger, 126-127
traditional caches, 15, 86-87
trail markers (navigation tip), 223
travel (geotourism), 255
  destination caches, 260-264
  GeoTours
    Extraterrestrial Highway,
      259-260
    historically themed,
      257-259
    local tours, 256-257s
  international considerations,
    270-271
  trip planning tips, 264-266

vacations, 266-269
  local treasures, 267-268
  packing tips, 268-269
Travel Bugs, 110
  Chain Chomp, 118
  Cindy (the Cinder Block), 118
  creating, 116-117
  Darth Vader TB1, 125-126
  defining characteristics, 24
  evolution, 119
  finding, 112-115
  Mary Proppins, 118
  Pet Rock, 118
  relocating, 115
  Sysop, 126
  Tigger, 126-127
treasures
  choosing items, 20-21
  hiding locations
    cities and suburbs, 29
    parks, 28
    wide-open spaces, 27
  prohibited items, 26-27
  replacing, 21
  signature items, 25-26
Treasure Trackers, 304
triangulation
  navigation tips, 223
  search technique, 74-76
Trimble Geocache Navigator
  application, 194
trips
  overnight trips, 32-33
  packing tips, 268-269
  planning tips, 264-266

U–V

Unite for Diabetes Trackables,
  123
usage guidelines (GPS receivers),
  270-271

vacationing (geotourism), 255
  destination caches, 260-264
  GeoTours
    Extraterrestrial Highway,
      259-260
    historically themed,
      257-259
    local tours, 256-257
  international considerations,
    270-271
  local treasures, 267-268
  packing tips, 268-269
  trip planning tips, 264-266
vehicle-based GPS receivers, 155
View Carre' geocache, 262
virtual caches, 16, 94

gear and equipment, 285
  overview, 284-285
  Wherigo Builder, 288-289
  zones, 286-287
Wide-Area Augmentation
  System. *See* WAAS
wildlife, safety precautions, 79-81
Windows Phone 7,
  Groundspeak's Geocaching
  Application, 190-192
Worldwide Challenges, 275
Write Note log, 64

zone (Wherigo), 286-287
Zoom button (GPS receivers),
  165

W-X-Y-Z

WAAS (Wide-Area
  Augmentation System), 138
wanderlust, 301-302
watch lists (Geocaching.com),
  52-53
water-resistant GPS receivers,
  149, 161
waymarking, 279-283
  locationless caches, 280-281
  search tips, 282-283
  waymark category directory,
    282
waypoints (GPS receivers)
  averaging, 149
  defining characteristics, 24
  saving, 173-177
webcam caches, 95
Wherigo, 283-289
  caches, 91
  components of play, 287-288